FAITH AND
"LITTLE SPACE GRACE"

B J S M I T H

ARPress
ILLUMINATING IDEAS
EMPOWERING VOICES

ARPress
45 Dan Rd., Suite 36
Canton MA 02021

Hotline: 1(800) 220-7660
Fax: 1(855) 752-6001

Ordering Information:
Quantity sales.Special discounts are available on quantity purchases by corporations,associations,and others.For details,
contact the publisher at the address above.

Printed in the United States of America.

Library of Congress Control Number
ISBN-13:   Paperback   979-8-89389-057-0
                   eBook   979-8-89389-058-7

Rev. date: 06/30/2017

About the Author

This book, "Faith and Little Space Grace" began with my desire to share God's word. In August, 2014 I sat at my desk pondering how to spread the word of God to a larger audience.

I was born in West Helena Arkansas; the fourth child of my parent's seven. As to faith, my life was structured in the teachings of the word of God. Many hours of church life, interacting with the people of God and growing in the knowledge of his word. My love for the word developed early in life; perhaps because I always wanted to understand what the preachers were preaching. This led me to searching and studying the scriptures on regular bases.

To learn faith and to live by faith is rewarding. God answer prayers because he loves us and he is merciful. But we must understand that God creates the time, place and the circumstance we experience. God work all things for the good of those that love him and who are called according to his purpose. It is by the counsel of His will that all things exist. Tests and trials may cause our faith to waver; but they are the building materials of character, strength and virtue.

For a period of thirty years plus, I have taught Bible classes to small groups. I love the study in the word and I love sharing the word with others. But at my desk, the desire to reach out became my motivation to write this book. Once the desire was planted in my heart, God approved it by several witnesses. A few days later I received a CD from a young minister and his wife; Bro. Marcus & Sister Falon McIntosh. The title of the CD is "The Grace Place" I heard the message and later made comments to Bro. Marcus. He taught was from Ezra 9:8. At that time it wasn't known to him what was in my heart. Prior to, I had begun to study and to meditate on the faith of Abraham. The portion of the verse of Ezra 9:8 got my attention: *"And* *now for a **<u>little space grace</u>** hath been showed from the Lord our God, to leave us a remnant to escape, and to give us a nail in his holy place, that our God may lighten our eyes, and give us a little reviving in our bondage."* I realized that the approval to write this book was sanctioned by the words of this scripture.

It has been a pleasure to write, to express and to learn as I study the love of God.

His mercy is forever, and he has given us access to his grace by faith in his word. There is nothing too hard for God: he governs the impossible. But the journey of faith is to walk before him and to perfect all of his commands given to you. It is the life of Faith and Little Space Grace from God.

ACKNOWLEDGMENT

I would like to acknowledge and give thanks to God for all his benefits. Without God I could do nothing; neither could I have experienced love from others who have encouraged me along life's journey. Special thanks to my husband, Harold for keeping me on task. Thanks to my children, Nina /Albert, Nicholas/Elisha for their love and support. Also I am thankful for my siblings and other relatives that have always given me their kind thoughts. My thank s to all could fill this page, but they are from my heart. Thank You All!

BJ Smith

Contents

Introduction

My prayer is for you to gain spiritual increase in the things pertaining to your salvation. This book shares wisdom, knowledge and understanding of things that are most often taught and preached concerning faith and grace. Faith and grace abounds in every facet of your life. The focus of this book is to expound on the beauty of God's mercies and how faith grants access to the grace of God.

To me, the best example of the life of faith is learned from the chosen people of God known and recorded in the Bible. The scriptures provide to the readers and hearers of the God's word, doctrines, instructions, rebuke and corrections. The words of God furnish believers the right course to follow. Every book has an author, and so does Faith. This book teaches the origin of faith. It also teaches about hope; which is the anchor of faith. God's grace is mentioned many times: expressing to you his love and mercy. Grace is the reward of faith that is given because you keep his word.

Faith and Little Space Grace connects you to God and to his promises. The Believer is on a faith journey; and God grants his mercy along the way. The path is already foreordained and established by the wisdom of God. On the journey God has provided rescue, redemption, and restoration out of all the distresses experienced. This is His "little space grace' to the Believers: a little reviving along life's journey. Surely His goodness and the mercy will follow us all the days of our life.

"For by grace are ye saved through faith; and that
not yourselves: it is the gift of God."
Ephesians 2:8

This book presents to you the origin of faith which begins with the hearing of God's word. You will read about the father of faith, who is Abraham and his walk before God. The doctrine of faith is taught by the life Abraham lived and his experiences as a sojourner chosen by God. The word of God is his plan, purpose, preparation, proclamation, promise, place, performance, prosperity and his pleasure. Faith in God will establish his dwelling place in you.

FAITH AND THE REWARD

A Believer's walk with God is a journey of faith. Without faith it is impossible to please God. Believers adhere to the word of God, because they believe God is God. They learn that God is the Almighty and the Lord of all. Believers trust and rely on his promises, because they have hope in knowing God reward faith in him. Some people may think that by saying 'I believe God' makes it faith. But faith connects us to a relationship with God through his word. Faith is knowledge of him; and this knowledge is based on his word. The word is the substance of things pertaining to him. This kind of faith is evidence of things not seen. Things not seen are made possible by faith. The words of God give witness of the unseen. And the unseen is what the believer seeks after. Therefore, what is sought after is deliverance from sin, disease, suffering and distress. Rightly dividing the word of God, and applying the word to the situation, will bring deliverance.

Everybody love receiving a reward for the effort and time involved in a task they desire to see accomplished. Some may call the reward the goal desired. On a journey, the sojourner expectation is to arrive at the desired end by remaining stedfast and following the right path. God's grace is given to the humble: those who fear him and keep his commandments. His favor is the reward men will receive. When faith pleases God, "little space grace" is given.

Consider Abraham, the sojourner of faith; he was blessed to view the Promised Land. He looked for a city whose builder and maker is God. Throughout Abraham's life, because he pleased God, he obtained God's grace. Abraham received a measure of "little space grace" from God as he experienced situations in his life. He was called the father of faith; and God made him the father of many nations. Those who pattern after his obedience are called the children of Abraham by faith. God chose Abraham and his seed to be an example for all others to follow. *"Therefore being justified by faith, we have peace with God through our Lord Jesus Christ. By whom we have access by faith into this grace wherein we stand, and rejoice in hope of the glory of God."*

The faith journey leads to the Promised Land. What God has promised in his word can be obtained by faith. We have access to the grace of God by faith. As illustrated in the Scriptures, the children of Israel, who were Abraham's seed possessed the land of promise because they obeyed the command of God. This is God's grace place. A place obtained when we allow the word of God to direct our path. Every time the children of Israel came in subjection to a dilemma, it was the word of God they adhered to that delivered them. God is pleased with his dwelling place: for we are his temple that he desire to dwell in.

THE GRACE PLACE

*"And now for a **little space grace** hath been showed from the **LORD our God,** to leave us a **REMNANT** to escape, and to give us A NAIL in his Holy PLACE, that our God may lighten our eyes, and Give us a little Reviving in our bondage."* Ezra 9:8

The above scripture was written by the scribe Ezra. The children of Israel were reminded of God's mercy shown them. Around the year of 468 B.C. EZRA, who was "the priest and the scribe of the law of God," had returned from Babylon, among a small remnant of the children of Israel. Ezra's name means HELP. He served the people by advancing the people to pure worship in Jerusalem. As a priest, Ezra taught the laws of God handed down by Moses. He understood what a clean and acceptable worship unto God was. Ezra desired to return the children of Israel back to true worship. His efforts were not unfruitful; because he sought after the things of God, and found God's favor. God granted Ezra favor with king Artaxerxes, who made voluntary contributions out of his treasure to assist Ezra with those things needed to set up worship. The buying of sacrificial animals, grain and drink offerings was purchased with the king's money. Vessels for the temple service were delivered to Jerusalem. The need of additional funds could be obtained from the king's treasury. In preparing for worship, Ezra appointed magistrates and judges. That which Ezra sought to accomplish as a leader of the people, he first proclaimed a fast," *that we might afflict ourselves before God, to seek of him a RIGHT WAY for us, and for our little ones and for our substance.*" Ezra 8:21 After 70 years of the Babylonian Captivity, it would seem that the children of Israel had learned obedience to God. But 69 years after coming out of captivity, Israel began to intermingle and marry the pagan people of that land.

Ezra knew the old landmarks: the forefathers, the work and promises of God in the life of Abraham, Isaac and Jacob. The children of Israel were not ignorant as to why they had suffered greatly because of their own disobedience to God. But Ezra called the people to repentance and to return to the right way. Israel was in need of going back to the foundation that was established for them in the life of Abraham. They were to hear the instructions of father Abraham, and not to forsake the nurturing of the law which would crown them with grace from God. The wonderful works of God were wrought in Israel, because of His covenant made with Abraham.

> "*The Lord did not set his love upon you, nor choose you, because ye were more in number than any people: for ye are the fewest of all people.: But because the Lord loved you, and because he would keep the oath which he had sworn unto \your fathers, hath the Lord brought you out with a mighty hand, and redeemed you*

3

Out from the hand of Pharaoh King of Egypt. Know therefore that the Lord thy God, he is God, the faithful God, which keepeth covenant and mercy with them that love him and keep his commandments to a thousand generations."

Deuteronomy 6:7-9

DIVINE ASSISTANCE

Grace is FAVOR, entreaty; it is from the word 'make supplication' In other words, to bend or stoop in kindness to an inferior; *bestow.* (Move to favor by petition) be merciful; have pity on. The word little, is defined as something small in degree, amount number or condition. The word Space implies an interval of Time; (a duration of). Space is 1-2– or 3 dimensional> Distance, Area and Volume.

WHY God showed "little space Grace"? Note first of all, Jesus came to fulfill the Law and the Prophets. Various times in history, God spoke to the forefathers in different manners by the prophets. But in the fullness of times, He speaks to men by his Son, Jesus Christ. The space between the forefathers and Jesus aided men with the mercies of God. In each experience grace assisted man. The promises of God to Abraham were sure. *"For when God made promise to Abraham, because he could swear by no greater, he sware by himself, Saying, surely blessing I will bless thee, and multiplying I will multiply thee. And so, after he had patiently endured, he obtained the promise. For men verily swear by the greater: and an oath for confirmation is to them an end of all strife. Wherein God, willing more abundantly to show the heirs of promise the immutability of his counsel, confirmed it by an oath: That by two immutable things, in which it was impossible for God to lie, we might have a strong consolation, who have fled for refuge to lay hold upon the hope set before us: Which hope we have as an anchor of the soul, both sure and steadfast,* Hebrews 6:13-19

God kept Israel as the apple of His eye. In Judah was God known and His name was great in Israel. His great works delivered them out of all their distresses when they called upon him. *"Marvelous things did the Lord in the sight of their fathers, in the land of Egypt, in the field of Zoan. He divided the sea, and caused them to pass through: and he made the waters to stand as an heap, Behold, he smote the rock, that the waters gushed out, and the streams overflowed; For their heart was not right with him, neither were they steadfast in his covenant. But he, being full of compassion, forgave them their iniquity, and destroyed them not: yea, many a time he turned his anger away, and did not stir up all his wrath."* Psalm 78:12-13; vv. 20, 37-38 God is merciful and His mercy endureth forever. Every day in the life of men, God "little space grace" is given to redeem men out of their distress. This is His measure of mercy given to all people.

Jesus came to fulfill the promises of God. Grace is given because of obedience to the law or command of God. When his commandments are kept, God is pleased and he will reward. Therefore, the fulfilling of the law is to obey his law. Each law carries a promise of good and life. If the law is broken, the outcome is the suffering of evil and death. A transgressor is lost from the way that leads to life; he is in need of rescue, redemption, restoration and refuge. But where sin abound, the grace of God much more abounds. Faith gives access to the grace of God. And men will find redemption and deliverance because of his grace.

The Law said, *"Thou shalt not see thy brother's ox of his sheep go astray, and hide thyself from them: thou shalt in any case bring then again unto thy brother."* Deuteronomy 22:6. The good that come from this law is showing love to thy neighbor which pleases God. The act of Mercy was shown; and redemption happened.

The PROPHET said, "All *we like sheep have gone astray; we have turned everyone to his own way; and the LORD hath laid on him the iniquity of us all.*" Isaiah 53:6. The realization of knowing that one has strayed from the right course places the person in need of redemption, and salvation. The iniquities that lead us astray, Jesus have forgiven by taking the guilt upon him. He became the sacrifice for sin, to redeem us from under the law of sin and death. *"For the wages of sin is death; but the gift of God is eternal life through Jesus Christ our Lord."* Romans 6:23

JESUS said, *"For the Son of man is come to save that which was lost. How think you? If a man have a hundred sheep, and one of them be gone astray, doth he not leave the ninety and nine, and goeth into the mountain, and seeketh that which is gone astray? And if so be that he find it, verily I say unto you, he rejoiceth more of that sheep, than the ninety and nine which went not astray. Even so it is not the will of your Father which is in heaven, that one of these little ones should perish."* Matthew 18:10-14

The Apostle Paul said, *"For by GRACE are ye saved through faith; and that not of yourselves: it is the gift of God."* Ephesians 2:8. This gift came because the covenant was made with the father of faith, Abraham. (Read Genesis 17:1-14). God first changed his name from Abram, *which means* "exalted father" to Abraham, *which means,* "father of a multitude." All who are of faith are counted as the multitude of the children of Abraham. This is the plan of God to save all people through the promised seed: and that seed is Christ. God said, *"For a father of many nations <u>have I made thee</u>."* Notice the words are past tense; not the future tense, 'I will make thee'. This was God's sure word of prophecy: already established. "Have I made thee."

The Grace of God is the reward of Faith in God. The everlasting covenant God made with Abraham was the cause for God showing the people "a little space grace." "Many *times did he deliver them; but they provoked him with their counsel, and were brought low of their inequity. Nevertheless he regarded their affliction, when he heard their cry; and He remembered for them his COVENANT, and repented according to the multitude of his mercies. He made them also to be pitied of all those that carried them captives. Save us O Lord God, and gather us from among the heathen, to give thanks unto thy holy name, and to triumph in thy praise."* Psalm 106:43-47. The children of Israel fell captive to Babylon because

7

they transgressed the commandments and laws of God. They were in captivity 70 years for their sins. Moses prophesied to Israel that they would fall into this captivity. He spoke in the Book of Deuteronomy chapter 28, the blessings for obedience, and the punishment for disobedience.

"The Lord shall bring thee, and thy king which thou shalt set over thee, unto a nation which neither thou nor thy fathers have known; and there shalt thou serve other gods, wood and stone." The prophecy came to pass when the king of Babylon, Nebuchadnezzar besieged Jerusalem. He took Jehoiachin the king of Judah, the king's mother, the king's wives, and officers of the land. Also from Jerusalem were taken all the princes, all the mighty men of valor, craftsmen, and smiths; none remaining but the poorest sort of people.

Moses further said to the children of Israel, *"And among these nations shalt thou find no ease, neither shall the sole of thy foot have rest: but the Lord shall give thee there a trembling heart, and failing of eyes, and sorrow of mind: and thy life shall hang in doubt before thee; and thou shalt fear day and night, and shalt have none assurance of thy life. In the morning thou shalt say, Would to God it were even! And at even thou shalt say, Would to God it were morning! For the fear of thine heart wherewith thou shalt fear, and for the sight of thine eyes which thou shalt see. And the Lord shall bring thee into Egypt again with ships, by the way whereof I spake unto thee, Thou shalt see it no more again: and there ye shall be sold unto your enemies for bondmen and bondwomen, and no man shall buy you."* Deuteronomy 28:65-68. The prophecy is true: and in the time of Jeremiah, the prophecy came to pass. *"So they came into the land of Egypt: for they obeyed not the voice of the Lord: thus they came even unto Tahpanhes."* Jeremiah 43:7

Jeremiah warned the people that destruction was coming from the north; implying that Nebuchadnezzar, king of Babylon will come and smite the land of Egypt. You may ask, why the land of Egypt? The children of Israel had called on Egypt for help. Isaiah said, *"Woe to them that go down to Egypt for help; and stay on horses, and trust in chariots, because they are many; and in horsemen, because they are strong; but they look not unto the Holy One of Israel, neither seek the Lord! Yet he also is wise, and will bring evil, and will not call back his words: but will arise against the house of evildoers, and against the help of them that work iniquity. Now the Egyptians are men, and not God; and their horses flesh, and not spirit. When the Lord shall stretch out his hand, both he that helpeth shall fall, and he that is helped shall fall down, and they shall fail together."* Isaiah 31:1-3.

The captivity of Judah occurred more than one-hundred years after Isaiah spoke this prophecy. Years later Jeremiah prophesied, saying, *"O thou daughter dwelling in Egypt, furnish thyself to go into captivity: for <u>Noph</u> shall be waste and desolate without an inhabitant."* And the Prophet said, *Egypt is like a very fair heifer, but destruction cometh; it cometh out of the north."* Jeremiah 46:19-20

The city of Noph in the Hebrew scripture is the name for Memphis; an ancient Egyptian city. The metaphor, *"very fair heifer"* was to remind Israel of the acceptable sacrifice they once offered to God. The heifer was selected as a sacrifice for sin offerings and for guilt offerings. Judah did not recognize nor take heed to the message given to them. Israel once bowed down to the sacrifices offered unto God. In Egypt, Israel served other gods: symbolized as the fair heifer. Israel had backslidden from true worship. God brought judgment upon Egypt by sending Nebuchadnezzar against Egypt. Judah became captives in Babylon resulting from this destruction of Egypt. Jeremiah said, *"The daughter of Egypt shall be confounded; she shall be delivered into the hand of the people of the north. The Lord of hosts, the God of Israel, saith; Behold, I will punish the multitude of No, and Pharaoh, and Egypt, with their gods, and their kings; even Pharaoh, and all them that trust in him. And I will deliver them into the hand of those that seek their lives, and into the hand of Nebuchadnezzar king of Babylon, and into the hand of his servants: and afterward it shall be inhabited, as in the days of old, saith the Lord."* Jeremiah 46:24-26

But God is faithful to his promises. He did not totally forsake his people. As Jeremiah concluded in his prophecy, he said, *"Fear thou not, O Jacob my servant, saith the Lord: for I am with thee; for I will make a full end of all the nations whither I have driven thee: but I will not make a full end of thee, but correct thee in measure: yet will I not leave thee wholly unpunished."* Jeremiah 46:28

God's "little space grace" kept Israel from being totally destroyed. This was the mercy and promise of God. God remembered his covenant with Abraham: and because God is faithful, Israel was redeemed. In the day of her redemption, Israel shall sing unto the Lord this praise: *"And in that day thou shalt say, O Lord, I will praise thee: though thou wast angry with me, thine anger is turned away, and thou comfortedst me. Behold, God is my salvation' I will trust, and be not afraid: for the Lord Jehovah is my strength and my Song; he also is become my salvation. Therefore with joy ye draw water out of the wells of salvation."* Isaiah 12:1-3 Notice, the wells are plural in the above verse of Scripture. Wells of water satisfy thirst; the implication is that there are many places and situations in life the sojourner of faith will need "little space grace. Water is a little reviving and restoration for the soul. Recall, David said, *"The Lord is my shepherd; I shall not want. He maketh me to lie down in green pastures: le leadeth me beside the still waters. He restoreth my soul."*....Psalm 23:1-3. The children of God will find the waters of salvation. Thirst is satisfied by daily drinking water to live by. We know that water refreshes and restores the soul. Faith allows us to draw spiritual water from the wells of salvation.

God's grace place is sought after by the sojourners of faith. In his place, there is redemption, restoration and a little reviving for the soul. By his word we are lead in the pathway of his righteousness. He maketh us to rest in green pastures: comforting us along the way. God has prepared for us his laws to partake of; so that we might overcome the enemy. Jesus said, "Give us this day our daily bread." In another place he said, "Man shall not live by bread alone, but by every word that proceedeth out of the mouth of God." His goodness and mercy follows us ever day of our life. To walk before him and to know that his protection surrounds us is to know his grace place.

Grace is God's Divine assistance to the sojourner of faith. He has provided all things pertaining to life and good for us.

HIS MERCY

Mercy with a Purpose: *"to leave us a remnant to escape, and to give us a nail in his holy place,"* Ezra spoke these words to the children of Israel. They returned to Jerusalem from Babylonian captivity to rebuilt Jerusalem again. The people were reminded that they, *"were bondmen, yet our God hath not forsaken us in bondage, but hath <u>extended mercy </u>unto us in the sight of the kings of Persia, to give us a reviving, to set up the house of God, and to repair the desolations thereof, and to give us a wall in Judah and in Jerusalem."* Ezra 9:9. What a beautiful discourse to hear after seventy long years of suffering. Judah had lost her kingly dynasty, her city, the temple and the wall that stood as a sign of God's protection over Israel. The captives were no more in captivity; but free to reestablish their lives in Jerusalem. The purpose for mercy placed within Judah the spirit to rebuild. That which has been downcast is weakening, without strength and no courage to go forth. Mercy revived the spirit of Judah; and gave Judah courage and strength to follow the commandments of the Lord. Mercy left Judah, a remnant who was delivered or escaped. Mercy extended herself to Judah; but mercy required gratitude in returns. Gratitude encompasses the full measure of giving thanks. Judah was obliged to repair the desolate city, the wall and the temple of Jerusalem. Following Ezra's message, the praises Judah would show the Lord, reflected his glory in them. Obedience to the will of God caused Judah to shine forth his accomplished work in them.

Mercy left a Remnant: After years of suffering, it was good news to know that a remnant was left. Judah' life was not totally consumed and taken way. Judah was the remnant left of Israel. They knew that God preserved them and kept his promise to them. Returning to Jerusalem, the seed of Abraham would have the opportunity to become fruitful, multiply, replenish, subdue and have dominion once again. Their experience taught Israel the love of God, his care, protection and deliverance. These things they should have learned and kept in their hearts. But they turned to the other gods and fell into judgment from God. To be the remnant made Judah see themselves as separated ones; special unto God. Mercy left a Remnant was the act of God staying his hands against Israel for full destruction of his people. It was in his power to do so; but it was his word which he upheld. *"For thou shalt break forth on the right hand and on the left; and thy seed shall inherit the Gentiles, and make the desolate cities to be inhabited. Fear not; for thou SHALT not be ashamed: neither are thou confounded; for thou shalt forget the shame of thou youth, and shalt not remember the reproach of thy widowhood any more. For thy Maker is thing husband; the Lord of hosts is his name; and thy Redeemer the Holy One of Israel; the God of the whole earth shall he be called. For the Lord hath called thee as a woman forsaken and grieved in spirit, and a wife of youth, when thou wast refused, saith thy God. For a small moment have I forsaken thee; but with great mercies will I gather thee. In a little wrath I hid my face from thee for a moment; but with everlasting kindness will I have mercy on thee, saith the Lord thy Redeemer."* Isaiah 54:2-8

Mercy Established God's Presence: Not only does Mercy have a purpose, but mercy brings together God and his people. If there had been any doubt from Judah that God had forsaken them, mercy changed the thought. Judah probably had horrific thoughts in their mind during the seventy years of captivity. They suffered mental distress because of the great lost of their land, families and their goods. Judah lost out with God; they lost their liberty of religion and their position among the heathens. Reputation, health, prestige, and freedom of enterprise were all lost by the devastating judgment of God upon Judah. Their spirits brought low; they were without hope as to a helper other than God. They were like a person placed in a dungeon with no redeemer to rescue them. But after seventy years of captivity, Judah was to understand the *"little space grace"* given them. Mercy had given them strength and courage to rebuild Jerusalem. Then mercy put within their mind assurance and confidence. Ezra said to them concerning mercy," *to give us a nail in his holy place"* The Nail was used in building to fasten together, so that the building become fashioned. They realized that the nail helped in establishing the building. The nail in his holy place alludes to God's dwelling place, His Temple. Judah knew that the holy place was where sacrifice and worship to God was held. They knew that God's presence is in his holy place. The nail assured Judah that mercy directed them to the presence of God. *"Therefore say, thus saith the Lord God; although I have cast them far off among the heathen, and although I have scattered them among the countries, yet will I be to them **a little sanctuary** in the countries where they shall come."* Ezekiel 11:16. God's dwelling place is in man. His mercy connects us to his presence.

Mercy Restoreth: Mercy is the love passion of God for his creation; mercy bonds God to men. His love is great, his love is virtuous, pure and the effective life giver, forever abounding towards men. Therefore, mercy works to restore that which is turned out of the way. Restoration is God's ministry of healing, which repairs and renew again. This is why Jesus did healings and cures; he was restoring that which was bruised, broken, diseased and in captivity. Jesus came to seek and to save that which was lost. Mercy brings the transgressor back to the former condition of the relationship God ordained for man in the beginning. A person may be a sinner, who hasn't known the gospel of salvation. All have sinned and came short of the glory of God. Mercy works without respect of person, to give life to all. The sin condition is the condition resulted from the transgression of Adam. Because of sin, people experiences pain, sorrow and death. Before Adam transgressed, he had no mental, emotional or physical discomfort. All things were provided for him; he was not in want, or desiring to pursue something out side of Eden. He was living a blissful life until he disobeyed the command of God. Sin caused enmity, the separator that breaks the fellowship men should have with God. In the day of Adam and Eve, God prophesied the Seed shall come and rule over the power of the serpent. The first time revealed in scripture, the **true mercy** of God. Transgression was committed in Eden; but by the grace of God sin would be done away with. The word went forth from God to give men hope for a restoration. The grace of God came through Jesus; the manifestation of the word of God that was spoken to Adam. *"And I will put enmity between thee and the woman, and between thy seed and her wed; it shall bruise thy head, and thou shalt bruise his head."* Genesis 3:15 God revealed to Adam the conflict of good and evil and the victory over the enmity through Christ. This word is the gospel of salvation: his mercy bringing restoration. Men were sold under sin through Adam's transgression; but redeemed from sin by the mercy of God. From that time in the history of Adam, the chief corner stone was set in place for the building of God's house. The word is the stone that the builders rejected, but that stone became the head of the corner. The Stone is Christ, who was with Moses and the children of Israel in the wilderness. The stone altar Abraham bowed and submitted to God is the symbolic stone, who is Christ. *"And he removed from thence unto a mountain on the east of Bethel, and pitched his tent, having Bethel on the west, and Hai on the east: and there he builded an altar unto the Lord, and called upon the name of the Lord."* Genesis 12:8 Jacob later built himself an altar of stone and called that place Bethel. *"And Jacob rose up early in the morning, and took the stone that he had put for his pillows, and let it up for a pillar, and poured oil upon the top of it. And he called the name of that place Bethel: but the name of that city was called Luz at the first. And Jacob vowed a vow, saying, If God will be with me, and will keep me in this way that I go, and will give me bread to eat, and raiment to put on, So that I come again to my father's house in peace; then shall the Lord be my God: And this stone, which I have set for a pillar, shall be God's house: and of all that thou shalt give me I will surely give the tenth unto thee."* Genesis 28:18-22

The wisdom of God was setting in place his word for the building of his dwelling place. The chief corner stone was laid in the beginning.

From that time onward, God spoke to the men of old. These men became precious stones in the building of his word in the earth.

The true mercy of God upholds his word: for he is not a man that speaks a lie. God assures men through his word that he never fails. The sufferings experienced by people do not negate or disallow his tender mercies. Many suffer because of unbelief: ignorant of the word of God, or disobedience to the word. The children of Israel did not go unpunished, but on the other hand, they also were not without hope for the mercies of God. In understanding true mercy it should greatly increase a person's faith. True mercies will impact the heart with confidence that God is love and a life giver. He restoreth the soul, the broken hearted, he sets the captives free and he give sight to the blind. His restoration work will heal, because his grace is sufficient in all the conditions of living.

Now the gift of God and the mercy of God for salvation to all men is Jesus Christ. God's word is fulfilled in Christ. After he had risen from the dead, he said, *"Father, the hour is come; glorify thy Son, that thy Son also may glorify thee: As thou hast given him power over all flesh, that he should give eternal life to as many as thou hast given him. And this is life eternal, that they might know thee the only true God, and Jesus Christ, whom thou hast sent."* **John 17:2-3** He fulfilled the promise of salvation; and he brought men into fellowship with God. His Mercy restoreth our souls.

4

"To Alter It. . ."

The time line of human life continues since Adam: God's little space grace always abounding with men from generation to generation. With Ezra's ministry, he called on the children of Israel to true worship after 70 years of freedom from their captivity. He taught Israel that little space grace by God was shown them. To the Gentiles around them, Israel may have been looked on as the forsaken; but they were God's remnant that returned. The prophecy spoken by Isaiah came to pass; *"And it shall come to pass in that day, that the remnant of Israel, and such as are escaped of the House of Jacob, shall no more again stay upon him that smote them; but shall stay upon the Lord, the Holy One of Israel, in truth."* Isaiah 10:20

Ezra wanted the Jews to realize that they were redeemed by God's grace. Moses said to the people, *"For thou art an holy people unto the Lord thy God: the Lord thy God hath chosen thee to be a* special people *unto himself, above all people that are upon the face of the earth.. The Lord did not set his love upon you, nor choose you, because ye were more in number than any people; for ye were fewest of all people: But because the Lord loved you, and because he would keep the oath which he had sworn unto your fathers, hath the Lord brought you out with a mighty hand, and redeemed you out of the house of bondmen"* Deuteronomy 7:7-8 Remember, the fathers are Abraham, Isaac & Jacob.

Many times the children of Israel were reminded of God's wonderful works which delivered them and led them along the way. Moses said, *"But because the Lord Loved you, and because he would keep the oath which he had sworn unto your fathers, hath the Lord brought you* *out with a mighty hand, and redeemed you out of the house of bondmen, from the hand of Pharaoh king of Egypt. Know therefore that the Lord thy God, he is GOD, the **faithful God,** which keepeth COVENANT and MERCY with them that love him and keep his commandments to a thousand generations.*" Deuteronomy 7:6-9 Read: Psalm 105:8-10 Luke 1:55, 72 Exodus 32:13-14 Hebrews 6:13-20

EZRA knew of the promises God made with Abraham, Isaac and Jacob. God promised to establish the covenant he made with Abraham and his children after him for an everlasting covenant. When a contract is made between two parties; usually a consideration of equal value is the bargaining chip for trade. Ask the question; what did Abraham have to trade with? The word TRADE is used in commerce; for the exchange of goods. Moses in the law said,

"*. . . And if it be a beast, wherefore men bring an offering unto the Lord, all that any man giveth of such unto the Lord shall be holy. He shall not **alter it**, nor change it, a good for a bad, or a bad for a good: and if he shall at all change beast for beast, then it and the exchange thereof shall be holy.*" The principle of this law is that the offering's value must be holy unto the Lord. Faith is the thing that pleases God: it is a true offering unto the Lord in worshipping him. By faith, "*we have access unto this Grace.*" By grace are *we saved through Faith*," Read the following scriptures; → Leviticus 27:9-10 Romans 5:2 Ephesians 2:8

In The Book of Ezekiel, the prophet said, "*And they shall not sell of it, neither exchange, nor alienate the first fruits of the land: for it is holy unto the Lord.*" Ezekiel 48:14. The first fruits of the land is increase: a parallel to the Blessings God spoke of in creation. "*Be fruitful, multiply, replenish, subdue and have dominion over the earth.*" Genesis 1:28. God said he, "*will establish his covenant*" made with Abraham: the Promised SEED. Without the seed, there are no Firstfruits or increase. Jesus said, "*Verily, verily, I say unto you, except a corn of wheat fall into the ground and die, it abideth alone: but if it die, it bringeth forth 'much' fruit*" {many nations}. John 12:24

It is written, *"They shall NOT SELL of it."* In Hebrew, the word sells [makar] *means, lit. Like as a merchandise, a daughter in marriage, into slavery)* or fig. *To surrender* Is a form of selling. The children of Israel violated God's law by intermingling marriage with the nations of the land? The prophet said, *"neither exchange" The Hebrew word meaning,* **to alter**; by implication to *barter, to dispose of; to* remove.

Did the people alter the word of God? The Prophet Isaiah said, *"Wherefore the Lord said, Forasmuch as this people draw near me with their mouth, and with their lips do honor me, but have REMOVED their heart far from me, and their fear toward me is taught by the precepts* {doctrines} *of men."* Isaiah 29:13. Today this kind of practice of religious exchanging of God's word is known.

The damnable doctrine of men, church covenants, ceremonial rites, creeds and codes alters the "Holy Covenant" of God. The first commandments of the law said, *"Thou shalt have no other gods before me. Thou shalt not make unto thee any graven image* (church ordinances or church by-laws, so to speak) *or any likeness of anything that is in the heaven above,* {mythology, horoscope,} *or that is in the earth beneath,* {all sort of earthly images} *or that is in the water under the earth."* (Many heathens worshipped fish and the power of the waters.) *Thou shalt not bow down thyself to them, nor serve them:* {submit to them, serve them, make alliance with them} for *I the Lord thy God is a Jealous God, visiting the iniquity of the fathers upon the children unto the third and fourth generation of them that hate me;"* Exodus 20:3-6 But God will show MERCY unto thousands of those who "LOVE ME, and KEEP MY COMMANDMENTS."

The blessing of Abraham, «a father of many nations" READ: Galatians 3:14-16. To alter the word of God: *"Men going about to establish their own righteousness; and have not submitted themselves unto the righteousness of God."* Romans 10:3-8. But the Firstfruits of God are produced from the word of God. Jesus Christ, who is the Firstfruits, was resurrected after obeying the word of God. Jesus said, "I come to do the will of my Father." And the voice from heaven said, "This is my Beloved Son, in him I am well pleased."

In the Book of Jeremiah, it is written, *"The priest said not, where is the Lord? And they that handle the law knew me not: the pastors also transgress against me, and the prophets prophesied by Baal, and walked after things that do not profit.* {In commerce, profit is the term used} *Wherefore I will yet plead with you, saith the Lord, and with your children's children will I plead. For pass over the isles of Chittim, and see; and send unto Kedar, and consider diligently, and see if there be such a thing. Hath a nation changed their gods, which are yet no gods? But my people have changed their glory for that which doth not **profit**. Be astonished O ye heavens, at this, and be horribly afraid, be ye very desolate, saith the Lord. For my people have committed two evils; they have forsaken me, the fountain of "living waters," Jeremiah* 17:13. This scripture support Ezra proclamation for true worship in Israel.

Israel Committed 2-Evils: Jeremiah 2: 8-14; 17:13 *"They that trust in their wealth, and boast themselves in the multitude of their riches; None of them can by any means redeem his brother, nor give to God a ransom for him: For the redemption of their soul is precious, and it ceaseth forever: That he should still live forever, and not see corruption." But God will redeem my soul from the power of the grave: for he shall receive me."* Read: Psalm 49: 6-9 & 15

Jesus said, *"Whosoever will come after me, let him deny himself, and take up his cross, and follow me. For whosoever will save his life shall lose it; but whosoever shall lose his life for my sake and the gospel's, the same shall save it. For what shall it **profit** a man, if he shall gain the whole world, and lose his own soul? Or what shall a man give in exchange for his soul?* Mark 8:34-37

The prophet said, *"Nor alienate the first fruits of the land,"* The Hebrew word for alienate_is Abar→ *and used widely of any transition:* by definition, To cross over; To cover; deliver, do away, escape, fail, get over, go beyond, go away, go forth, proclamation, perish, provoke to anger; raiser of taxes, <u>remove,</u> take away, <u>make to transgress,</u> translate, <u>turn away.</u>

Notice, the words that defines the word <u>alienates;</u> these words also reflect the transgressions of the children of Israel. Another expression of the word alienate, is to commit TREASON; and treason is a betrayal of trust. Malachi spoke of a conspiracy found with the children of Israel. They committed treason by turning away from the things of God. Read Malachi chapter two, and note what was spoken concerning the treacherous acts of the priesthood. And the prophet Jeremiah said, *"And the Lord said unto me, A <u>conspiracy</u> is found among the men of Judah, and among the inhabitants of Jerusalem. They are turned back* [the act of alienating] to *the iniquities of their forefathers, which refused to hear my words; and they went after other gods to serve them:* ↔ [they committed treason; they were traders] the *house of Israel and the house of Judah have broken my covenant which I made with their fathers."* READ: Jeremiah 11:9-11; Malachi 2:11-17; Ezra 10:1-5. The children of Israel played the harlot; they committed spiritual adultery. The priests of God were to teach the law to Israel.

Malachi pleaded with the priests, saying, *"And ye shall know that I have sent this commandment unto you that my covenant might be with Levi, "My covenant was with him of life and peace; and I gave them to him for the fear wherewith he feared me, and was afraid before my name. The law of truth was in his mouth, and inequity was not found in his lips: he walked with me in peace and equity, and did turn many away from iniquity. For the priest's lips should keep knowledge, and they should seek the law at his mouth: for he is the messenger of the Lord of hosts. But ye are departed out of the way; ye have caused many to stumble at the law; ye have corrupted the covenant of the Levi, saith the Lord of hosts. Therefore have I also made you contemptible and base before all the people, according as ye have not kept my ways, but have been partial in the law. "Judah hath dealt treacherously, and an abomination is committed in Israel and in Jerusalem; for Judah hath profaned the holiness of the Lord which he loved, and hath married the daughter of a strange god, "For the Lord, the God of Israel saith that he hateth putting away: for one covereth violence with his garment, saith the Lord of hosts: therefore take heed to your spirit, that ye deal not treacherously."* Malachi 2:4-16

Malachi was the last Old Testament prophet of scripture. He called upon Israel to take heed to the commandments of the law. Malachi also prophesied that a messenger will come; preparing the way of the Lord. Four-hundred years after Malachi, John the Baptist came preaching repentance and remission of sins. Israel was the people of God who had gone astray. In the time of Malachi, Israel dealt treacherously and committed abominations against the holy covenant of God. *"Behold, I will send you Elijah the prophet before the coming of the great and dreadful day of the Lord: And he shall turn the heart of the fathers to the children, and the heart of the children to their fathers, lest I come and smith the earth with a curse."* Malachi 2:5-6. And Jesus said *"For all prophets and the law prophesied until John. And if ye will receive it, this is* ELIJAH, *which was for to come."* Matthew 11:13-14

5

ORDAINED

Many events in the Bible will teach men that "Little Space Grace" was shown by God to his people. One reason for his grace is because God is faithful to his promises: he cannot lie. 'Heaven and earth may pass away, but His word will remain.' When the covenant was made with Abraham, God said that he will ESTABLISH it forever. READ: Genesis 12: 3; 17:7; 18:18; 22:18; 22: 2-5; 28:13-22; Acts 3:11-26 closely read verses 24-26; Galatians 3: 7-9 Genesis 18: 3-5 Genesis 24: 42-44 1Kings 17: 8-24; 2Kings 4: 8-17; Ezekiel 11: 16-17; John 13:35; & 14: 15-21 Acts 1:7-10; John 16: 5-16; The Hebrew word establish is *quwm* [koom] >> *To rise — abide, accomplish, confirm, continue, decree, endure, enjoin, get up, make good, help, lift up, make newly, perform, pitch, raise up, rear up, ordain, set up, stand up, stir up, strengthen, succeed, uphold.* The merciful acts of God are seen in the words describing, "God will ESTABLISH it"

To establish a thing, there must be a plan to accomplish the desired goal. Foundation is the ground work for the Builder to construct his work. God chose Abraham to establish his plan of salvation. Abraham was the foundation to the children of Israel; the origin of their lives. The work God performed will create children of faith through Abraham. He believed God, and it was accounted unto him as righteousness. He was called "The Father of Faith." The things Abraham encountered, illustrated the plan of God; God's "Little Space Grace" and mercy was with him throughout his faith journey. His mercy followed Abraham, and gave him hope in the promise of God as he walked before him.

Abraham's experiences prophetically illustrated the destiny of the children of Israel. The children of Israel were in the loins of their father, Abraham. To understand the plan of God working in Abraham, envision the process of human fertilization. With conception, things are growing and developing for the purpose of coming to maturity, [birth]. Understand what happens in the womb. MOVEMENT - MOTION - ACTION these are the activities of the word in the earth; in particularly, in Abraham's heart and his faith walk.

The early stage of producing children of faith; the seed or word of God was planted in Abraham. Surely, movement was the greater part of Abraham's faith journey. He left his homeland; travelled to various places, sojourning as God led him. Each experience strengthened his character, and added to his faith virtues of righteousness.

God said unto him, *"Get thee out of thy country, and from thy kindred and from thy father's house, unto a land that I will show thee." "And Abram took Sarai his wife, and Lot his brother's son, and their substance that they gathered, gotten in Haran; and they went forth to go into the land of Canaan;"* Genesis 12: 1 & 5 Abraham moved from the land of Ur; and this move was his early response to the voice of the Lord. He went on a journey that was directed by God. In this scripture, the MOTION words of action with Abraham are, Get thee out; unto a land; they went forth; God's word can be compared like the human germ cell. It is microscopic in size (too *small for the eye to see*) but it is the substance of things hoped for. Spiritually so, in the heart the process of germinating God's plan is at work. His covenant made with Abraham was being fashioned. God sent out his word to accomplish his will. The word activity was in motion. To *"get thee out,"* to move Abraham from the place he was in. *"Unto a land"* pointed Abraham in the direction he should follow: showing motion was happening. *"They went forth"* obedience to the word was the motion. The same land Abraham went to was the land the children of Israel possessed. When the human egg is fertilized, it travels in the womb and makes a bed to begin its growth. In the womb is growth, and being nourished until the appointed time. The promises of God to Abraham were being fertilized by every movement that brought Abraham unto the PLACE he sojourned to. He was called a Hebrew; this word means, sojourner, or to cross over. Abraham was a foreigner or traveller. The scriptures testify of his movement upon the land: the motion that kept alive the word that would come to pass. *"By faith Abraham, when he was called to go out into a place which he should after receive for an inheritance obeyed: and he went out, not knowing whether he went."* Hebrews 11:8

Abraham and the PLACE called Egypt

While in Canaan, Abraham experienced a grievous famine. He left Canaan and went south. In his sojourning, Abraham and his wife went to Egypt to be sustained there. The reason Abraham went to Egypt was because there was no food or substance in the land of Canaan. This motion led to another degree of God's plan forming in Abraham's life. God told Abraham that his seed would be servants in the land of Egypt. Abraham's seed entered the land by the selling of Joseph the son of Jacob in Egypt. There was a famine in the land in Joseph day. The dream of the Egyptian Pharaoh was how God remembered Joseph affliction. God revealed the interpretation of the dream to Joseph. There would be seven years of plenty and the seven years of lean. Joseph had favor with the king, and became the second man in his kingdom. Joseph managed the affairs of preparing the land to survive the famine. The famine was God's plan to bring the seed of Abraham into Egypt: and in so doing, the prophecy of Genesis 15:13-16 was fulfilled. But what happened in Egypt with Abraham and Sarah was a similitude of God's deliverance. Faith was traveling the path by which the word of God would come to pass. The deliverance of the children of Israel out of Egypt happened 400 years later. Read about the dream Joseph interpreted. Genesis 41:15-36; *Pharaoh made Joseph a Ruler:* Genesis 41:37;

WHILE IN EGYPT:

1. The people admired Sarah's beauty.
2. The princes of Pharaoh chose Sarah to be in Pharaoh's house.
3. For Sarah's sake, Pharaoh entreated Abraham well.
4. God brought plagues on Pharaoh and his house because of Sarah, Abraham's wife.

Abraham experience in Egypt: Genesis 12:10-20 Pharaoh governed Egypt; and his ruling was not by laws, but rather by his decree to have things done. As Abraham entered Egypt, he considered Sarah's beauty; and that the Egyptians would desire to kill him and take her. He said to Sarah, *"Say, I pray thee, thou art my sister: that it may be well with me for thy sake; and my soul shall live because of thee."* Many comments are made about Abraham hiding his marriage relationship of his wife. As a man of faith, his words were prophetic. He knew Sarah would become a bondwoman in Pharaoh's house. But Sarah was not to be in bondage to another. During the time in Abraham's life, it was not mentioned that God told him to travel to Egypt. But there are times when the integrity of a man's heart will guide him in the right choice to make. His faith didn't waver because he left the land of promise to seek food in Egypt. As a provider for his home, he sought to sustain his wife and nephew. The situation he was in at the time did not shake his faith. The grace of God was with him because of his faith. Someone may ask why God didn't have Abraham to remain in Canaan during the famine. The famine caused Canaan to be a barren place. Canaan was a land of heathen rulers and the other nations of people lived there. The Sojourner of Faith left Canaan typified the trying of his faith working patience. Longsuffering is experienced when on a journey. Faith is more than just a confession of belief. With faith, there will come a time of trials to test the love of God in you. But faith is strengthened by patience, experience and hope. Patience was a virtue added to Abraham on his journey.

Sarah, as a type of the "freewoman" *For Jerusalem from above is free, "which is the mother of us all."* Sarah is represented as Jerusalem:

and in the Book of Revelation, New Jerusalem is the city of God. The promise of God to Abraham, God said that Sarah will be the mother of nations. Abraham promised son came through his wife Sarah. Abraham referred to Sarah as his sister because he believed God would make her the mother of nations through him. A sister is a member of the same family: Sarah was both a sister to Abraham in the flesh as well as a sister in the spiritual kingdom of God. In the kingdom of God, Jesus said, *"Ye do err, not knowing the Scriptures, nor the power of God. For in the resurrection they neither marry, nor are given in marriage, but are as the angels of God in heaven."* Matthew 22:29-30. Some preachers judged Abraham to have told a lie. They err in not understanding the mystery or plan of God, or the purpose of his work. God works everything after the counsel of his own will. Read about *"The Freewoman"* from Galatians 4: 22-27; Hebrews 12:22; Romans 7:1-2; Sarah! Read Genesis 17:19

Faith in Abraham's heart prevented a deferment of the promise. He said to Sarah, *"that it may be well with me for thy sake; and my soul shall live because of thee."* This was a strong word of prophecy; the words "shall live" are future tense. The first time the word 'Prophet' appeared in Scripture was when God called Abraham a prophet. The word of God in Abraham enabled him to speak a "sure word of prophecy." This prophetic statement anchored hope in Abraham concerning the things God promised him. If Abraham's HOPE had been deferred, then there would also have been a forfeiting of the covenant promise of God. But Faith" is the substance of things hoped for…" Read about A Sure Word 2Peter 1:19; Genesis 12:13; God remembered Luke 1: 69-74; Hebrews 6:13–19; "God Confirmed His Oath Genesis 26: 1-5; Genesis 28: 10-14; Genesis 35: 9-15; St. Luke 1: 71-75; Hebrews 6: 17-18;

> **HOPE deferred maketh the <u>heart</u> sick: but when the desire cometh, it is *A TREE of LIFE*."** Proverbs 13:12

Sarah obeyed the voice of her husband. She honored his judgment and submitted to his request. Sarah is honored in the New Testament in

Apostle Peter's letter to the early church. His advice to the wives and husbands: "Likewise, *ye wives, be in subjection to your own husbands; that, if any obey not the word, they also may without the word be won by the conversation of the wives;* (the **conversation** is a person life style or character.) *While they behold your <u>chaste conversation</u> <u>coupled</u> with fear. Whose adorning let it not be that outward adorning of plaiting the hair, and wearing of gold, or of putting on of apparel; But let it be the hidden man of the heart, in that which is not corruptible, even the ornament of a meek and quiet spirit, which is in the sight of God of great price. For after this manner in the old time the holy women also, who trusted in God, adorned themselves, being in subjection unto their own husbands: Even as Sarah obeyed Abraham, calling him lord: whose daughters ye are, as long as ye do well, and are not afraid with any amazement. Likewise, ye husbands, dwell with them according to knowledge, giving honor unto the wife, as unto the weaker vessel, and as being **heirs together of the GRACE of life**; that your prayers be not hindered.*" 1 Peter 3:1-6. In this passage of scripture, Abraham was justified in calling Sarah his sister: they are heirs together of the Grace of Life. In Paul's teachings, he said, *"Wives, Submit yourselves unto your own husbands, as unto the Lord. For the husband is the head of the wife, even as Christ is the head of the church: and he is the SAVIOR of the body.* (Like Abraham, Sarah was his wife) *Therefore as the church is subject unto Christ, so let the wives (be) to their own husbands in everything."* Ephesians 5: 22-24

"O ye seed of Abraham his servant, ye children of Jacob his chosen. He is the Lord our GOD: his judgments are in all the earth. He hath remembered his COVENANT forever, the word which he commanded to a thousand generations. Which COVENANT he made with Abraham and his oath unto Isaac; and confirmed the same unto Jacob for a law and to Israel for an everlasting covenant: Saying, unto thee will I give the land of Canaan, the lot of your inheritance: When they were but a few men in number; yea, very few, and strangers in it. When they went from one nation to another, from one kingdom to another people; He suffered NO MAN to do them wrong: yea, he reproved kings for their sakes; Saying, Touch not mine

anointed, and do my prophets no harm." Psalm 105: 6-15 **Scriptures:** Hosea 12: 12-13; Genesis 28:5 & 29: 20, 28; Deuteronomy 26:5; Genesis 43: 1-9; 45: 45:

"SARAH'S BEAUTY"

"The Egyptians beheld the woman that she was "very fair." The natural beauty of a woman would mean that she has no flaws, no wrinkles, no spots or blemishes. Her beauty would be pleasing to the eye and a delight to the heart. The woman being **"very fair"** is a reflection, and foreshadows the Bride of Christ. God saw his finished work; the Bride of the Lamb in the likeness of Sarah's Beauty. The activity of God's word in motion in Sarah's life, but not yet fulfilled. As we will learn from the covenant God made with Abraham, included God's selection of Sarah as the "mother of all nations." Genesis 17: 19-21. The blessings of Abraham, being the father of many nations are how God granted salvation to all men through Abraham. Sarah is represented in scripture as "Jerusalem" King David called Jerusalem, his city 'ZION' → 1Kings 8:1; 2Chronicles 5:2 Psalm 2: 6-7; ZION is the city of God. Jerusalem is from above, "the mother of us all." Abraham's Sarah will be the mother of all nations. All people of the faith of Abraham is Blessed with the inheritance promised him; who is Christ in you the hope of glory. ——>

THE GLORY of ZION *Psalm 48: 1-14*

"Great is the Lord, and greatly to be praised in the city of our GOD, in the mountain of his holiness. BEAUTIFUL for situation, the joy of the whole earth is mount ZION, on the sides of the north, the city of the great King. "God is known in all her palaces for a refuge. For, lo, the kings were assembled, they passed by together. They saw it, and so they marveled: they were troubled and hasted away." Continue reading to verse 14; Read: Genesis 12:14-17

Notice the word <u>Beautiful</u> in this scripture in the left hand box. Then consider the words spoken by the Egyptians concerning Sarah. **"The woman was very fair."** The spiritual implication is that God saw,

"That he might sanctify and cleanse it, (the church which is the bride of Christ) *with the washing of water by the word* {the WORD is Christ} read John 1:14 *That he might present it to himself a **glorious church, not having spot, or wrinkle, or any such thing: But that it should be HOLY and without blemish."** Ephesians 5:26-27

The glorious church will be seen in her Beauty; complete and made ready, as a woman adorned for her husband. The church will appear with Christ when he returns to set his kingdom in the earth. The Spirit of God revealed to man his plan and his accomplished work. His word is sure; the substance of what he desires: known in types and shadows. Many accounts in the Old Testament were foreshadowing the heavenly things of God. But faith is the evidence of things to be revealed. Ephesians 5:26-27

Events in the life of Abraham were the foundational spiritual stages of development; Christ is the Seed, who came the 4th-millenium day to fulfill the covenant promised. Abraham was more than 2-millenium days from Christ. God allowed a time period given to create a people. Then the people were a number large enough to be called a city. The people were the children of Israel. Jesus came to fulfill the "law and the prophets." **Matthew 5:18** And in the fullness of times, God sent his word; the word *(which is Christ)* to accomplish what he please. The word prospered in the things where unto God sent. God's saving grace, because He so loved the world that he gave his only begotten Son. Therefore man's redemption is through the blood of Christ, and the forgiveness of sins, according to the riches of his grace. Isaiah 55: 10-11; Isaiah 51: 4-7; Romans 1: 16; Psalm 72: 1-20;

6

MADE READY

Sarah became the mother of nations: but symbolically she was a reflection of the Bride of Christ. Her beauty is the finished work of the word; cleansing and purifying the soul of men. Spots, blemishes, wrinkles or any such like, will be changed. The word of God working in men makes them chaste unto the Lord. Long ago, God established his laws with Moses, that Israel might learn sanctification and purification. God is Holy, and he commanded: *"For I am the Lord your God: ye shall therefore sanctify yourselves, and ye shall be holy; for I am holy: neither shall ye defile yourselves with any manner of creeping thing that creepeth upon the earth."* Leviticus 11:44

Sanctification and purification is the cleansing process; therefore the word assignment for all people is to **SANCTIFY** and PURIFY. Moses taught the children of Israel to sanctify themselves and to make pure all things offered by sacrifice {or worship}. To be cleansed so that the church is presented without spot, wrinkle or blemish or any such like. The body of Christ will become the glorious church through sanctification and purification. Read: Luke 3: 18; Malachi 3: 3; Leviticus 8: 13-21; Numbers 19: 1-9; Thessalonians 4:3-4; 2 Thessalonians 2: 13; Leviticus 16: 1-19; Hebrews 9: 11-15; "*SPOTS*": Colossians 3: 5-10; Galatians 5: 14-26; Ephesians 4: 22-32 (selfishness) 1Corinthians 10: 24, 33; Romans 15: 1; 1Corinthians 22-23;

Three appearances of the unclean are mentioned: the Spots, Blemishes and Wrinkled. These are stated by Paul in his letter to the church of Ephesus. He wrote concerning the relationship of the church with Christ; using the analogy of the husband and the wife. *"Therefore as the church is subject unto Christ, so let the wives be to their own husbands in everything. Husbands love your wives, even as Christ also loved the church, and gave himself for it; that he might* **sanctify**, *and* **cleanse** *it with the washing of the water by the word. That he might present it to himself a glorious church, not having spot, or wrinkle, or any such thing: but it should be holy and without blemish."* Ephesians 5:24-27

What are SPOTS? The Greek word 'spiko,' *means > a stain or blemish (fig)* DEFECT. Spot is *an imperfection; something that prevent from functioning correctly.* DISGRACE *(bad behavior)*

SPOTS!

Envy	Malice	Uncleanness	Bitterness
Evil concupiscence	Blasphemy	Pride	Selfish
Inordinate affection	Jealousy	Covetousness	Or any such like!

Galatians 5:19-22; Romans 3:14; Ephesians 4:31; Titus 3:3; 1Peter 2:1; Mark 7:20-23;

Spots are removed by washing or cleansing; in other words, sanctifying and purifying. If something unclean comes in contact with that which is clean, a spot or stain is created. Like so, the unclean becomes engrafted into the spirit of man; occupying the place that should remain clean.

Paul and other apostles taught the early church to live godly. The church was to practice pure religion; abstain from worldly lusts; love one another; encourage unity and self-denial. The teachings were to turn men away from carnality: that which wars against the Spirit!! For the church to make her ready, she must undergo sanctification and purification. Like as with Sarah, the church must become subject to the will of God.

Are ye not CARNAL, and walk as men?" 1Corinthains 3:3 Paul spoke this to rebuke those who were causing division. But the glorious body of Christ will have No Spot, No Wrinkle or any such like. Spots are the attack on the body. An example of the effect of spots, consider by contrast, the natural elements. These will allude to spiritual implications. First air, which is the exchange of gases; air empowers, and propels motion. Fire, causes the consuming away; fire transform and purify things. And without water all things will become dust. Water is the cohesive agent that holds things together. What about earth? Earth is the natural substance or the building material of all visible things that are formed. Earth is the weakest element; and it is dependent on the other three elements. Dust alone has no power to do anything; even the wind can move dust about. For we know that men are of the earth. Dust we are and to dust will every man return to the earth.

Spots are visible to the natural eye; they attach to material or fleshly beings or things. Therefore, spots affect the carnal nature of man; called the body or flesh. Moses taught that the sacrifices and offerings to God are burned with fire: the process of purification. The bodies of rams, goats and heifers (used for sin offerings), were fleshly bodies, placed on the altar. Paul said," *present your bodies a living sacrifice, HOLY; acceptable unto God, which is your reasonable service.*" Romans 12:1 The SPOT of envy, malice, bitterness, uncleanness and any such like, finds the carnal nature to attack. Consider how the earthly materials when they are bound together can be made many things in the natural. An unclean spirit may have derived from mingling with things that are not of God. An ungodly character will be the outcome. The person defiled by the unclean may behave violently, ruthless or uncaring toward others. The vices of the devil are mingled with in (DUST); then enmity against God. But in Christ, men are sanctified through the TRUTH. Jesus prayed, "And *for their sakes I sanctify myself, that they also might be sanctified through the Truth.*"

Recalling the serpent in the Garden of Eden; he lied to Eve. She heard his voice and following her own logic, submitted to his words. Satan defiled God's words that Eve recited to him, by implying something God had not given. In so doing, Eve was deceived in thinking that she will not 'surely die' if she partook of the tree. From that time, enmity is the warfare of flesh and spirit. Enmity blemished the relationship with God because of the transgression. The end to transgression is death. But the Spirit of God and his Truth is the victory over death.

Submitting to the voice of Satan is the law of sin and death. A law is a principle or a rule which governs the action of a person. To go beyond the limit of what is commanded, is to violate the law. The transgression is the law of sin; being governed by the voice of the devil. Death is the law of separation and the enmity against God. This punishment was put upon man because of transgression. But the grace of God through Jesus Christ, men are given life. The penalty placed on sinful man is death. Men are being made ready for God's acceptance by the washing of the water of the word. Sanctification and purification came by the laws of God; typified by the institution of a blood sacrifice. These laws of God typified and foreshadowed Christ sanctifying and purifying his body {the church}. Supporting Scriptures: Romans 7:14; 8:7; 1 Corinthians 3:1; 2Corinthians 4:10; Colossians 1:5-19

What are Wrinkles?

The Greek word 'rhutis' *means > a fold (as drawing together) (espec. on the face). This* word implies aging; the appearance resulting from an outward show of what lies within. It is said, "There is a cause to every effect" Not at all times will the cause be known; but the implication is that wrinkles are indicators. Wrinkles reveal to the sight and to the understanding that sin is having an attack on the nature of man. Natural wrinkles come from aging, exposure to the sun, perhaps an unintentional fold in the fabric; or some detail overlooked. Spiritually so, wrinkles are the results of having been exposed to sin. Sins which may lay dormant or hidden a period of time. But that which is hidden in the dark, the light will reveal. Notice the descriptions that follows;

wrinkles are things recognizable to the natural eye. **WRINKLES!!**
<u>The Outward Appearance</u>

BITTER and sometimes violent conflict or dissension; struggle,
fight,

FURY or Hostility is overt acts of warfare. A person may display
antagonism, or to be in opposition, or to be Resistance in thought.
The Principle is ENMITY. DISCORD is the lack of agreement
or harmony. Disagree, Clash, conflict, contention, Dissension,
Difference, and Variance.

Read: Genesis 13: 7-8; Proverbs 15:18 & 9:22; 1Corinthians 1: 10-13; 3:1-9
Ephesians 2: 11-22; James 4: 1-10; 1John 2:15-17; John 15: 18-23; John 17: 12-22.
To walk in carnality is to walk in the flesh. *"They that worship him must worship
him in Spirit and in Truth."* John 4:24

Wrinkles are undeniable to the natural sight. They are displayed
in the actions that are contrary to the word of God. Wrinkles are
removed by being cleansed by the word of God. When people repents
of sin and obey the word of God; the process of cleansing starts.
The washing of the water of the word continues this process. The
person must continue to be a hearer and doer of the word. Heeding
to the teachings of the word will provide godly doctrine, reproof,
instruction and correction. As a new babe in Christ, the word will
nurture the new Believer, leading the way to the holiness of God.
Along the faith walk, the Believer move away from the unclean.
With Abraham, he left the land where the people worshipped idol
gods. He left his father's house, his kinsman's and his country. He
became separated from the old path of life; the abominations that
was around him. Sanctify is the act of separating from the practice of
sinning. The effect of washing is for the purpose of removing the dirt,
and the unclean things which are spots. To practice sanctification,
Believers are becoming adorned with the garments of righteousness.

7

"LET US MAKE MAN"

Highlighting the **FORMED DUST:**

A 'man is a triune being; meaning that man is *body, soul & spirit.*
First > the body is the fleshly, physical aspect of a man. Shaped
and formed from the dust of the earth. The flesh is the physical and
weaker part of the triune man. The body might benefit or suffer
any form of attack from natural elements. Air benefits the body
with respiration: needed for circulation and brain function. Fire
maintain warmth for the body, and is needed in preparation of food.
Water is beneficial to the body for hydration, and cleansing. Like the
earth, that makes contributions through agricultural, and all natural
resources usable to the body. Natural elements as earth, air, fire and
water are created for the sustaining of the body. For instance, if water
is not part of living things, those things will decay and become dust.
The natural gas, oxygen is needful for the body. Heat is necessary
to keep things alive. All four elements given to creation sustain life.
God created man from the dust of the earth; then man became a
living soul by the breath of God. Before the foundation of the world,
God saw man in his perfection; then God decreed, *"Let us make man
in our image, after our likeness."* Supporting scriptures: Colossians 3:9-10;
Hebrews 1:1-4; 3:1-4; Proverbs 42:3 & 9:1 Psalm 122:1-9; Ephesians 2:19-22;
The natural benefits for the body are provisions God made for man
in the beginning. But the spiritual things of God benefits the body
of Christ are, purification [fire], cleansing/sanctification [water], and
his word [air] the life giver. These constitutes the spiritual formation
of man; bearing witness to the image and likeness of God.

The **Second** aspect of triune man is the SOUL. The Soul is the nature, character, and personality of man. If sin rules in the flesh; sin will defile the character, change right behavior and defame the innate nature of a person. The effect of the sin is reflected or seen as spots, "wrinkles" and blemishes. A person might know the character of another by seeing their sinful behavior. This is why the soul is in need of being transformed and conformed into the image of Christ. Sin damages the soul, but living godly is the renewal of the soul.

God breathed into Adam's nostrils, *"He became a living SOUL."* Prior to this, the formed dust of the earth was Lifeless: without intellect or a mind. He was without power and judgment to act upon. The natural wonders and great works of men happened because of intellect, power and judgment. These things are acquired learning through the process of time. God formed and fashioned man with soul, this begun the process to make man in the image and likeness of God. The word created all things, endowing man with character traits. But sin entered into the world, causing the soul to lose the spiritual nature of God. The sinful nature of man was not the original form of man. Sin corrupted the soul; but by the grace of God, man can become a new creature having God's image and likeness. Through Jesus the soul is redeemed, repaired, restored, and reconciled to God. *"If so be that ye have heard him, and have been taught by him, as the truth is in Jesus: That ye put off concerning the former conversation the old man, which is corrupt according to the deceitful lusts; And be renewed in the spirit of your mind; And that ye put on the new man, which after God is created in righteousness and true holiness."* Ephesians 4:21-24. The word that created all things will make men in the image of God and after his likeness. *" For the WORD of God is quick, and powerful, and sharper than any two-edged sword, piercing even to the dividing asunder of soul and spirit, and of the joints and marrow, and is a discerner of the thoughts and intents of the heart."* Hebrews 4:12

The process of the Soul becoming saved is through <u>sanctification</u> and <u>purification.</u> *"Let this mind be in you that was also in Christ Jesus."* Be not *conformed to this world, but be transformed by the renewing of the mind."* The scripture speaks of this MIND as intellect, *"to know."* Man is to first HEAR the word; *"faith cometh by hearing the word."* Romans 12:2

God's word is <u>wisdom</u>, <u>law</u>, <u>judgment</u>, <u>statues</u> and the <u>guide</u> (the way) in which to act upon. God is faithful to his word: he called men unto the fellowship of his Son Jesus Christ. Realize that the condition of the soul is ungodly; the soul is in need of cleansing. Notice the little word <u>unto;</u> it is of a 2-fold condition. **UN** > > is a prefix that means, do *the opposite; deprive of; remove; NOT towards or contrary to.* The word TO > > is a functional word: it is in motion {acting}. The movement or motion is towards a person, place or thing. The children of Israel were taught to sanctify and purify themselves. They were to set <u>apart, lay aside</u>, and to <u>consecrate.</u> Israel was taught the laws by Moses and by the priesthood. This was a foreshadowing picture of Christ sanctifying and purifying the church. Israel offerings were to be without spot or blemish. To follow the word in obedience to God's word, will change men from their sin condition. Obedience to God moves men UNTO!! Men are brought in fellowship with Jesus Christ. (Corinthians 1:9)

Another blessing given for the soul is empowerment from the word of God. The apostle Paul said, *"I am not ashamed of the <u>gospel of Christ:</u> for it is the **Power of God** <u>unto</u> salvation,"* *Romans* **1:16.** Holy Ghost power, as people may express it, is the gospel of Christ. Someone may say, "I got the power" but, the work and power of the gospel is to bring deliverance to the people. Looking at the preaching today, some people wonder if Christ's gospel is preached? With Moses, the laws of God were given to the people; but because of their stiffneckness, they remained in sin. Today sin and wickedness is on the increase. There is also an increase of ministries, who all claim to be of God. Media has increased the access for preaching the gospel. But salvation and deliverance to people aren't increasing. The gospel of Jesus hasn't lost its effect; obviously the problem is with the message that is going out. Then there are excuses by some that today is a new changing age for the church. But the word of God never changes. From the beginning of man, God foreordained and established his laws for men to obey. If the quote, "new day" is calling for something else new, then men are deceived.

God is not on his throne in our day, sitting and writing new laws to accommodate the 'new day' we live in. The "new day" is not new, because sin and wickedness has ruled in the earth for thousands of years. The prophet Isaiah proclaimed to Israel, *"Behold, the Lord's hand is not shortened, that it cannot save; neither his ear heavy that it cannot hear: But your iniquities have separated between you and your God, and your sins have hid his face from you, that he will not hear. For your hands are defiled with blood, and your fingers with iniquity; your lips have spoken lies, your tongue hath muttered perverseness. None calleth for justice, nor does any plead for truth: they trust in vanity, and speak lies; they conceive mischief, and bring forth iniquity."* Isaiah 59:1-5 What Isaiah spoke of are the same kinds of sinful living in this 'new day.' Sin is an old activity in the lives of sinful men. That which is old will eventually rot, decay and be done away with. The true "New Day" is reserved for the people of God when Jesus returns to rule. John said, *"And I saw a new heaven and a new earth: for the first heaven and the earth were passed away: and there was no more sea."* Revelation 21:1

Understanding the power of the gospel is like knowing that natural power is a force. Because power is of multiplicity; and power is numerically enlargement. Think about a small crowd of demonstrators versus a military force of a thousand: Which group has more power? We realize that the force with the greater number has power. If Christians are to become empowered, they are to increase in the knowledge of the word of God. Spiritual power, is strength and might; the soul's catalyst to act or to go forth with.

The next thing for Soul is JUDGMENT: and this is the nature of God's word. Judgment is the discerner, which pierce and divide asunder soul and spirit. Is this not the work of a sanctifying and purifying process in the Believer? The word of God will give insight to the things that are good or evil, right or wrong; or what is truth and what is false. The scripture said, *"Rightly dividing the word of truth."* That which is divided is set apart, separated or taken away. Using for an example, God wrote his laws on stone; therefore they were being engraved upon. The stone's surface underwent a cutting away in order for the words of the law to be seen. But God's laws are now written in the heart of men. A cutting away of the flesh, which is true circumcision {circumcise} and then the nature of Christ is revealed. The process of sanctifying and purifying the soul of man; done by the word of God. *"There is no condemnation to those that are in Christ, who walk not after the flesh, but after the spirit."* Romans 8:1.

The word of God cleanses men from unrighteousness and sin. *"If we say that we have fellowship with him, and walk in darkness we lie, and do not the truth: But if we walk in the light, we have fellowship one with another, and the blood of Jesus his Son cleanseth us from all sin."* **1John 1:6-7 Scriptures:** Omnipotent- Omnipresence & Omniscience: Ephesians 4: 6; *Genesis 2: 7* INTELLECT-POWER-JUDGMENT Philippians 2: 1-5; Romans 7: 24-25; 1Corinthians 2:14-16; *The Soul that sinneth':* Ezekiel 18: 20; John 5: 18; Proverbs 13: 14 ; 8: 33; 10: 8, 14; 12:15 ; 21:11; Matthew 7: 22-22; 1Corinthians 1: 19-27; *The Sure Mercy:* Psalm 100: 5; 145: 8-9; Isaiah 1: 27; Joel 2: 25; Matthew 17: 11; Colossians 1: 19-23; *The Power of the WORD:* Hebrews 4:12; Proverbs 10: 29; 24: 5; Luke 1: 49-55; Psalm 24: 7-10; 89:13-18; Matthew 3: 11-12; *Hearing:* Romans 10:13-21; Hebrews 11:6; Luke 1: 37; Matthews 17: 20; *The Discerner:* Hebrews 5: 14; 1Corinthians 2:14; 1Corinthians 1:18-24; *"Hear O Israel, thou shalt love the Lord thy God with all thy heart, with all thy soul, and with all thy mind, and with all thy strength: this is the first commandment."* LOVE GOD: Mark 12:30; SOUL: Genesis 2:8; Romans 7: 5-25; Hebrews 4: 12; 1Peter 1: 13-25; (1) The Heart is the WILL or desire; purpose to act. (2) The Soul is the true person; self, {I, me}. (3) Mind; the thoughts, reasoning & judgments (4) Strength; power and ability to perform.

SOUL is the spiritual or moral force in man: a living soul that breathe to actuate itself. The word inspiration is from the root word inspire; meanings to breathe or blow in. Man became a living soul when God breathed into his nostrils. For spiritual life in God, Paul said, *"All Scripture is given by the inspiration of God,"* 2 Timothy 3:16. In the image and likeness of God, men must receive the Spirit of God to actuate this life. The word of God breathes upon men his life. Jesus said unto Nicodemus, "ye must be born again; of water and of the Spirit. Intellect, power and judgment are of the soulish nature in men. God endowed within men the ability to think, reason, recall and retain knowledge. He acts out of his will; the seat from which motives are bred. The outcome of his actions is determined good or evil as to the law that he follows. *"For we know that the law is spiritual: but I am carnal, sold under sin. [v.18] "For I know that in me (that is in my flesh), dwelleth no good thing: for (to) will is present with me; but how to perform that which is good I find not." [v.25] "I thank God through Jesus Christ our Lord. So then with the mind I I serve the law of God; but with the flesh the law of sin."* Romans 7:17-25

By one man's transgression, sin entered into the world; as a result, all men are born with the Adamic nature. *"But not as the offense, so also is the free gift. For through the offense of one many be dead, much more the GRACE of God, and the gift by Grace, which is by one man, Jesus Christ, hath abounded unto many."* Romans 5: 12-21. The process of sanctification and purification conform man into the image of Christ and after his likeness. Genesis 1: 26. The soul of men that sinneth shall die. For this cause Jesus came to save men from sin. *"<u>For this corruptible must put on incorruption, and this mortal must put on immortality.</u> "As we have borne the image of the earthly, we shall also bear the image of the heavenly."* I Corinthians 15: 53, & 49 *"I will greatly rejoice in the Lord, my soul shall be joyful in my God: for he hath clothed me with the garments of salvation, he hath covered me with the robe of righteousness, as a bridegroom decketh himself with ornaments, and a bride adorneth herself with her jewels."* **Isaiah 61: 10** Read: Revelation 21: 2

The <u>**Third**</u> part triune of man is <u>SPIRIT:</u> Spirit is life; like the wind, invisible, in motion and vital for life. The body and soul of man is dependent on the spirit to live. When a person hears the word of God, the soul should conform to the word. It is the Spirit of the word that quickens and bringeth life to men. If the people continue in sin, the

41

spirit in man remains alive in sin. The man remains unclean, unholy and unchanged. But men are conformed and transformed by the dividing asunder of soul and spirit. *"Wherefore gird up the loins of your mind, be sober, and hope to the end for the grace that is to be brought unto you at the revelation of Jesus Christ." As obedient children, not fashioning yourselves according to the former lusts in your ignorance: But as he who hath called you is holy, so be ye in all manner of conversation."* 1Peter 1:13. It is written, "Be ye holy; for I am holy." *ye know that ye were not redeemed with corruptible things, as silver and gold, from your vain conversation received by traditions from your fathers; But with the precious blood of Christ, as a lamb **without blemish** and **without spot."*** 1Peter 1:18 ***"Seeing ye have purified your souls in obeying the truth through the Spirit*** *unto unfeigned love of the brethren, see that ye love one another with a pure heart fervently:"* 1Peter 1:22

The Word of God works with the SOUL: "the loins of your MIND" We are called to "be sober {rational, temperate} allowing his "Revelation of," being made known. For "in your ignorance" is the condition of the man without the knowledge of God's word.

God fashioned man with a body; formed from the dust of the earth. God breathed into man the breath of life. God's breath or word endowed formed man and he became a living soul. These things are pointed out to teach the process of Genesis 1:26. All other created things were in full perfection to the law spoken by God. But with man, his essence of becoming the god man in the earth started with formation. Next, man will experience conformation, and then transformation. All men are formed: and learning from Abraham, faith creates the likeness of being conformed. In Christ men will become transformed by the renewing of their mind (soul). Remember, the soul that sinneth shall die; but the gift of God is eternal life. Men without the sinful nature can now obtain newness through faith. This is the grace of God given to actuate his life in us. The spiritual likeness and image of God is taught in the life of Abraham and Sarah. They are the spiritual parents of faith and their lives received from God "little space grace."

8

NOT A FLAW

Reading and learning the foundational structure of the father of faith is like going on an amazing journey. First the beginning of the journey is authorized by God establishing faith in the heart of Abraham. God made Abraham the origin of faith so that all men can become children of faith through his Seed. Christ is the promised Seed of Abraham: his son Isaac was the type. *"Now to Abraham and his seed were the promises made. He saith not, and to* <u>seeds</u>, *as of many; but as of one, and to thy **seed** which is Christ."* Galatians 3:16 Faith journey led Abraham from place to place as he increased in the virtues of God by the things he experienced.

Nothing experienced was for naught; but God's work was for the good of Abraham, because he believed in God. The events of Abraham's life are recorded in scriptures with great spiritual messages. They are not just stories told; but hidden within are the mysteries of the will of God for the salvation of men. In the New Testament, Paul received the revelation of the will of God; Paul said, *"According as he hath chosen us in him before the foundation of the world, that we should be holy and without blame before him in love: Having predestinated us unto the adoption of children by Jesus Christ to himself, according to the good pleasure of his will, to the praise of the glory of his grace, wherein he hath abounded toward us in all wisdom and prudence; Having made known unto us the mystery of his will, according to his good pleasure which he hath purposed in himself: That in the dispensation of the fullness of times he might gather together in one all things in Christ, both which are in heaven and which are on earth: even in him."* Ephesians 1: 4-10

In another scripture, Paul said, *If ye have heard of the dispensation of the grace of God which is given to you-ward: How that by revelation he made known unto me the mystery; as I wrote afore in few words, Whereby, when ye read, ye may understand my knowledge of the mystery of Christ."* Ephesians 3:2-3 And v. (9) *"And to make all men see what is the fellowship of the mystery, which from the beginning of the world hath been hid in God, who created all things by Jesus Christ."*

The events of Abraham›s life contained the hidden mysteries: the types and shadows of what would be revealed in Christ. In the fullness of times, the types and shadows of Christ are revealed by his light shining through the word. He is the light of the world; in him is no darkness at all. To be in darkness is to be void of light; that is being without the knowledge of his word. But God saw the beauty of his creation in man. God illustrated his vision in the beauty of Sarah: for the woman was "very fair." She is the mother of the children of faith. Sarah represents God's New Jerusalem, which will come down from heaven as prophesied by John.

A GLORIOUS CHURCH

The beauty of Abraham's wife revealed the purpose of Christ in you. Abraham said to her, **"I know thou art a fair woman to look upon," God** see the church in her beauty; like as the vision of John in the Book of Revelation. Without Spot, Wrinkle or Blemish: holy unto the Lord. *"As he hath chosen us in him before the foundation of the world*, that we should be **holy** and **without blame** before him in love."* Ephesians 5: 24-32; 2 Corinthians 11: 2; Colossians 1: 21-28; Luke 1: 74 & 75; Song of Solomon 1:1

Behold thy art fair my love, thy art fair. . ."

"For thy Maker is thine HUSBAND the LORD of hosts is his name; and thy Redeemer the Holy One of Israel; the God of the whole earth shall he be called." Isaiah 54: 5

Supporting scriptures: Proverbs 12: 4; Joshua 24: 17-21; Deuteronomy 6: 13-15; Exodus 20: 5; *When the wife becomes unclean* →Hosea 2: 7 –13; God promised to wash away *The filth of the daughter of Israel* → Isaiah 4: 4-6; Malachi 3: 2-3; Psalm 51: 1-13 Isaiah 1: 18 Revelation 7:13 –15; Ephesians 1:4

People may read about Spots and Wrinkles: learning that they pertain to things unacceptable to God. Some people disregard what God calls unclean, unholy and unacceptable. But the test of faith changes people, when faced with becoming a living sacrifice unto the Lord? But the godly standards of righteousness never change. It is in the carnal nature of men to resist the commandments of God. The body of Christ, which is the church, is to be presented holy unto the Lord. Therefore spots and wrinkles are removed by the washing of the water of the word.

God has given men the pattern of things in heaven which were first taught by Moses. The first covenant had ordinances of divine service; the furnishing of the tabernacle and the using of each vessel ordained. The responsibilities of the priests were to offer sacrifices for themselves and for the sins of the people. All the gifts and sacrifices of the priests' service could not make them perfect; for they did not understand the pattern. A time was appointed when the meat and drink offerings, diver's washings, and carnal ordinances would be done away with. Read: EXODUS chapters 25 –28: EXODUS chapters 28-29; and chapters 30-31

Christ is the high priest who was offered once for the sins of the world. He fulfilled the law of the old covenant; showing that his sacrifice done away with the old covenant. Jesus fulfilled the types and shadows of the old covenant. Jesus said, "*Think not that I am come to destroy the law, or the prophets: I am not come to destroy but to fulfill.*" Matthew 5:17. "*Christ is the end of the law for righteousness to everyone that believeth.*" Romans 10:4. Men are not cleansed from spots and wrinkles nor blemishes by the offerings the old covenant taught. The apostle Paul wrote that a man must be a doer of the whole law. It was impossible for Israel to keep these ordinances; because the law was weak through the flesh. Read Romans 8:3. The Savior came to redeem men from under the law. Read the following scriptures: _The Old & New Covenants:_ Hebrews 7: 19-28; 8:1-13; 9:1: 10; 11-22 & 23-28; Jesus, the Great High Priest is Savior and the Redeemer. Jesus priestly ministry is to be a Refiner and Purifier of the soul of man. He sits in the temple of God, purifying the sons of Levi. _A Refiner & Purifier:_ Malachi 3: 3; I Corinthians 6: 8-11; Isaiah 1: 25; 1 Peter 1:6-7; Psalm 66: 10; 2 Peter 2: 5-12 ; Therefore, through Christ is redemption and forgiveness of sins by the washing of the water by his word. Jesus is the Son of David and the Seed of Abraham. Through him all nations of the earth are blessed.

As for spots, wrinkles or blemishes the emphasis also mentioned, _"or any such thing: but it should be holy and without blemish."_ Ephesians 5:26-27 The Greek word **HOLY** is defined as _sacred: pure,_ [morally] blameless _or religious;_ [ceremonially] consecrated:—_most holy; saint._ The Hebrew word **HOLY** is defined as a sacred _place or thing: Sanctify— consecrated hollowed (thing) holiness; dedicated (thing) holy_ day, holy portion; holy (thing) saint, sanctuary.

The word Holy appears many times in the Old and New Testaments. One of the first time the word HOLY appear in scripture is Exodus 3:5 _**"And he said, Draw not nigh hither; put off thy shoes from off thy feet, for the place where on thou standest is HOLY ground."**_ God was speaking to Moses in this verse of scripture. Moses was chosen as a Leader over the children of Israel. A Leader is the one who guide or lead others the way in which to go. Moses shoes represented the place he occupied; his occupation was shepherding in Midian. When God told him to take off his shoes, this brought on a new occupation for Moses. He stood on holy ground: and this place or position was sacred to the Lord. Moses understood that if the ground be holy, then his stand and walk was to be holy unto the Lord. At that time God was calling Moses to a position of leadership. God's calling for leadership are principles that the apostle Paul taught. Read: 1Timothy. 3:16

JESUS came and fulfilled the HOLY place:

John the Baptist spoke of Jesus by saying, *"This was he of whom I spake, He that cometh after me is preferred before me: for he was before me. The law was given by Moses, but grace and truth came by Jesus Christ. "He it is, whose coming after me is preferred before me, whose <u>shoe's latchet</u> I am not worthy to unloose."* John 1:15 & 27. With the old covenant pattern, the high priest entered the most holy place once a year to atone for the sins of the people. Jesus entered in the holy place and now sits on the right hand of the Father in heaven. He told his disciples, *"I came from the Father, and am come into the world: I leave the world, and go to the Father."* John 16:28. The **Holy place** is in the presence of the Father. *"And now, O Father, glorify thou me with thine own self with the glory which I had with thee before the world was."* John 17:5. Jesus came down from heaven to do the will of the Father who is in heaven. To be holy is to be in the <u>holy place</u> with God. Read about a better sacrifice than that which the pattern of heavenly things known in the old covenant. Hebrew 9:23-28; 12:2; Romans 12:34; Luke 24:26

Moses was the Deliverer God chose for the children of Israel. God directed him in setting up the tabernacle for worship. He made all vessels of the Tabernacle according to the command God had given him. These vessels were holy unto God; they signified all that Christ would reveal and fulfill as to the purpose of God, and he deemed as holy. Jesus fulfilled the holiness of God; he sits on the right hand of the Father. But Jesus is also in his temple of the Believers. For an example of the fulfillment of the old, recall the time Jesus was brought to the temple by his parents for dedication. There was an old man named Simeon in Jerusalem who spoke of Christ, saying, *"Mine eyes have seen thy salvation, which thou hast prepared before the face of all people; a light to lighten the Gentiles, and the glory of thy people Israel."* Luke 2: 30-32

In the Old Covenant, only the high priest could enter the second veil of the tabernacle, which is called "the most Holy Place." ***But Christ*** *being come a high priest of good things to come, by a greater and more perfect tabernacle, not made with hands, that is to say, not made of this building;" For Christ is not entered into the holy places made with hands, which are the figures of the true; but into heaven itself, now to appear in the presence of God for us:"* Hebrew 9:11 & 24 Christ is in the most holy place which is the presence of God.

"So *Christ was once offered to bear the sins of many; and unto them that look for him shall he appear the second time without sin unto salvation."* Hebrews 9:28. During the day of ascension, Jesus was taken up and a cloud received him back into heaven. Other scriptures speak of Jesus is on the right hand of the Father. He is in the presence of God: the 'Most Holy Place." It was the shedding of blood; the true sacrifice which Jesus alone could fulfill the patterns of things spoken in the law. His obedience pleased the Father: it is written, *"This is my Beloved Son in whom I am well pleased."* **John 3:22**

When Jesus, *"ascended up on high, he lead captivity captive and gave gifts unto men."* The purpose, *"for perfecting the saints, "for the work of the ministry, for the edifying of the body of Christ: till we all come into the unity of the faith and the knowledge of the Son of God, unto a perfect man, unto the measure of the stature of the fullness of Christ."* Ephesian 4: 8-13 Men are freed from the bondage of sin and death: once in captivity but now rescued by the blood of Christ. But there are some who try to find excuse, by saying "no body is perfect." This statement is void of knowing the work of transforming and conforming to the word. His word being perfected in us is not slack concerning his power to accomplish his will. Jesus not only prayed for his disciples, he also promised to send them the Comforter. The Comforter will guide, teach and lead men in the path of Truth. Jesus led captivity captive: he gained victory over the works of the devil. If sin is man's captivity; this captivity is overcome by the Victor, who is Christ. Captives are the spoils taken after the battle or warfare is won. Remember with Abraham, he rescued Lot; as a similitude, so has Christ redeemed men from the bondage of sin. Sin is the enemy or enmity of righteousness. To become the sons of God, men must follow the way, the truth and the light. Jesus is the guide to follow. With Christ there is no Spot, Wrinkle, Blemish nor any such like that will remain. We are "Washed by the Word."

"WITHOUT BLEMISH"!!

The church which Christ will receive is a glorious church. Glory is always the crowning of a work or an accomplished goal. In the Greek word, **without blemish** is defined, as > *(lit. or fig.)* It is to be without blame; *blemish, fault, spot faultless, unblameable.* The definition should illustrate to you a life that is true, innocent and just. Is this not what the Bible teaches as the Nature and character of Jesus Christ? He is the Truth, he is Just, and he is without sin or guile. BLEMISH is a spoiling mark or flaw; a mark of imperfection that spoils the appearance of something. In the time of Abraham, his wife's beauty reflected the glory that would be revealed in God's accomplished work in the body of Christ. Sarah's beauty symbolized the appearance of the glorified body, the church. The expression, *"she was a very fair woman to look upon"* The word "very" placed emphasis on the distinguished appearance of Sarah. This is like so with the body of Christ: she will become "very fair" to look upon.

Beauty always glorifies the work of the master designer. Beauty has symmetry, form, and all that the work presents: found acceptable. God sent out his word and the word accomplished where he please. The word prospered in the thing where unto it was sent. Isaiah 55:11 God sent out his word: but when it was sent, what did the word bring? The word brought God's thoughts and his ways to men to hear and obey. God is the Creator of all things; and the "Same" word which was with Him in the beginning was made manifest to men. *"We beheld His glory, the glory as of the only Begotten of the Father, full of Grace and Truth."* John 1:14

BLEMISHES

FALSEHOOD	DECIET	REBELLIOUS	PERVERSE	REBELLIOUS
QUARREL	DEBATE	OVERTHROW	PREJUDING	DISRESPECT
QUARREL	DEBATE	DISREGARD	NEGLECT	UNJUST
OVERTHROW	PREJUDING	GOSSIP	DISCORD	CONFLICT
DISRESPECT	DECEPTION	PERVERSE	DISSENSION	PERVERSE

Blemishes are character defects of those who walk after the things of the flesh. We cannot please God; neither can we glorify God in the flesh. These are the weights and sins that so easily beset us. But through obedience to the word of God we are washed and cleansed. Blemishes are flaws in the spirit of man when a man practice offending in the law of God. All the above blemishes are overt actions against "thy neighbor." The law commanded that we love our neighbor as our self. No one commits division, injustice, disrespect, deception and other things against themselves. But flaws are removed by the keeping of the word of God.

The grace of God will repair and restore that which became marred. Sin marred the children of Israel in their day; and people of the earth today are marred by sin. But by God's power, men can be made into vessels he will place his glory in. The scripture referring to this example is found in Jeremiah 18:16; the Lord spoke unto Jeremiah to observe the work of the potter. "...*and behold, he wrought a work on the wheels. And the vessel that he made of clay was marred in the hand of the potter: so he made it again another vessel, as seemed good to the potter to make it.*" The potter or Creator is God; his work ('in his hand') was fashioning man to be in his image and after his likeness. When Adam transgressed, the work of God was blemished by sin. But the true mercy of God chose to make it again: it 'seemed good to the Creator to make it.' What seemed good to God was his desire to save man, to repair man, to restore man to his unblemished form. By faith, God has given men access to his grace. Being transformed by the word will present men in the image of Christ, having no spots, wrinkles or blemishes. "Not a Flaw!"

The New Testament church is blessed to be the precipitant of what the children of Israel kept falling short of. The Old Testament laws of sanctification and purification are what the priests tried to teach Israel. Even after their captivity, the message was a call for true worship. Ezra declared a fast that the people would cleanse themselves from the unclean things of the heathens. The message of cleanliness adheres to, clears away blemishes, spots and wrinkles.

In 468 B.C. Ezra taught the remnant people of Judah to worship God. As a priest, Ezra knew that leading the people in worshipping God was his service. Ezra was a scribe who wrote the laws of God. The First and Second Book of Chronicles were written by Ezra. There would not have been any success in the work of Ezra if God had not shown him "a little space grace." Ezra 7:6-11. God was working out his promise and covenant he made with Abraham. His 'little space grace' was a measure of his mercy enabling his will and purpose. The activity of God's word is known in the life of his holy prophets and servants who came before Christ. They were favored by God because of their obedience to his word. Ezra was chosen to help in aiding God's grace to the captives. God was behind the scene, blessing Ezra through the Persian king Artaxerxes; who granted Ezra "all his requests" to carry out the work.

The work in respect of things needed for pure worship. Ezra 7:11-28. The 70 years of captivity was over; and the children of Israel were free to return to Jerusalem. The restoring and rebuilding of Jerusalem was in progress. The word of God, spoken by of Jeremiah, Ezekiel and Daniel and other prophets concerning Jerusalem was being fulfilled. READ: Jeremiah 30:1-3 Ezekiel 39:25 Hosea 10:1-11; Isaiah 27: 17-20; & 44:24-28

None of the vexations that the children of Israel underwent altered the covenant God made with Abraham. But the mystery of God's covenant was fulfilled through Jesus obeying the Father's will. He was the one to come and reconcile man unto God. Jesus is the grace of God, the Redeemer of men who came to "revive us again." Isaiah 22:20-25; Psalm 13:1-6; Joel 2:25-30; Hosea 6:1-5; Hebrews 2:9-18; Luke **13:32;** John 11:25, 26; As stated, "little space grace" was shown to the children of Israel many times; this if found throughout the scriptures. Abraham's life experiences illustrated "little space grace" to the children of God. His life provided the example of the origin and guide of faith. We are justified by faith if we walk in faith.

Faith give us access {a door or entrance way} to the Grace of God. Jesus said, *"I am the way, the truth, and the life: no man cometh unto the Father, but by me."* **John 14:6** In another scripture, Jesus said, *"Verily, verily, I say unto you, He that entereth not by the door into the sheepfold, but climbeth up some other way, the same is a thief and robber. But he that entereth in by the door is the shepherd of the sheep. To him the porter openeth; and the sheep hear his voice: and he calleth his own sheep by name, and leadeth them out. And when he putteth forth his own sheep, he goeth before them, and the sheep follow him: for they know his voice. {v.7} Verily, verily, I say unto you, I am the door of the sheep."* John 10:1-4. The promised Seed, who is Christ brought grace and truth to the world. God's grace has appeared unto all men.

His "little space grace" will restore, revive, and rescue men out of their afflictions. The accounts in the Old Testament testified to "little space grace" delivering the children of Israel out of many troubles. In the Old Testament, the children of Israel heard from God through the men of God for their deliverance. It was in that Israel heard the word of God; the guide to follow for deliverance. Today, we gain access to the grace of God through Jesus Christ by faith. God's standard of righteousness hasn't changed from his standards given to Israel. Today, his laws are written in men hearts by the hearing of the gospel. This is another reason why faith pleases God: because his word in the heart issuing forth righteousness. Read: Galatians 4: 22-29; Genesis 17: 15-16; Revelation 21:2 & 10; Romans 4: 20-25; Genesis 12: 15;

Learning about Abraham's faith brings light to the mystery of God's will. Everything Abraham encountered in his faith journey has a spiritual implication to the plan of God. Thus far, we see Sarah in the spiritual light of being "Jerusalem from above." Her beauty reflects the image of the Bride of Christ that is mentioned in the Book of Revelation. *"Let us be glad and rejoice, and give honor to him: for the marriage of the Lamb is come and his wife hath made (herself) ready. And to her was granted that she should be arrayed in fine linen, clean and white: for the fine (linen) is the righteousness of the saints."* Revelation 19:7, 8

9

GRACE PROTECTS

IN PHARAOH'S HOUSE:

Not only was Sarah "very fair" to look upon; the princes of Pharaoh Chose Sarah to be in Pharaoh's house. Abraham's faith was being tested while in Egypt. The very thing that was dear to Abraham was in danger of being taken from him. The "help mete" as a co-builder in her husband's house; building a life together was taken. A wife is ordained to bringforth children, to nourish, to assist and reflect the strength of her husband. But to be in Pharaoh's house meant that Sarah would be under a different system of laws. Pharaoh was the title given to the rulers of Egypt. The people of that day viewed Pharaoh as a god. The test of faith for Abraham was that he would be up against an authority contrary to the law of God. The same conflict Believers in Christ face in their faith walk today.

Abraham believed the covenant of God; and this was his victory over the rule of Pharaoh. Abraham did not bargain with Pharaoh for Sarah; he did not waver in his faith. It is not recorded Abraham thought that being in Egypt was out of the will of God. The scripture said, *"He staggered not at the promises of God."* Romans 4:20

The princes of Pharaoh chose Sarah to be in Pharaoh's house. Apparently the princes could influence Pharaoh in decision making. They *"commended her before Pharaoh."* In other words, the princes bragged on Sarah's beauty. Pharaoh was influenced by the princes and out of a lust to have Sarai brought to his house. He coveted what was not his; and God sent *"great plagues* to Pharaoh's house" *because of Sarai Abram's wife."* Genesis 13:17

Sarai' beauty reflected her anointing and endowment from God. The name Sarai is, dominative, which is to say a position of dominance; deriving from the word dominates and domicile: and to Reside. Therefore, Sarai name *means,* "to have a commanding or preeminent place or position." By this Sarai can be seen in a spiritual understanding as God's ordaining and selection for the church. God chose the place or position for Abraham and Sarai to be in. It may be predominant, paramount and superior to all others in power, influence and importance. The bride of Christ will be arrayed with such beauty, like as Sarai. She symbolized the spiritual image of the church; the New Jerusalem from above. God chose the children of Abraham; he called them His anointed ones. ↔Psalm 132:17 Ezra wrote, *"Be ye mindful always of his covenant; the word which he commanded to a thousand generations." Saying, Unto thee will I give the land of Canaan the lot of your inheritance; When ye were but few, even a few, and strangers in it. And when they went from nation to nation, (*Egypt) *and from one kingdom to another people; He suffered no man to do them wrong; yea, he reproved kings* (Pharaohs) *for their sakes, Saying, Touch not my anointed, and do my prophets no harm."* **1Chronicles 16:15 & vv. 19-22.** Sarai's presence in Pharaoh's house caused God to reprove Egypt, because she was his anointed. Although Abraham left the land of Canaan because of the grievous famine; his faith granted him "little space grace" while in Egypt. If he had stayed in Canaan at that time, he would have died without food and water. In need of survival, Abraham went to Egypt because it provided an oasis for him and his wife. His tribulation worked patience, and patience experience and experience hope. He was not left stricken because God commended his love toward him while experiencing his trial. To walk by faith brings on patience; a suffering that will cause the Believer to surrender his or her will unto God. God taught and illustrated His principles of faith in Abraham's sojourning. READ: James 4:7-10; Romans 5:3-5; 2 Peter 1: 2-8; Genesis 12:16; Genesis 12:: 14-17;

Ecclesiastes 7: 7; Psalm 25: 14; & 56 :1 1; Proverbs 1: 7; & 16: 7; Luke 1: 50; Matthew 10: 26-28; Hebrew 13: 6; 2 Corinthians 7:1; 1 Peter 1:15-17

Sarah was taken into Pharaoh's house, but no harm was done unto her. It was by divine interventions, God protected Sarah from being violated by Pharaoh. In Pharaoh's house, his servants were preparing Sarai, or making her ready for the ruler. Apparently there was a time of preparation for a woman to be given to the king. And during that time period, Pharaoh entreated Abraham well for her sake. Genesis 12:16. This might remind you of the account in The Book of Acts, when a man named Simon saw the signs that followed the apostles. He coveted their power and offered money *"Saying, Give me also this power, that on whomsoever I lay hands, he may receive the Holy Ghost."* Acts 8:18. The beauty of Sarai had a powerful effect on the man. Pharaoh did not understand the glory of God upon Sarai; he desired her for himself. Because Abraham said that Sarai was his sister, Pharaoh used gifts to show accommodations to the woman's kin. If he had discovered Sarai to be other than Abram's family member, he also would not have given gifts. His gifts masked off the true corruption of his covetous heart. But God saw the iniquity that was in Pharaoh's heart.

For SARAH'S sake, Abraham was entreated WELL!!

Sarah was in a place and position for God to show his protection to his anointed ones. Pharaoh gave to Abraham sheep, oxen, he asses, menservants and maidservants, also she asses and camels. Pharaoh did not know that all things were working for the good of Abraham and Sarai. God's wisdom is justified of its children. The gifts provided Abraham with food, and a position of authority, to manage his household and others. Abraham acquired riches from the hand of Pharaoh; more than a "red cross" relief. With sheep and cattle he would learn pasturing. Sheep and oxen provided meat, milk and cheese; their wool and hides for tents, clothing or shelter. Men servants and maidservants placed Abraham in the position of leadership and to govern. Camels carried burdens and had great endurance with travel. The trial of Abraham's faith brought on spiritual blessings. Faith substance is with sacrifice, being fruitful, multiplying, replenishing, subduing, and having rule in your life. All the gifts from Pharaoh brought Abraham natural blessings; which stood to witness God's "little space grace" was with Abram.

The trial or tribulation period of Abraham's patience was working experience. Experience is a direct participation with the events or trials we may undergo. From these experiences, knowledge is gained though the trying of faith. What is made manifest is the divine nature of Christ, known in the virtues Abraham exemplified. With this knowledge Abraham became invested with things that would pertain to priestly service. There would come the time when he would be asked of God to offer up his son Isaac for a sacrifice. Years later, out of his lineage, the tribe of Levi would be the priesthood. Abram didn't see the covenant being fulfilled by the experiences of his sojourning: for he walked by faith, not by sight. This was God's vision and plan. The life of Abraham was only the image of the vision; therefore the substance of things hoped for. It was a test of Abraham's faith to experience his wife being taken into Pharaoh's house. Abraham's affection for Sarah was a love relationship. When the situation occurred, the tempter's temptation was making an appeal to his human emotion. Abraham's moral standing was tested; but the king's gifts did not turn his heart from the righteousness of God.

The word of God was firm in Abram's heart. The scripture said of Abraham, *"He staggered not at the promise of God through unbelief, but was strong in faith, giving glory to God; and being fully persuaded that, what he had promised, he was able also to perform. And therefore it was imputed to him for righteousness."* **Romans 4:20-22.** Having this hope in him, he was delivered out of his trials by God. *"For wisdom is a defense, and money is a defense: but the Excellency of knowledge is, that wisdom giveth life to them that have it."* Ecclesiastes 7:12. The scripture teaches, *"The fear of the Lord is the beginning of wisdom."* Proverbs 9:10

Abraham experienced, "Little Space Grace" in Egypt; whereby God gave him a place of escape. As for Sarai' deliverance, it foreshadowed the children of Israel being redeemed out of their afflictions four hundred years later. The message or teaching Abram passed on to his son Isaac, and grandson Jacob was establishing the way in which Israel was to follow. *"Give ear, O my people. To my law: incline your ears to the words of my mouth. I will open my mouth in a parable: I will utter dark sayings of old: Which we have heard and known, and our fathers* (Abraham, Isaac & Jacob) *have told us. We will not hide them from their children, showing to the generation to (come) the praises of the Lord, and his strength, and his wonderful works that he hath done. For he established a testimony in Jacob, and appointed a law in Israel, which he commanded our fathers, that they should make them known to their children: That the generation to come might know them, even the children which should be born; who should arise and declare them to their children: That they might set their* **hope** *in God, and not forget the works of God, but keep his commandments:* Psalm 78:1-7

Pharaoh's house Plagued because of SARAH: There are three particular instances in the scriptures that the house of a Pharaoh King was plagued by God. At two separate accounts, God delivered his people by sending plagues in the land. When Sarah was in Pharaoh's house the Lord greatly plagued Pharaoh's house. In Genesis 12:17 the term **PLAGUED** (a verb, past tense word)_*means,* >> *to touch; to lay the hand upon (for any purpose); by impl. To reach [fig. to arrive, acquire]; violently, to strike (punish, defeat, destroy, etc.) Beat, - able to bring down, cast down, come down, smite.*

Also in the same verse of scripture, the word PLAGUES, (a noun– and plural {with an's'}) means, > > *a blow (fig. infliction); also by impl. A plague is a spot, sore, straitened, stripe, wound.*

In Moses writing concerning Abraham and Sarah, the kind of plagues Pharaoh suffered are not named. The inferences would be to realize that the plagues were direct blows to the physical bodies of those in the king's house. The plagues in Egypt were God's judgment to deliver his righteous ones out of their afflictions; he honored his covenant made. His oaths and counsels are immutable: unchanged and certainly they will fulfill his will. READ→ Psalm 22: 19-22; JOB 5: 19-27; *Plagued:* Genesis 12: 17; Genesis 20: 14; 1Chronicles 16: 21; Psalm 105: 14-23

Since the transgression of Adam, all people will experience trouble, sorrow and distress of some sort. But overcoming afflictions are the work of being conformed to the righteous nature of Christ. God's commanded, *"let us make man in our image, and after our likeness."* With the father of faith, Abraham was excelling in the nature of Christ. The faith walk leads to the way of acquiring the divine nature of Christ. The apostle Peter encouraged the church, by saying, *"add to your faith virtue; and to virtue knowledge and to knowledge temperance; and to temperance patience; and to patience godliness, and to godliness brotherly kindness; and to brotherly kindness charity."* 2Peter 1:5-7; Genesis 1:26; & 13:8

This scripture was written by the Apostle Peter. In it, Peter named 7-virtues that are acquired by faith. To some extent the same in understanding the 7 are also of the nine fruit of the Spirit. The Fruit of the Spirit are love, longsuffering, gentleness, goodness, faith, meekness and temperance. When the Believer walks in obedience to the will of God; the seven virtues are their actions.

The two fruits not named are JOY and PEACE: because joy and peace are the reward of faith. The Believer doesn't add to faith joy and peace. What faith does is to access "little space grace" of God. Grace is given, and the Believer experiences the joy and peace from the redemption. Therefore, peace is not added to your faith in the same manner as adding knowledge. It is in being very courageous in spiritual warfare to overcome the conflict {battle}. When the battle is won, then there is peace. The situation is resolved concerning the thing that was the test. As with JOY; it happens because God is pleased when his word is accomplished in you. JOY, because you gained strength in overcoming the conflict. Study this closely, and you will see that every instance of discomfort in Abraham's life, virtues was added because of his faith in God. The increase of virtue caused decrease in the distress, sorrows and troubles in Abraham's life. In other words, God's word had rule over Abraham's circumstances, adversities and his enemies. Galatians 3:13-18; Genesis 17: 5-7 & 12:3;

There should be no doubt about whether the test was allowed by God, as concerning Abraham and Sarah. Doubt is disbelief: and it is being void of the knowledge of God. We must learn to judge things by the word of God. His word is a discerner of the thoughts and intents of the heart. If the word is abiding in us, we can allow His wisdom to judge all things. His laws are so well established, they will correct any misdeed. His word instructs any course of learning. His word teaches righteousness. His word rebukes any offense. Nothing is new under the sun that the word of God has not the rule over. The carnal mind judges the outward appearance of a thing. But the wisdom of God judge after the inner man.

A man in captivity is the one with a physical circumstance; for he is bound. But the circumstance does not necessarily make the soul in captivity. On the other hand, the soul of a free man can be bound by sin. In Egypt, Abraham added to his faith knowledge, patience, and godliness. Soon would come in his life, <u>brotherly kindness </u>which stood out when recalling the account of Abraham and his nephew LOT. Abraham settled the dispute of their herdsmen: "And *Abram said unto Lot, Let there be no strife, I pray thee, between me and thee, and between my herdsmen and thy herdsmen; for we be brethren."* Genesis 13:8 Abram spoke the principle of God: "love thou neighbor." Matthew 19:19 He used the word of God to judge the strife between the herdsmen.

Abraham's life was a live illustration of "faith, the substance of things hoped for." There is no circumstance experienced by man that God has left unaddressed. This is why <u>hope</u> keeps the connection of faith for the deliverance desired. God has given us his word to assess his Grace; Jesus Christ the Righteous One is the grace of God. He is the Promised Seed of Abraham: in him all nations of the earth are blessed. *"For the grace of God that bringeth salvation {deliverance} hath appeared to all men, Teaching us, that denying ungodliness and worldly lusts, we should live soberly, righteously, and godly, in this present world."* **Titus 2:11, 12**

Something about PLAGUES:

Plagues literally occur to express God's anger; they are given to point out His judgment upon sin. Following the accounts of God punishing a people or the land with plagues, happened as resulting from sin and transgression. The effect of being smitten or touched by plagues is a manner of defeating and exacting power over the enemy. Plagues in scripture seemed to fall upon those who were in authority; they who usurped evil control over others. When people are greatly oppressed by the government of others, God will execute his judgment upon the evil rulers. Great plagues such as pestilences, earthquakes, storms, floods, diseases, and famines are sent by God. To suffer the punishment of plagues, a king and a nation of people are broken. Plagues will break the grip of human power; plague defeats the purpose of evil rulers and often will take away their control.

Disaster affects the natural elements of the land, air and water: damaging blows to physical things. Devastation can change the will and pride of humans as well. The restoration and repair that society is in need of will bring on a consideration for charitable means to aid in relief from disaster. Pharaoh fell into this kind of dilemma; he was touched by plagues and needed relief. Note the three questions Pharaoh asked Abraham. One question was in the form of blaming Abraham for the plagues. He asked why Abraham didn't tell him that Sarah was his wife.

Implications in Pharaoh's 3-questions: He asked, *"Why saith thou, she is my sister?*

1. Pharaoh questioned Abraham to find **FAULT**. Sometimes when people are in distress they seek to blame someone else for their problem. Since Pharaoh could recognize that there must be a cause for the plagues; he was implying that a wrong had been committed. As a ruler in Egypt over many people, why would he single out one man to blame for his troubles? Genesis 12:18 Pharaoh had coveted a man's wife. **Read:** → Deuteronomy 5:21; Luke 12:15; 1 Timothy 6: 7-12; Proverbs 21: 26; Proverbs 15: 25-29; Proverbs 12: 13; 2 Peter 2: 9-10;

2. Pharaoh questioned Abraham to find **JUSTIFICATION**. It seemed right in Pharaoh's mind to take Sarah into his house; as a king, he had that authority. Pharaoh was suffering from the plagues, and he sought to justify himself. He said unto Abraham, *"why didst thy not tell me that she was thy wife;"* Pharaoh was implying that his actions were right; and that he was being wrongly punished. **Read:** → Proverbs 12: 15; Proverbs 14: 12; Proverbs 21: 1-3

3. Pharaoh questioned Abraham to find **REPROACH:** Pharaoh asked, *"Why saith thou, She is my sister? So I might have taken her to me to wife:"* Reproach is defined, as > <u>A cause or occasion to blame, discredit or disgrace; an expression of rebuke or disapproval.</u> Pharaoh posed this question to discredit Abraham's character. But the plagues exposed Pharaoh as the one found to have faults; he was unrighteous and a man of disgrace in the eyes of God. **His fault** <u>was</u> coveting another man's wife. **He was unjust;** *<u>his unrighteousness</u>* was the wrongful use of his authority; and **his reproach** was because he did not handle his matters wisely.

The plagues in Pharaoh's house served as God's rebuke and disapproval of the king. Everything that Pharaoh sought to judge Abraham by became the judgment met back to him. His questions exposed his condemning heart. He had a heart of lust, unrighteousness and pride.

Pharaoh touched by the plagues showed God's righteous judgment against his evil heart. "Judge *not, that ye be not judges. For with what judgment ye judge, ye shall be judged: and with what measure ye mete, it shall be measured to you again.*"

Pharaoh judged Abraham to have fault; he blamed Abraham for his troubles. Pharaoh was pointing the finger at Abraham, instead of seeing his sin. He was unrighteous in trying to appear innocent of his actions: a self-righteous attitude. Not knowing Abraham's background caused Pharaoh Shame and disgrace because of his own actions. Also he breached the security of his house; his lack of skill or effectiveness as king. God sent the plagues to reprove and defeat Pharaoh's control. Three things Pharaoh may have learned because of the plagues; [1] learn not to covet. [2] Learn that God righteousness prevails and [3] He should have learned that the Lord is the Almighty. Pharaoh witnessed God's favor and deliverance to Abraham and Sarah from his control.

From the wise, it is written: *"A sound heart is the life of the flesh: but envy the rottenness of the bones. He that oppresseth the poor reproacheth his Maker: but he that honoreth him hath mercy on the poor. The wicked is driven away in his wickedness: but the righteous hath hope in his death. Wisdom resteth in the heart of him that hath understanding: but that which is in the midst of fool."* Proverbs 14:30-34

SARIA was returned to her Husband:

To resolve the problem in his house, Pharaoh released Sarah back to Abraham. His power and control was defeated by the hand of God. Pharaoh said unto Abram, *"Now therefore behold thy wife, take her, and go thy way."* Genesis 12:19 Pharaoh was dumb-founded and afraid of the man of faith. The plagues God sent, forced him to make peace with Abraham. He was afraid and without power to harm Abraham; therefore Pharaoh was compelled to let Sarah go. She was once coveted by Pharaoh because of her beauty; but now, Sarah became the object of his displeasure. He spoke in terms like as a person scorned: his voice resonated anger. There was no apology from him, having coveted Abram's wife; but rather words to disdain. Pharaoh's pride was hurt and he wanted to make Abraham feel belittled and to lessen Abraham sense of pleasure for his beloved Sarah.

This is a lesson Believers today experience in their faith walk. A wicked person will attack the faith of those who stand on the word of God. They are reproached and evil spoken of like as known with Abraham. But give thanks unto the Lord, *"Remember his marvelous works that he hath done, his wonders, and the judgments of his mouth; O ye seed of Israel his servants, ye children of Jacob, his chosen ones. He is the Lord God; his judgments are in all the earth. Be mindful always of his covenant; the word which he commanded to a thousand generations; Even the covenant which he made with Abraham, and his oath unto Isaac; And he confirmed the same to Jacob for a law, and to Israel foe an everlasting covenant, "And when they went from nation to nation, and from one kingdom to another people; He suffered no man to do them wrong; yea, he reproved kings for their sakes, Saying, touch not mine anointed, and so my prophets no harm."* 1Chronicles 16: 20-22; Psalm 105: 15;

Only a few words spoken by Pharaoh, but the words were to bring reproach and to attack the man of faith. The wicked ruler was blind and he didn't understand God's purpose or the faith of Abraham. Therefore he lashed out to Abraham, *"behold thy wife."* The vision of God is what kept Abraham from staggering at the promises of God. Abram had no problem beholding Sarah: for she represented the vision of God, the "New Jerusalem."

Pharaoh *"commanded his men concerning Abraham."* He passed on his responsibility to others to send Abram and Sarah away. It is in the power of the king to command others to do things under his rule. With Pharaoh, he solicited the help of others to carry out his actions. Actually, he found no fault in Abraham: therefore he cast out an innocent man. *"And Pharaoh commanded his men concerning him: and they sent him away, and his wife, and all that he had."* What king would allow an offender to leave his country with all his belongings? The implication in this scripture shows that Abraham was <u>innocent</u>; but Pharaoh was trying to ease his conscious by allowing him to take all his belongings. He did not do this out of pity or compassion for Abraham; it was Pharaoh's pride and guilt that he was covering. Genesis 12:20

Abram obtained "Little Space Grace" the measure of God's favor to him while in Egypt. The covenant God made with him was developing in the womb of the spirit; not yet ready to come forth. In the process of time the promise would fulfill. *"Blessed be the God and Father of our Lord Jesus Christ, who hath blessed us with all spiritual blessings in heavenly places in Christ: According as he hath chosen us in him before the foundation of the world, that we should be holy and without blame before him in love."* Ephesians 1:3

The faith walk continued to move Abraham in other places. Little Space Grace was the measure Abraham received in all places of his sojourning. The scripture said, *"God has given to every man a measure of faith."* Ezra the priest highlighted this measure with the words 'little space' in the sense of a place or locale that the faith travelers are brought to. In fact, Believers will go through many places on their spiritual journey: and God's grace will be sufficient for them.

10

Expanding Faith

ABRAHAM in BETHEL

After Abraham left Egypt with his wife and his nephew Lot; he came to a place between Bethel and Hai; the location *"where his tent was at first."* This would mean that when God sent Abraham out from Haran, he established a dwelling place near Bethel. Genesis 13:3 Bethel is in the land of Canaan; the central location of the land. This place was later called the city of David, and also called Zion. Abraham left Egypt: and as a metaphor, he was brought out of his **"straits."** This was his experience of being in a narrow place in his life. Of himself, he did not go to the right or to the left to find the way. An indication that he did not waver in his faith: God brought him into a large place; "Bethel" Note the description of the place Abraham came to: *"between Bethel and Hai" this* implies a larger place in his experience. Abraham moving forward expanded his life and experiences. Before men began to know the reality of God's word, His word was already performing and establishing His purpose. The word go forth to activate the fulfilling of His will, which is to be revealed in due season.

For an example of "straits" - The scripture speaks of Job's afflictions; many of which people also might experience in their lifetime. JOB lost his children, his riches and his health. He was in 'straits' but God sent his word by Elihu, that he may know the righteousness of God. The word straits is found twice in the Bible; *"Because he hath oppressed and hath forsaken the poor; because he hath violently taken away a house which he builded not; Surely he shall not feel quietness in his belly, he shall not* *save of that which he desired. There shall none of his meat be left; therefore shall no man look for his goods. In the fullness of his sufficiency he shall be in **straits**: every hand of the wicked shall come upon him."* **Job 20: 22** The first Hebrew word' strait' means, *to press; be narrow; fig. be in distress. Be distressed, be straitened, and be vexed.* The word <u>straits</u> means, *something tight; (fig.)* trouble, pain, distress. Written by Jeremiah, the prophet, *"Judah is gone into captivity because of affliction, and because of great servitude; she dwelleth among the heathen, she findeth no rest: all her persecutors overtook her between the **straits**."* Lamentations 1:3

Abraham' was in straits; his affliction in Egypt because Sarah was taken by Pharaoh. Abram encountered the rule of Pharaoh's house; a place that he had no power over to change. This kind of circumstance could only be changed by the hand of God. The physical place of afflictions in Egypt placed Abraham in the "Grace Place" with God. He suffered a loss of personal value; no power to rise up against Pharaoh. These straits prevented him from going forward in his life without Sarah. Of a truth, afflictions will touch that which people take pride in; or things that they dearly cherish. Afflictions can render a person without the human ability to bring about change. An affliction slow down and brings a halt to the progress the person is trying to gain in life. But it is the Grace of God that delivers men out of their afflictions.

Read→ Job 33: 1-24; Job 36: 1-6; Psalm 102: 19-21; Genesis 41: 49-52; Exodus 4: 31; Deuteronomy 26: 5-11; Psalm 34:19; The Psalmist said, *"He sent from above, he took me, he drew me out of many waters. He delivered me from my strong enemy, and from them which hated me: for they were too strong for me. They prevented me in the day of my calamity; but the Lord was my stay.*

He brought me forth also into a large place; *he delivered me, because he delighted in me. The Lord rewarded me according to my righteousness; according to the cleanness of my hands hath he recompensed me. For I have kept the ways of the Lord, and have not wickedly departed from my God.*

For all his judgments were before me, and I did not put away his statues from me." Psalm 18: 16-22. Although these are the words of the Palmist: resonating the testimony of Abraham. God's word is active; sent out to perform his deliverance: even before David wrote this Psalm. Read also: Psalm 32:7; 41:1; Joel 2: 32; Obadiah 1: 17;

Another Psalm that also testifies of Abraham's deliverance: *"I called upon the Lord in distress: the Lord answered me, and set me in a large place."* Psalm 118:5 "Little Space Grace" is the deliverance God granted Abraham; for he was in 'straits'. This was God's measure of Grace, when Abram was afflicted and in his place of straits. "Little Space Grace" brought Abraham to a 'large place'. Like a man that is no longer in captivity: his freedom relinquished the restraints that were about him. Abraham left behind Egypt, 'The House of Bondage" and he moved forward in his life. His experience illustrated the deliverance of the children of Israel: they too, were delivered out of Egypt and they moved forward. Note the above scripture, *"he set me in a large place."* No more in straits, no more in distress, nor vexed or in trouble: but delivered.

BETHEL: a LARGE PLACE, Bethel appeared first in Genesis 12:8; the place Abraham *"builded an altar unto the Lord."* Bethel means, **House of God.** And years later with Jacob, the grandson of Abraham, established an altar in that place. To be in that place, Abram built an altar for sacrifice; a figure of God's dwelling place. Read: Genesis 12: 8; Genesis 28: 18-22; Psalm 90: 1; Psalm 76: 1-2; Joel 3: 16-21;

Abraham left the "House of Bondage" and came to" The House of God." In Pharaoh's House or kingdom, he governed by decrees, rules and pride. His house had boundaries that restricted his control beyond the territory he presided over. He had limited power, strength and ability to excel, especially if a greater than he would arise. Only in his domain could he exercise authority; and for a time limited to his lifespan. The Pharaohs were not rulers by inheritance or blood lineage; they were tyrants. God sent plagues to Pharaoh's house; and

Pharaoh had no control over the natural elements that came against him.

There's no power that can subdue the hand of God. To experience being in a large place excites human emotions and physical ability. Like the early pioneers of this country, they explored the territories, made new pathways, and settled in the lands they believed to be resourceful and good. A large place is liberty: experienced in having opportunity to pursue, conquer and establish a ruling hand in that domain. Visionary goals become more than possibilities; they are reachable and acquired. As the story of Abraham's faith journey continue; by the words of Jesus Christ, he said *"And Jesus looking upon them saith, with men it is impossible, but not with God: for* **with God all things are possible.***"* Mark 10:27. And the prophet Jeremiah said, *"Ah Lord God! Behold, thou hast made the heaven and the earth by thy great power and stretched out arm, and* **there is nothing too hard for thee:***"* Jeremiah 32:17

God sent Abraham out from his country, from his relatives, and his father's house. Abraham obeyed the voice of God. When he was in the land of his nativity, he was familiar with laws, traditions and customs of the land. Among his relatives, Abraham had the same common family life and history. In his father's house, Abraham was accustomed to authority, management, and ruling over a household. But to leave that place, Abraham became a sojourner; he walked by faith. All the familiar things of his life were left behind. He entered into new relationships, new places and the government of God.

"And Abram went up out of Egypt, he and his wife, and all that he had, and Lot with him, into the south, "And he went on his journeys from the south even to Bethel, unto the place where his tent had been at the beginning, between Bethel and Hai." Genesis 13:1, 3 He returned back to the area he was living in before he went to Egypt because of the famine. Bethel is the *"house of God"* the place Abraham found to be the dwelling place of God. The word 'house' can be used synonymous

with the word "kingdom." In contrast to the government of God, Abraham had the experience of his father's house and the rule of Pharaoh. But God's House is greater: no boundaries or captivity. No injustice or unrighteousness; no falsehood or breach of promises. A kingdom ruled in righteousness and established forever. The faith walk brought Abraham a large place. It is written, *"God is in all, above all and through all."* He is all-powerful; all knowing and exists everywhere. Ephesians 4:6

GOD'S HOUSE: {A Large Place}

Hebrew, *bayith* A HOUSE: (in the greatest var. of applications, espec. Family) <u>court</u>, daughter, d<u>oor</u>, + dungeon, <u>family</u> x great as would contain hangings; [winter house] <u>palace</u>, place, + prison, + <u>steward</u> + <u>tablet,</u> web > **Bayith** means, *place*. Note: every word that defines house is also in the scriptures. These words are like metaphors relating to the activity of God working with man. Each of these words became the fabric of man's history. Men are the tapestry God has woven together. God's house reflects images of a bigger picture telling the story from the beginning to the end of the work of salvation. They also are prophetic in that each word foretells the plan, purpose, performance, provisions, pattern, power and prosperity of the kingdom rule of God.

More explanations on God's house will be given later in this book. For now the focus is on the layout of the spiritual House God foreordained in the beginning of creation. First take a look at the shadow of things that Abraham experienced. The particular way Moses worded these accounts in Abraham's life are like fragments of the spiritual building God is fashioning. The revealing of the things ordained for man's salvation is made known in the New Testament. *"Consider the Apostle and High Priest of our profession, Christ Jesus. Who was faithful to him that appointed him, "For this man was counted worthy of more glory than Moses, inasmuch as he who hath builded the house hath more honor than the house. For every house is builded by some man; but he that built all things is God.* "Herein *is the mystery of God's will, that he predestined us to be the children of God. For Grace and Truth came by Jesus Christ,* "That *in the dispensation of the fullness of times he might gather together in one, all things in Christ, both which are in heaven and which are on earth; even in him.*" Hebrews 3: 1-3 Proverbs 9:1; Zechariah 6:12, 13

The Builder of the House is God: we are the temple of God, his dwelling place. And his place is to be holy unto him. The Large Place is more than a four walled structure: it is "the kingdom of God" In the Old Testament pattern; Moses commanded the priest and the children of Israel to obey the commandments, ways, judgments and statues of God. The tabernacle, the vessels used at the altar, the covenant, and laws were foreshadowing the spiritual house that God has ordained. Moses lived in the shadow of the House; he served God by those ordinances and commandments.

Give attention to the Builder of the House, and expound on the mystery of God's will. It is written to reveal that the salvation of man was in the foreknowledge of God before the creation of the world. God ordained men before the creation of Adam, to be his children. Some people make statements like, "God knew; or that we are human;" which are excuses for sinning. Some may say, "God knew I was going to do this; or God knew this would happen." But God is Just and Righteous; not willing that any should perish, but that all men repent. A person that disdains God and his purpose is a person void of understanding the mystery of salvation. The love and mercy of God is so awesome, that even the unlearned and defiled can come to the knowledge of the truth. The Light of his word will dispel their darkness or ignorance. When light shines upon them, they are without excuse. Jesus Christ is the light of the world: he is the Grace of God, and the salvation of men. **Read:** Romans 5: 2, 15, 17; Ephesians 4: 3–7; Romans 5: 20-21;

If the question is asked, how did God Build His House to dwell in? The answer can be understood in the following verses of scripture. *"Wisdom hath builded her house, she hath hewn out her seven pillars; she hath killed her beasts: she hath also furnished her table. She hath sent forth her maidens; she crieth upon the highest places of the city."* **Proverbs 9: 1-3**

From the Book of Proverbs, chapter 8, wisdom was with God from the beginning of creation. *"Doth not Wisdom cry? And understanding put forth her voice? "Counsel is mine, and sound wisdom: I am understanding: I have strength. The Lord possessed me in the beginning of his way, before the works of old. When he prepared the heavens, I was there: when he set a compass upon the face of the depth: When he established the clouds above: Then I was by him, as one brought up with him: and I was daily his delight, rejoicing always before him. Rejoicing in the habitable part of his earth: and my delights were with the sons of men."* **Proverbs 8: 1, 3, 14, 23, 27, 30 & 31** Wisdom is personified as woman: the word of God figuratively is expressed as the mother of all things. All things created, once unseen because they were in the mind of God; now seen by the things created. The images or visions of what God desired to create were first his thoughts. Like as a builder who has a plan to the completion of his work. Wisdom, like a woman, brings forth or manifests those things that are in the heart of God.

But what is this wisdom? Wisdom is the Word of God. The scripture said, *"In the beginning was the Word, and the Word was with God, and the Word was God. The same was in the beginning with God. All things were made by him; and without him was not anything made that was made. In him was life; and the life was the light of men."* John 1:1-4. Notice, John said the word was **"with God"** to express the equality, identity, agreement and performance of God and his word. Wisdom was with God in the beginning. The nature of Himself is Just, therefore he is righteous and he is truth. *"The heavens are thine, the earth also is thine: as for the world and the fullness thereof, thou hast founded them. "Justice and judgment are the habitation of thy throne: mercy and truth shall go before thou face."* Psalm 89:11, 13 The Word and God are Oneness: identical and sameness. The Word and God have harmony in opinion, action and character. The nature of God is peaceful, gentle, kind and it is love.

The past tense word **"was"** is a term saying that something had been accomplished. The performance of God's word resulted in things that are created. **"Was"** also marks a measure of time; the starting point of God uttering his word and the things manifested show a space between beginning and ending. God said, "Let there be," and it was so. *"All things were made by him; and without him was not anything made that was made. In him was Life; and the life was the Light of men."* John 1:3-4. The word of God is wisdom: the word of God is life: the word of God is light {the knowledge of him}. Without knowledge, men could not build, establish or advance in any undertaking they seek to accomplish. To adhere to God's wisdom {word} all things are possible. There's no area in a person's life that the word of God cannot restore, reconcile, redeem, resolve and recover.

In another scripture, the prophet Isaiah wrote, *"For my thoughts are not your thoughts, neither are your ways my ways, saith the Lord. For as the heavens are higher than the earth, so are my ways higher than your ways, and my thoughts than you thoughts. For as the rain cometh down, and the snow from heaven, and returneth not thither, but watereth the earth, and maketh it to bring forth and bud, that it may give seed to the sower, and bread to the eater: So shall my word be that goeth forth out of my mouth: it shall not return unto me void, but it shall accomplish that which I please, and it shall prosper in the thing whereto I sent it.* Isaiah 55:8-10

In the mind, thoughts are the word activity within the mind not yet made known. Thoughts direct and guide us in every action of life. But humans' thoughts cannot excel the vastness of the heavens. Therefore, Isaiah described the unreachable place of God's thoughts. Because he is the Eternal, and man can never find his neither beginning nor end. So as with the ways of God; they are higher than the ways of men. God's thoughts and ways are His word uttered forth to accomplish and to prosper in His purpose. Where do thoughts come from? At the time someone is thinking, the conscious mind is analyzing, making judgments, reasoning and recalling information. But no one knows what the thought will be the next five seconds away. God knows the thoughts of men, even before they are formulated in the mind.

In school, students are taught that a sentence is a group of words that gives a complete thought. Thoughts are words gone forth; words are the builder of thoughts. This is why "the fear of the Lord is the beginning of wisdom" Words must be spoken to bringforth knowledge. By definition, wisdom is knowledge, judgment and insight: a wise attitude or course of action.

The previous verses of scripture, note God's Word and Wisdom have the same position in creation: the Word is first with God; Wisdom is first with God. It is written, *"For there are three that bear record in heaven, the Father, the Word, and the Holy Ghost: and these three are one"* **1John 5:7** Jesus and the Father are one; he was the word made flesh, and dwelt among men. The Holy Ghost bear witness of him. *"But when the Comforter is come, whom I will send unto you from the Father, even the Spirit of truth, which proceedeth from the Father, he shall testify {bear record} of me. And ye also shall bear witness, because ye have been with me from the beginning."* **John 15:26-27** The Words Jesus spoke are spirit and life. *"And now O Father Glorify thou me with thine own self with the glory which I had with thee before the world was. . .' And the glory which thou gavest me I have given them; that they may be one, even as we are one."* John 17:3, 22

The position of WISDOM: she is→ first or foremost in time, place and rank. Recalling wisdom with God in the beginning of the creation of heaven and earth, show wisdom rank. Wisdom place was in heaven; she is Truth. God is the Eternal and origin of life; His Word is his wisdom and the Holy Spirit is life; the agent that causes His word to accomplish and prosper.

Wisdom → First **in Time:** Wisdom was with God in creation: Wisdom said, "<u>The Lord possessed me in the beginning of his way,</u> "<u>I was set up from everlasting, from the beginning, or ever the earth was."</u> Wisdom was ahead of time; the measure of time came about the fourth day of creation. *"And God said, let there be lights in the firmament of the heaven to divide the day from the night; and let them be for signs, and for seasons, and for days, and years."* Time marked the beginning of history for humans and the created things. With God, he is eternal; and he is endless life. In the beginning of creation, the Word was with God and the Word was God.

In the Book of John 1:1, the Greek word is *logos,* defined as: something said; by implication a topic, subject of discourse. Also logos is reasoning, or motive; account, cause, communication concerning doctrine, preaching, question, saying, shew, speaker, speech, talk, treatise, tidings, utterance, word, work. Meditate on these words and notice that they are in activity; words sent out. Next consider that these words are effective because they produce life to those who receives them.

The profession of faith is to know that God established and predestined man's salvation. His words went out, and they will not return unto him void. *"According as he hath chosen us in him before the foundation of the world, that we should be holy and without blame before him in love. (God) predestinated us unto the adoption of children by Jesus Christ by himself, according to the good pleasure of his will. "Having made known unto us the mystery of his will, according to his good pleasure which he purposed in himself: That in the dispensation of the fullness of times he might gather together in one all things in Christ, both which are in heaven, and which are in the earth: even in him:"* Ephesians 1:4, & 9-10

The work of Christ is known by the words which define *'logos'* His "Good Pleasure" is what he accomplished; because it is the will of God. *"And the Holy Ghost descended in a bodily shape like a dove upon him, and a voice came from heaven, which said, Thou art my Beloved Son; in thee I am well pleased."* Luke 3:22

Wisdom → First **in Place:** *"One God and Father of all, who is above all, and through all, and in you all."* **Ephesians 4:5** God is above all, in all and through all. He assumes all positions of being in, above and through. <u>Above all</u> is his omnipotent position; authority, power and control. <u>In all</u> is God's omnipresence position; existing everywhere, present. And <u>through all</u> is God's omniscience position; because his word is the truth, the way, and it is in movement all the time. From this domain, is found wisdom, knowledge and understanding.

Wisdom adorned and ordered the place, space, and dimensions of created things. Surface, plane and dimension proves the physical manifestation of created things. There is nothing that the naked eye can behold that wisdom was not the origin of. Place is position, whether the place is in, out, around, above or under. Place is arrangement and the order that occupies created things. Place is the spiritual and physical environment or atmosphere. It is area, region or a particular dwelling: like as a house. If a man intends to build a house, he must have an image or blue print of the building plan. He must know the surface, the plane and dimensions of everything that is to be fitly framed together. The man must be able to judge the quality of the materials that are used. He must have an understanding of the foundation; *determining* if it will be durable or not. Many things are considered by the Builder in the work of building.

Time, money, physical strength and power to complete the task, the Builder must possess. By Wisdom, knowledge, judgment, and skill to produce all created things are possible. Judgment is the nature of wisdom that discerns, distinguish and determine all processes of the work. *"But where shall wisdom be found? And where is the place of understanding? God understandeth the way thereof and he knoweth the place thereof. For He looketh to the ends of the earth, and seeth under the whole heaven: Then did he see it, and declared it: he prepared it, yea, and searched it out."* JOB 28:12, 23-24 & 27 [read] JOB chapter 28

Wisdom → First **in Rank:** When God said "Let there BE" in the creation, His command established his law (s) upon everything that is created. God's command ranks as the first order wisdom responded to. The law or nature of what is created, never change. A bird, for instance, has the ability to fly, chirp, and to build a nest for her chicks, because these are laws in the bird. The fish of the sea were created with another set of laws by God. The RANK of wisdom is the position of order and formation of things. Wisdom's first position in creation was being with God in the creation of heaven and earth.

Wisdom said, *"I was set up from everlasting, from the beginning, or ever the earth was: "When there were no fountains abounding with water. Before the mountains were settled, before the hills were, I brought forth; while as yet he had not made the earth, or the fields, or the highest part* of the dust of the world. *When he prepared the heavens, I was there: when he set a compass upon the face of the depth: When he established the clouds above; when he strengthened the fountains of the deep: When he gave to the seas his commandment: when he appointed the foundations of the earth; Then I was by him, as one brought up with him: and I was daily his delight, rejoicing always before him; Rejoicing in the habitable part of his earth; and my delights were with* the sons of men." **Proverbs 8: 23-31;** [read] Genesis 1: 3-5; Psalm 119: 105; Proverbs 6: 23;

The first physical arrangement in creation is light. God spoke, and light appeared; and God said that it was good. To have the knowledge of God is to have light. Light equates to knowledge; and this light came by spiritual bread; the wisdom from above. And in Christ was Life: and his life was the Light of men.

In the Lord's Prayer, *"Give us day by day our daily bread."* Luke 11:3. The first order in man's day should be light. *"For with thee is the fountain of life: in thy light shall we see light."* Psalm 36: 9 read Genesis 1:3-5; Psalm 104:1-9; 119:105.

The knowledge of God is the light that man should walk in. Wisdom rank is in formation, distinction and durability; it is foremost with God. *"The law of the Lord is perfect, converting the soul: the testimony of the Lord is sure, making wise the simple. The statues of the Lord are right, rejoicing the heart: the commandment of the Lord is pure, enlightening the eyes."* Psalm 19: 7-8

Everything that is formed has the identity to what it is. God said, "Let there be" and it appeared because wisdom performed His command. The law which uttered from His mouth in the beginning made all created things. Wisdom expressed God's judgments. And every law given to His creation never changes; wisdom ranks eternally superior to all things.

11

THE PLACE

Returning to BETHEL, God's House: It is written, Wisdom "hath" builded her House. House was defined earlier, as having various applications of use in the scriptures. Twelve words, that are synonyms will be used to represents God's House. These words are illustrated by life experiences of the men of God in the Old Testament. The following will speak of each word, to show wisdom building Bethel. Also the biblical use of the word {Bethel} which is God's House can be used synonymously with the word Kingdom of God. Remember, Abraham was brought into a "large place" and he dwelled in Bethel. It may be significant to note that the number 12– represents the ministry of kingdom. Kingdom is government composed of laws, rules, judgments, ordinances and statues. Jesus spoke of the <u>Kingdom of Heaven</u> and the <u>Kingdom of God</u> several times in his parables. The parables pointed to the government of God in the earth and in heaven. Read: Matthew 13: 45-46; 13: 47-50 & 52; 19: 13-15; Mark: 26-29

FAMILY: to represent God's House

Family is the first word in the definition of 'house' from the Hebrew text. The dictionary defines 'family' as "a group of people united by certain convictions; fellowship; A group of people of common ancestry. A family is a group of people living under the same roof, and under one head; household. A group of people regarded as deriving from a common stock: race. The origin of the family evolved from a father and mother. In the beginning God said, "let us make man in our image and after our likeness." The law is the plan of God spoken in creation. Adam and Eve were driven out of the Garden of Eden because of transgression. From that time onward, man was in need of a way back into fellowship with God.

The order of family relationship began with the union of man and woman; it was sanctioned by God. When Adam knew his wife Eve, children were born unto them: the first human family. Sin separated man from his abode in Eden: then God's plan began to evolve through the ages until the "seed of the woman "won victory over the seed of the serpent. The Christ to come changed the course of human life: and his work will produce the sons of God. The father of faith is Abraham; and those of faith are the children and inheritors of the promises God made with Abraham. The promised Seed" who is Christ, will make man in God's image and after his likeness. Jesus said, *"Except a corn of wheat fall into the ground and die, it abideth alone: but if it dies, it bringeth forth much fruit."* **John 12:24** Jesus spoke this of himself; being the SEED that must die, so that many will come forth. This is the covenant Abraham was given, *"Through thou **seed,** I will make thee a father of many nations."* {Much fruit} came from the seed.

The origin of the human family is the father. The law given to him is to be a provider, protector and to govern the affairs of his house. In every home of today, not all are governed by a man. But this does not change the established laws of God. There is no family or family unit without a father as the origin of their existence. If a father is not abiding in the law pertaining to being a father, his house suffers neglect and lost. Recall Adam, the father of the human race who was to keep and dress the garden. Like as with Adam, so also with a husband and father today, he is the keeper of the household. This is the law of God men should abide in.

Transgressing and disobeying the laws of God are very wide spread today; many people think that it is the norm. The effect of sin brings on sorrow, sickness, suffering and death of the family unit. The remedy for these conditions brought on by sin is to obey the laws of God wholeheartedly. God commanded Moses to speak unto the children of Israel these words: *"And now, Israel, what doth the Lord thy God require of thee, but to fear the Lord thy God, to walk in all his ways, and to love him, and to serve the Lord thy God with all thy heart and with all thy soul, To keep the commandments of the Lord, and his statues, which I command thee this day for thy good? "And the Lord commanded us to do all these statutes, to fear the Lord our God for our good always, that he might preserve us alive, as it is at this day. And it shall be our righteousness, if we observe to do all these commandments before the Lord our God, as he hath commanded us."* Deuteronomy 10:12-13 & 6:24-25

Abraham, Isaac and Jacob are the forefathers of the children of Israel. They were chosen to be a peculiar people unto God in the earth. Israel's life was to foreshadow by example the family of God. He is the Father of all; and under his lordship shall his children obey. God is provider, protector and he governs his house by loving kindness, mercy and truth. The Psalmist wrote, blessed *is the man whom thou chooest, and causest to approach unto thee, that he may dwell in thy courts: we shall be satisfied with the goodness of thy house, even of thy holy temple."* And in another place, David said, *"How amiable are thy tabernacles, O Lord of hosts! My soul longeth, yea, even fainteth for the courts of the Lord: my heart and my flesh crieth out for the living God. Yea, the sparrow hath found a house, and the swallow a nest for herself, where she may lay her young, even thine altars, O Lord of hosts, my King, and my God. Blessed are they that dwell in thy house: they will be still praising thee. "*Psalm 65:4 & 84:1-4

Bethel is the place where Abraham first made an altar unto the Lord. This image was reflecting where God may be found; it represented what wisdom **hath** builded. The scripture spoke in past tense form, [hath]; God's word is sent out to accomplish his will. The past tense word shows that the plan of God was predestined and established by wisdom. Man awaits the manifestation of those things to fulfill. The Kingdom of God shall be revealed when Christ returns as king of kings and Lord of lords. It is not the material structure or the natural land that man should seek after. The spiritual message speaks of an eternal dwelling place. The Word of God shall establish his dwelling place.

PLACE: to represent God's House

With any Builder, the locale is selected for the purpose of being suitable to the plan. God brought Abraham out of Egypt into a large place. He left Egypt, being rich in cattle, silver and gold; his wife, all that he had and his nephew Lot with him. In this place, they dwelled together until strife came between their herdsmen. Abraham solved this dispute by saying to Lot, *"Let there be no strife, I pray thee, between me and thee, and between my herdsmen and thy herdsmen; for we be brethren."* **Genesis 13:8.** Strife over property or material substances hinders spiritual inheritance. Abraham, as the head of his house taught the principle of "love thou neighbor, as thyself."

The large place Abram had come to was Bethel; the scripture identifies it as the land of Canaan. Is not this the land of promise which Moses spoke of to the children of Israel? God planted the children of Israel, which is this "vine" in Canaan; that he would place his name there. {Read Psalm 80:8} Before the seed was born and became great in number; Abraham walked through that land. The substance of the thing hoped for was in Abraham's day; but the thing became a reality in Joshua's day.

Moses told the children of Israel that Canaan was a land "flowing with milk and honey" a good land they would possess. The land provided nourishment {milk} and the land provided sweetness {honey} Note that both milk and honey are foods; consumed and taken in by the mouth. Milk is drawn from the breast. For we know that babies need milk because they haven't developed teeth to chew meat. Milk serves to nourish the immature and maintain bone strength. Honey is sweet to the taste; and that which is sweet is pleasant and agreeable in its effect.

Understanding the shadow of how wisdom builded her house is known in the life of Abraham. Canaan, the good land promised to Israel; provided food and metals which enriched the possessors. Abraham had cattle, silver and gold; these things come from land flowing with milk and honey. The earth provides all the material riches of the land; that which is harvested of cattle and the material resources in the earth. The life of man is sustained by food. The pleasures that men pursue in life are acquired resources out of the earth. Those things may be metals, jewels, wood, silver or gold; all natural resources come from the land. People enjoy and love to taste the sweetness and pleasure of these things.

Moses said unto the children of Israel, *"And it shall be, when the Lord thy God shall have brought thee into the land which he sware unto thy father, to Abraham, to Isaac, and to Jacob, to give thee great and goodly cities, which thou buildedst not, And houses full of all good things, which thou filledst not, and wells digged, which thou diggedst not, vineyards and olive trees, which thou plantedst not; when thou shalt have eaten and be full; Then beware lest thou forget the Lord, which brought thee forth out of the land of Egypt, from the house of bondage."* Deuteronomy 6:10-12 *"Ye shall therefore keep all my statutes, and all my judgments, and do them: that the land, whither I bring you to dwell therein, spew you not out. And ye shall not walk in the manners of the nation, which I cast out before you: for they committed all these things, and therefore I abhorred them. But I have said unto you, Ye shall inherit their land, and I will give it unto you to possess it, a land that floweth with milk and honey: I am the Lord your God, which have separated you from other people. Leviticus* 20:22-24

But what is the spiritual implication of Abraham's cattle, silver and gold? What is the message that pertains to Bethel? Cattle are domestic animals; which implies that animals are tamed and governed by men or herdsmen. In God's House, there is growth and development: being nourished and pastured in good land. Read Psalm 23. Later the laws of sacrifice would be taught Abraham's children by Moses. Written in Proverbs 9:2, of wisdom, *"she hath killed her beast:"* which alludes to sacrifice or worship. Abraham, the father of faith, experienced the substance of the thing hoped for; the evidence of things not yet revealed. For clarification, the word **substance**, Greek > hupostasis' *means, a setting under (support) in a (fig.) Essence; objectively > assurance, subjectively >confidence.*

The following note is to explain more about the substance wisdom presented in the work of God. God worketh everything after the counsel of his own will. And his works are truth and righteous: always abounding in a good thing. Definitions:

1. Essence > the individual, real, or ultimate nature of a thing. It is something that exists; the properties or attributes by means of which something can be placed in its proper class or identified as being what it is.

2. Assurance > freedom from doubt; pledge; guarantee, security. It is being certain in mind; or something that inspires or tends to inspire confidence.

3. Confidence > the quality or state of certainty; a relation of trust; reliance on another's discretion.

Abraham's material wealth is a figure of the spiritual blessings in God's House. As children of God, we are blessed with spiritual blessings in heavenly places in Christ Jesus. Again, "The Place" of God where Abraham sojourned was flourished with milk and honey. Wisdom said, "Riches *and honor are with me: yea durable riches and righteousness. My fruit is better than gold, yea, than fine gold; and my revenues that choice silver. I lead in the way of righteousness, in the midst of the paths of judgment: That I may cause those that love me to inherit substance; and I will fill their treasures."* Proverbs 8:18-21

Faithful Abraham was subject to the will and plan of God. God's will for men is that they fear him and keep his commandment. The House of God {Bethel} is his temple; his place to dwell in. The prophet Malachi, the messenger of God, prophesied, *"And the Lord whom ye seek, shall suddenly come to his temple, And he shall sit as a refiner and a purifier of silver: and he shall purify the sons of Levi."* Malachi 3:1. Silver and gold are found in the earth: but refinement is necessary to make them of use. Both silver and gold are tried in the fire to remove the dross. They are heated for a length of time; made pliable for the making of vessels.

The word of God works in men; the word conforming them into the image of Jesus Christ. Faith will bring man to the place of silver and gold. Abraham acquired his gold and silver in Egypt: having undergone the trials of his faith. But it is not the natural treasures of the earth that men should lay up for themselves. Jesus said, *"But lay up for yourselves treasures in heaven, where neither moth nor rust doth corrupt, and where thieves do not break through nor steal: For where your treasure is, there will your heart be also."* Matthew 6:20. The durable treasure Jesus spoke of is not spoiled by moth or rust. What is this treasure? Jesus pointed to where a man's treasure is found: in the heart. The heart is the seat of a man's intellect; the place of passion and a receptor of knowledge. The heart issues forth or performs what is laid within it. But the man, who is a hearer and doer of the word of God, will lay up WISDOM {the word of God}.

In the Book of Job, it is written, *"Surely there is a vein for the silver, and a place for gold where they fine it." But where shall wisdom be found? And where is the place of understanding? Man knoweth not the price thereof: neither is it found in the land of the living. The depth saith it is not in me: and the sea saith it is not with me. It cannot be gotten for gold; neither shall silver be weighed for the price thereof. . . Whence then cometh wisdom? . . . And unto man he said, Behold, the fear of the Lord, that is wisdom; and to depart from evil is understanding."* JOB 8:1, & 12-28

The good land, the Promised Land, the land that floweth with milk and honey is the 'large place' faith brought Abraham to. He was rich in cattle, silver and gold. He went to Egypt because of a famine in the land of Canaan. He was delivered out of Egypt by the hand of God. The trials of his faith did not cause his hope to waver; "hope maketh no shame; because the love of God was in his heart." "Little space grace" was the large place Abraham walked in. Grace and truth followed him in all the places he sojourned.

Remember, Abram was called out of his own country; his name means 'exalted father.' God said unto him, *"And I will make thee a great nation, and I will bless thee, **and make thy name great**: and thou shalt be a blessing:"* Genesis 12:2. Abraham faith expanded; also did he increase in the knowledge of God. He became a man of a good reputation and honored by those around him and of his household. Abraham's walk of faith is understood in the words of Solomon, *"Wisdom is the principal thing; exalt her, and she shall promote thee: she shall bring thee to honor, when thou dost embrace her. She shall give to thine head an ornament of grace: a crown of glory shall she deliver thee. "Hear, my son and receive my sayings; and the years of thy life shall be many. I have taught thee in the way of wisdom; I have leaded thee in the right paths. When thou goest, thy steps shall not be straitened; and when thou runnest, thou shalt not stumble."* Proverbs 4:7-12. The children of faith are blessed with faithful Abraham; inheritors of the same promise God made to Abraham.

12

WISDOM BUILDED

COURT: to represent God's House The spiritual blue print of the work of Wisdom designed the <u>COURT</u>; diagramed in the plan of God. Usually the COURT is a fenced yard; and may be surrounded by walls. This implies a secret place, with restrictions and with a designated boundary. With Abraham, the locale that he was in was described as **Hai** to the east and **Bethel** to the west of his dwelling. This locale situated him between the two places. *"And he went on his journeys from the south even to Bethel, unto the place where his tent had been at the beginning, between Bethel and Hai."* Genesis 13:8. The Spiritual Court of Bethel is part of the structure of the House of God. Little is known about Hai, but the area is in Palestine, east of Bethel.

Two scriptures mentioned Hai in the Old Testament. {Genesis 12:8 & 13:3} The Hebrew, **Ay, 'Aya'** (Neh. 11: 31); or **Ayath** (Isa. 10:28) this name was derived from the name > **Iy; and** defined as RUIN [*as if overturned*]; a heap. God's <u>protection</u> is in Bethel, his House; but anything without protection will potentiate ruin. There are numerous scriptures that reference Court: and much attention was given to its design. God gave Moses the command to make the Court of the tabernacle to be situated by cubit measurements; southward, north side, west side and eastward. It is interesting to note that Abraham left Egypt, travelling from the south. He was traveling north when he came to the place where he had at first pitched his tent. This Place that he came to was Bethel. Faith spiritually etched out in his sojourning, the Court of the House of God. And Abram was before Moses; therefore the <u>court of God </u>was fore shadowed in the life of Abraham. In details the location of Abram can be seen as the picturing of a court. Nearly all houses built have a court area; some are fenced in.

In the Book of Exodus, Moses was given the command from God on the enclosure of the Tabernacle. *"And thou shalt make the court of the tabernacle: for the south side southward there shall be hangings for the court of fine twined linen of a hundred cubits long for one side: And likewise the north side in length there shall be hangings of a hundred cubits long: . . . And for the breath of the court on the west side shall be hangings of fifty cubits: And the breadth of the court on the east side eastward shall be fifty cubits. The hangings of one side of the gate shall be fifteen cubits." Exodus* 27:9-16

The Hangings in the Court of the tabernacle would prevent those on the outside from perceiving the things of God. This may remind you of the time Nicodemus came to Jesus by night to question the kingdom of God. Jesus told him, a man must be born of water and of Spirit to enter into the kingdom of God. [Read: John 3:1] Jesus said to his disciples, *"unto you it is given to know the mystery of the kingdom of God,"* Matthew 13:11. The Hangings in the Court of the tabernacle stood as a way of a restraint, to those who would enter in unclean. No unclean person or beast was brought into the tabernacle for an offering or sacrifice. The practice of washings and purification were high standards for those who served in the sanctuary.

The Hangings in the Court of the tabernacle veiled the way to the most holy place. It was the order of the Levitical priesthood to serve at the altar. But Jesus is the Great High Priest who entered in once; now sitting on the right hand of the Father. In the presence of God: a type of the most holy place was signified by the high priest; who went alone once every year, to offer a blood sacrifice for himself and the sins of the people. Behind the second veil of the tabernacle was the holiest of all. But the spiritual way of the holiest of all was not yet made manifest. The apostle Paul teaching to revealed the type and shadow of the tabernacle: he said, *"Having therefore, brethren, boldness to enter into the holiest by the blood of Jesus, By a new and living way, which he hath consecrated for us, through the veil, that is to say his flesh."* The former things *"Serve unto the example and shadow of heavenly things, as Moses was admonished of God when he was about to make the tabernacle: for See, saith he, that thou make all things according to the pattern showed thee in the mount."* Hebrew 8:5

Faith is wonderfully illustrated in the life of Abraham. Every event of his life being understood, signify to the children of God what faith is. If you have faith, you are like as Abraham, a sojourner, looking for that spiritual place with God. The old saints use to sing, "We come this far by faith, leaning on the Lord, Trusting in his holy name, for He never failed us yet." It is this assurance which will bring us unto the grace place before the throne of God.

The **large place:** Abraham came to a large place which brought him into the courts of God. His experience illustrated the workings of the Holy Spirit. The word of God was spiritually performing the course of faith that every man should walk in. Keep in mind that Abraham is called the father of faith. A father is a leader to his children; an example to go by. By the word of God, the spiritual law was already establishing faith through Abraham. In order to have children of faith, there must be a father of faith; even before Moses came with the law. This is the foreknowledge of God pertaining to man's redemption from sin through the gospel of Christ. For Jesus is the promised seed of Abraham. *"Know you therefore that they which are of faith, the same are the children of Abraham. And the Scripture, foreseeing that God would justify the heathen through faith, preached before the gospel unto Abraham, saying in thee shall all nations [heathen] be blessed. So then they which are of faith are blessed with faithful Abraham.* Galatians 3: 6-9

Jesus was reproached by the Jew because he said unto them, *"If a man keeps my saying, he shall never see death."* **John 8:51.** The Jews tried to find fault in Jesus, with those words, "Then said the Jews unto him, Now we know that thou hast a devil. Abraham is dead, and the prophets are dead; and thou sayest, if a man keeps my saying, he shall never taste death. Art thou greater than our father Abraham, which is dead? And the prophets are dead: whom makest thou thyself? Jesus answered, *"If I honor myself, my honor is nothing: it is my Father that honoreth me; of whom ye say, that he is your God: Yet ye have not known him; but I know him: and if I should say, I know him not, I shall be a liar like unto you: but I know him, and keep his saying. Your father Abraham rejoiced to see my day: and he saw it, and was glad."* Then said the Jews unto him, Thou art not yet fifty years old, and hast thou seen Abraham?" Jesus said unto them, *Verily, verily, I say unto you, before Abraham was, I am."* John 8:54–58

The Jews could not comprehend that knowing God is to know life; and **not** knowing God, is to taste death. Jesus said to Martha, *"I am the resurrection and the life: he that believeth in me, though he were dead, yet shall he live: And whosoever liveth and believeth in me shall NEVER die. Believest thou this?* Jesus raised Lazarus from the dead so that the people would believe his sayings. Jesus wept because of their unbelief: then having the grave stone rolled away, he raised Lazarus. The people believed on Jesus because the Light of God shined in their darkness. To know Christ, the darkness of man's mind is done away with. Lazarus knew Jesus: for he once had fellowship with him. Lazarus believed in Jesus; although he was dead, he was brought back to life. This miracle was preformed for those who watched on; it was to enlighten the people. The gates of hell or the grave can't prevail against the revelation of Jesus Christ. If death and darkness resides in the same place; when light is come, darkness is expelled. Jesus is the light of the world: and everyone that knows him has light: for he is the light of life. *"Then spake Jesus again unto them, saying, I am the light of the world: he that followeth me shall not walk in darkness, but shall have the light of life."* John 8:12

The Jews thoughts were void of light, because they saw Jesus as one honoring himself above father Abraham. They claimed to be established on the life of Abraham; and also holding to the words of the prophets. To the Jews, Jesus was a liar: because Abraham and the prophets were dead. To say that God is their God and to not know Jesus made the Jews out to be false. The forefather of the Jews and the children of Israel was Abraham. He heard God's word and he kept his sayings. This is what Jesus was alluding to with the Jews; to hear and keep "my sayings."

Therefore, faith is by hearing and doing the will of God. Hearing enlightens a man; and obeying show proof that the men know God. Jesus said, *"Abraham saw my day and he rejoiced and was glad."* God revealed to Abraham the salvation of the Lord: he saw The Day of the Lord. *"And Abram fell on his face: and God talked with him, saying, as for me, behold my covenant is with thee, and thou shalt be a father of many nations."*

Even as Abraham believed God, and it was accounted to him for righteousness. "Know *you therefore that they which are of faith, the same are the children of Abraham*." This scripture put to shame the false claim the Jews had in saying they knew God. But Jesus said unto them, *"Yet ye have not known him;"* He disputed their false claim of knowing God. The Jewish leaders could not comprehend, recognize nor honor the promised Seed. Their works of the law was not of faith. Faith is because of the righteousness that is in the law; that which Abraham kept. He saw the salvation of God; the Lord visited him at his tent. By faith Abraham saw Christ work: the promised covenant was to bless all nations through the Seed of Abraham.

You may think like the Jews in Jesus day; questioning how Abraham could have seen the day of the Lord? To see a thing is to come into knowledge of it. Experience is knowledge. Throughout Abraham's life, his faith was being exercised; acquiring the experience of knowing God. He knew rescue, redemption and restoration: he knew worship, sacrifice, and priesthood: he knew God had given him "little space grace," in all places he sojourned. Abraham lived four-hundred years before the Law. He performed those things pertaining to the laws God gave to Moses. Four hundred years before the law, God imputed Abraham's faith as righteousness.

The description of the 'large place' Abraham came to in his travel is an image of the tabernacle in the wilderness. In setting up the tabernacle, Moses was given details as to its size, furnishings, and the purpose of each division. The entrance way of the tabernacle was called the **court**. The court is situated, facing the east; like as with Abraham. He pitched his tent between Hai on the east and Bethel to the west. A courtyard is part of the territory of the house that followed, showed that he was a true worshipper of God.

Abraham dwelled in the land of Canaan: the same being the land of promise. The Prophet Isaiah wrote, *"He that walketh righteously, and speaketh uprightly; he that despiseth the gain of the oppressions that shaketh his hands from holding of bribes that stoppeth his ears from hearing of blood, and shutteth his eyes from seeing evil. He shall dwell on high: his Place of defense shall be the munitions of rocks: bread shall be given him; his waters shall be sure. "But there the glorious Lord will be unto us **a place** of broad rivers and streams; wherein shall go no galley with oars, neither shall gallant ship pass thereby. For the Lord is our judge, the Lord is our lawgiver, the Lord is our king; he will save us."* **Isaiah 33:15-16.** Little space grace, saved the herdsmen from destroying themselves. God's mercy and truth prevailed through Abraham, who upheld God's law of loving thy neighbor. What God purposed for the salvation of man, Wisdom, went forth establishing his will in the life of Abraham.

In Bible history, the family head acted as judge for those of his household. We know that God is Supreme Judge. Man is created to be in the likeness and image of God. The family's head as judge was reckoned accountable to God for his judgments. In the process of time, Moses set judges over the children of Israel: they handled smaller cases. The qualification for being a judge is that the man is capable, trustworthy, fearing God, and hating unjust profit. The head of the family was to be upright and judging according to God's law; because they represented God. Abraham was a householder, the head of the family: and he judged righteously.

Wisdom hath built her house; and the court of the Lord is at Bethel. *"But unto the place which the Lord your God shall choose out of all your tribes to put his name there, even unto **his habitation** shall ye seek, and thither thou shalt come."* **Deuteronomy 12:5** Abraham first entered Bethel long before David became king and ruled in Bethel. And in prophecy, the son of David was anointed to sit on his throne. This refers to Jesus as the one to sit upon the city of God: the scripture says, *"Yet have I set my king upon my holy hill of Zion. I will declare the decree: the Lord hath said unto me, Thou art my Son; this day have I begotten thee. Ask of me, and I shall give thee the heathen for thine inheritance, and the uttermost parts of the earth for thy possession."* **Psalm 2:6-8** *"Moreover he refused the tabernacle of Joseph and chose not the tribe of Ephraim: But chose the tribe of Judah, the mount Zion which he loved. And he built his sanctuary like high palaces, like the earth which he hath established forever."* **Psalm 78:67-68**

Mount Zion is the place of Bethel; the place of Jesus birth, Bethlehem of Judea. By lineage, Jesus came out of the tribe of Judah: the kingly tribe. Jesus was called the son of David: and the city of David is Zion. *"Yet have I set my king upon my holy hill of Zion. I will declare the decree: the Lord hath said unto me, Thou art my Son; this day have I begotten thee."* 'Emmanuel,' is God with us: Jesus Christ, and his name is placed in Zion. This same city is also Bethel, or Zion, the city of David. Bethel means the house of God.

"O sing unto the Lord a new song; for he hath done marvelous things: his right hand, and his holy arm, hath gotten him the victory. The Lord hath made known his salvation; his righteousness hath he openly showed in the light of the heathen. He hath remembered his covenant and his truth toward the house of Israel: all the ends of the earth have seen the salvation of God." **Psalm 98:1-3**

Wisdom built Bethel, "God's House:" In understanding the wisdom of God, realize His word is actively performing his work. Before the foundation of the world, God said, *"let us make man in our image, after our likeness: and let them have dominion over, Genesis* **1:26.** The character and nature of Christ was exemplified in faithful Abraham. As a man of righteousness, note Abram's character when the separation of him and his nephew Lot occurred. Abraham's character showed how love seeketh not her own. Love is the law of God, and love aided Abraham in solving the strife that was between the herdsmen. First he gave Lot a justifiable reason to not have strife. He said unto Lot, "we *are brethren."* In other words, we are of the same household, and the same blood line. Read: Genesis 13:1-13

When in father's house, brethren are to adhere to the rules of the house. Brethrens carry the same blood; therefore they usually portray common traits. Brethrens learn behavior, speech, and traditions form the country they live in. There are many brethren who fell into various covetous acts; like as with Lot's herdsmen. But mathematically speaking, Faith is the common denominator; it denotes and names the order to comply to. Children that are raised by parents obey the rules of the house; strictly out of laws imposed upon them. But faith speaketh in righteousness. You love the brethren because it is the right thing to do. This is what Jesus taught when he said, "Greater *love hath no man than this, that a man lay down his life for his friends.* **St. John 15: 13** *Ye are my friends, if ye do whatsoever I command you. "These things I command you, that ye love one another."* **v. 14** To be a Friend is to be in a relationship with another; like as a relationship of being brethrens. Wisdom said, *"A friend loveth at all times, and a brother is born for adversity."* Also wisdom said, *"A man that hath friends must show himself friendly: and there is a friend that sticketh closer that a brother."* And we know that the friend that is closer than a brother is Jesus Christ.

God spoke to Isaiah, the prophet these words, *"But thou, Israel, art my servant, Jacob whom I have chosen, the seed of **Abraham my friend."***

The brother of Jesus wrote, *"And the Scripture was fulfilled which saith, Abraham believed God, and it was imputed unto him for righteousness: and he was called* **the FRIEND of God.***"* **James 2:23**

Abraham allowed Lot to choose the land he desired without controversy. It is the nature of wisdom to be pure and peaceable. For Abram said unto Lot, *"Is not the whole land before thee? Separate thyself, I pray thee, from me: if thou wilt take the left hand, then I will go to the right; or if thou depart to the right hand, then I will go to the left."* *Genesis* **13:9.**

It is apparent; Abraham had no problem with a choice or seeking for directions. The reason is because his assurance was in the promises of God. Unlike a person that waver at the least uncomfortable situation in life. Abraham was anchored in truth: his defense was the word of God. The wisdom of God was a lamp to his feet and a light to his path. By faith, wisdom gave Abraham assistance. Through faith, wisdom gave him the course or path to walk in. The word of God was the truth Abraham kept in his heart. The word of God was the light Abraham followed.

Faith gave him access to the 'little space grace' of God; because he allowed wisdom to have her perfect work in him. Lot had not the wisdom of God in the choice he made; therefore he sought out for that which would satisfy and please his flesh. Lot's present state was of a carnal mind. Abraham was a man that delighted in the law of God after the inward man. Enmity brought on their separation; because one was walking after the flesh and the other after the Spirit. What does separate means? SEPARATE: parad– *to break through, i.e. spread (oneself)—disperse,* **divide***, be out of joint, part, scatter [abroad] sever self, stretch, sunder.*

The separation or dividing asunder of flesh and Spirit is the working of Wisdom. There must be a cutting away when forming or creating a thing. For instance, in the work of building a house, there must be a cutting away or hewing out. The blueprint of the house specifies every dimension for all the areas of the house. The master builder follows the blueprint so that all dimensions are fitly framed with building materials. The scripture said, *"Wisdom hewn out her seven pillars."* **Proverbs 9:1** The master plan is that God has ordained a place for his name to dwell in. Man is the temple in which God's name shall dwell. The temple of God has a chief corner: that chief corner stone is Jesus Christ. The vision Ezekiel had concerning the temple of God is in The Book of Ezekiel chapters 40-44. "And *the glory of the Lord came into the house by the way of the gate whose prospect is toward the east. So the spirit took me up, and brought me into the inner court; and, behold, the glory of the Lord filled the house. And I heard him speaking unto me out of the house; and the man stood by me. And he said unto me, Son of man, the place of my throne, and the place of the soles of my feet, where I will dwell in the midst of the children of Israel for ever, and my holy name, . ."* **Ezekiel 43:4-7**

Lot was like a person who is an opportunist. He followed his uncle for what he could gain for himself. When Lot seemly had acquired wealth: is because he had the opportunity to choose any part of the land to dwell in. He selfishly took the land he assumed was the best. Lot can be viewed as a man without faith. He lusted after the things of the flesh and the lust of his eyes. His journey happened for selfish reasons; he wasn't following a spiritual vision. From the time Lot left Haran, he was with Abraham. By separating, he made his dwelling in the wicked cities; he pitched his tent toward Sodom.

Picture the life of Abraham and Lot is like in a story told of two pastors. Both presided over possessions they obtained on their journeys. Abraham was a man rich in cattle, silver and in gold. His riches were given him because of God's favor with him. Lot traveled with Abraham from Haran unto the place where they separated from. Lot had flocks, and herds and tents. The spiritual connotation that is seen with each man substances are as follows. Rich is wealth; this would point to what things Abraham had in abundance. Rich in cattle; sheep and cows, are domestic animals. Contrast this with Bethel, God's House; a house of a multitude, or of a great host of people. Many times the prophets of the scriptures called God "the Lord of hosts". The "hosts" were his people Israel; a multitude. Cattle are raised close to the home site; they are not as wild beast of the field. These domestic animals are to be pastured; kept within the boundary of the land so that no stranger can lay claim on them. As a pastor, Abraham was the overseer. He provided grain and he also maintained a safe environment for his cattle. His natural life activities developed pasturing skills.

Abraham was also <u>rich in silver</u>; a valuable metal from the earth. Silver is purified with fire and polished to reflect the mirror image of the silversmith. Like as the children of God, Jesus sits in his temple as a silversmith; purifying the sons of God. The finished work is that they reflect the character of Christ. *"And he shall sit as a refiner and purifier of silver: and he shall purify the sons of Levi, and purge them as gold and silver, that they may offer unto the Lord an offering in righteousness."* **Malachi 3:3.** Jesus spoke the parable of the man who found a treasure hidden in the field. With any treasure, valuable items made of silver, gold and other precious metals are desired. Jesus is the man that sold all that he had and purchased that field. He gave his life and redeemed man from out of the pit. *"Again the kingdom of heaven is like unto treasure hid in a field; the which when a man hath found, he hideth, and for joy thereof goeth and selleth all that he hath, and buyeth that field."* **Matthew 13:44** God's people is his peculiar treasure in the earth; purchased by the blood of Christ.

Abraham was <u>rich in gold</u>; this metal also is found in the earth. The world's currency is measured by the value of gold. But gold in the hands of the Lord is tried in the fire; it is purified and molded into various vessels, and ornaments of honor. The children of God are as gold tried in a fiery furnace; being made and fashioned for his work and purpose. If earthly man can enjoy the pleasures that gold provides; much more does God take pleasure in his gold. Those that are acceptable unto God are tried in the fire; brought in submission to the will of God. This happens when a person submits to the word of God. They are to present themselves a living sacrifice unto the Lord: faith requires sacrifice. **Read:** Psalm 4:5; 27:6; 51:19; 107:22; Isaiah 56:7; Jeremiah **17:24-26;** Hebrews 5:1 13:13-16; & 11:6

Abraham's abundance of cattle pointed to the many "living sacrifices" that faith would bring to the altar of God. Consider all the sacrifices and burnt offerings from the time of Moses until the prophet Ezra. The number of children as the sand of the sea is the multitude counted for in God's promise to Abraham. The apostle Paul wrote, *"I beseech you therefore brethren, by the mercies of God, that ye present your bodies a living sacrifice, holy, acceptable unto God, which is your reasonable service."* **Romans 12:1** All who are blessed of Abraham are the multitude of people saved by the grace of God. Those that are of faith are the children of Abraham: the <u>exceeding great reward</u> God promised him. ↔read: Genesis 15:1

The hope Abraham held to was evidence of the abundance of the things not yet seen. The promised seed, who is Christ, fulfilled God's covenant made to Abraham. Therefore being rich in cattle, silver and gold were the images of the inheritance promised him. There are many rich people in the land today; but how many people are blessed by the rich? Earthly riches are temporal and do not answer to all things in a man's life. God's riches are durable: his living word and his eternal life to all that believeth on him.

The word of God was established in Abraham's faith walk. What God established became one of the seven pillars wisdom hewn out. **Faith** is one of the seven pillars the word of God hewn out. The dwelling place or temple of the Lord is supported by faith. Abraham lived by faith: he pleased God. *"He staggered not at the promise of God through unbelief; but was strong in faith, giving glory to God; and being fully persuaded that, what he had promised, he was able also to perform."* **Romans 4:20-21** Abraham's faith was like a strong pillar in his house. His faith was steadfast, nevertheless, moving him forward on his spiritual journey with God.

The pillar of Abram's house was faith. If conflict had remained in his house, then death and destruction would have been the outcome. The shield of his faith withstood the attack that came upon his house. Strife happened, because covetousness arose between the herdsmen over the cattle. The people that covet what belongs to his neighbor, is operating out of the carnal flesh. The root of covetousness is envy; and strife will keep this lust alive. The end of carnal lust brings forth death. But the wisdom of God teaches men to follow after the words of his law. God's wisdom will bring men to life and good. The temple of God must have the pillar called faith; for it supports His dwelling place. The virtue that stands out in Abram's experience is "*brotherly kindness.*" in which, charity is the work thereof. The end of obeying God's law is Love. Jesus said, "*If ye abide in me, and my words abide in you, ye shall ask what ye will, and it shall be done unto you. Herein is my Father glorified, that ye bear much fruit; so shall ye be my disciples.*" John 15:1-8

People may have heard that the fruit of the Spirit is Love; but the fruit is a product of the seed planted and allowed to mature in the heart. Jesus said that the heart was the good ground. The Sower that sowed the word of God in good ground was taught by Jesus in the gospels. In his parable, the seed carries the promise of what is hoped for. A matter to consider is that the people of God are to know this mystery. Concerning the parable of the Sower, Jesus said unto his disciples, "*Know you not this parable? And how then will ye know all parables?* "Luke 8:10 the connection of "*heaven came down, and glory filled my soul*" is His word went forth and accomplished his will. The parable spoke of the Sower who went out to sow seed. His word prospered where he sent it; bearing fruit and giving increase. God is glorified in his people who abide in his word. In the Old Testament, the glory of the Lord filled the tabernacle. And later with Solomon, God's glory filled the temple. But the future millennial Temple, God promised, *"The Latter glory of this house shall be greater than the former. And in this place I shall give peace saith the Lord of hosts."* Haggai 2:9

What is your answer to Jesus first question? {"Know you not this parable?"} He said to his disciples, *"Because it is given unto you to know the mysteries of the kingdom of God: but to others in parables; that seeing they might not see, and hearing they might not understand."* Matthew 13:11

It appears that **"seeing"** is twofold: the first seeing is to behold or look upon. The other 'seeing' is to regard; meaning to respect and have affection for. Nicodemus' question is an example of a person that wants to see and understand the "miracles" Jesus did. As a ruler of the Jews, Nicodemus had no spiritual insight or foundation to base his teaching on. How could he be an effective Ruler of God's people Israel, not knowing the mystery of the kingdom of God? There are men today who claim to be rulers of the people of God.

But like Nicodemus, they too are <u>seeing</u> might not see, and <u>hearing</u> might not understand the kingdom of God. Notice the word <u>might</u>; this implies a condition that may be contrary to what should be. The word **not** which follows the word *might* is emphatic in expressing the condition of Nicodemus' seeing and hearing. To change his condition would be to change his carnal nature. Jesus told him, *"Except a man is born again, he cannot see the kingdom of God."* The born again experience is that of water and of the Spirit. Traditionally taught, water is the baptism people follow to obey. But water baptism does not cleanse man from sin. Being born of water pertains to a cleansing. We are to be sanctified, purified and cleansed by the word of God. Jesus said, *every branch in me that beareth not fruit he taketh away: and every branch that beareth fruit, he purgeth it, that it may **bring forth** more fruit. Now ye are **clean** through the <u>word</u> which I have spoken unto you."* The word *<u>bring forth</u>* is underlined to draw attention to the birth activity. To be born is to bring forth, or bear fruit. Jesus taught about the Sower who planted the seed in good ground. The seed is ordained to produce, bring forth, birth out a new creature. The seed sown is planted in one form, but will come forth as a fruit if it abides in the vine. The fruit is the end of the law given to the seed. In the fruit, there is life; ordained to give life to those that desire it. The seed brings forth thirtyfold, sixty- fold and a hundred-fold harvest. This is true prosperity; an increase bearing fruit from the word. God' words accomplish what he pleases and prosper in the things where unto it is sent.

Next Jesus asked, *"And how then will ye know all parables?* It is the foundational doctrine of Christ for man to know the parable of the Sower in order to know all parables. Recall, wisdom hath built her house: in other words, the temple of God is established by His word. In the beginning of creation, was the Word. The Word was with God and the Word was God. *"All things were made by him."* The Seed sown is the Word of God. Jesus said, *"He that soweth the good seed is the Son of man;"* He explained the parable to the disciples. In God's house, Jesus is the stone that the builders rejected; he became the head of the corner. The temple of God is established on the word of God. READ:→Luke 8:10; Matthews 13:11; Mark 4:10-12; *BRING FORTH:* John 3:1-3; John 15: 1-8; Matthews 13:37; 24:42; Psalm 118:22; Isaiah 28:16; Mark 12: 10; Acts 4:11; Ephesians 2:20; 1 Peter 2:6-7

In other words, the temple of God is established by His word. From the beginning of creation, was the Word. The Word was with God and the Word was God. *"All things were made by him."* God commanded, *"Let the earth* **bring** *forth grass, the herb yielding SEED, and the fruit tree yielding fruit after his kind, whose SEED is in itself, upon the earth: and it was so."* Genesis 1:11 Jesus spoke about those who heard the parable of the Sower but did not understand it. Look at the words *might not* which are followed by the word *understand*. Hearing is to understand the parable of the Sower who went out to sow the seed.

There are several things that happen to cause understanding. The instance a sound is known, simultaneously the hearer becomes the audience. The hearing environment has an audience: and the audience would be the one who recognize, perceive and receive the utterance. What makes the sound or voice recognizable is knowledge gained. Knowledge is acquired from information, teaching and experience. The Jews were those that supposedly knew the law and the prophets' message. The Jews often defended their practices of the law. They would say, "We are the children of Abraham" or they may refer to the forefathers. Did not the Jewish leaders of Christ' day know his laws? The Scribes were interpreters' of the laws of Moses. They claimed to know the written laws, but they were not able to understand. The reason was because the Jews lacked perception.

If unable to perceive the voice or sound; the person is also unable to understand the sound. Perception is experienced when a person is enlightened: light must appear to reveal the mystery. In Jesus, is light, and he came to give men light in the knowledge of God. When light is come, the person can grasp the nature or the significance of what the voice or word is saying. *"For the Lord giveth wisdom: out of his mouth cometh knowledge and understanding." Give instruction to a wise man and he will yet be wiser: teach a just man, and he will increase in learning. The fear of the Lord is the beginning of wisdom: and the knowledge of the holy is understanding."* Proverbs 2:5 & 9:10-11 Read: John 8:33; Luke 11:52; Matthew 23:13; *THE LIGHT:* John 1: 4-5; 8:12-18; 1:8; & John 3:19-21;

Hearing is the continual perceiving of the utterance heard. The words hear is in activity; but the ("ing") forwards this activity. The hearer proceed, advance or progress in what is heard. This is a key of knowledge in understanding all the parables of Jesus. Hearing is effective only when the message or word of God is obeyed. In the Old Testament, long before men began to record on parchment the written word; men first heard the voice of God. To hear is a skill of discerning, recognizing, and comprehending the utterance. This is what was known about Abraham: he heard the voice of God. His action was first to build an altar; which illustrated his submission to the word. Then Abraham obeyed; his action was his confession of faith. The conviction of his faith in God was proven by his obedience. Paul said, *"Faith cometh by hearing, and hearing by the word of God."* **Romans 10:17**

The mystery of the kingdom of God is to SEE and HEAR the word of God. A mystery is something hidden or unveiled. But a heart that is open to the truth will receive the word. The good ground happened because it had undergone change. In preparing to sow seeds, the husbandman clears off the land. He will remove sticks and stones or debris that hinders the seeds that are being sown. In the parable, Jesus said that the good ground, *"is he that heareth the word, and understandeth it;" Matthew* 13:23. The good ground in a figure of speech, refers to the good heart. The good heart is respective to the word of God; having a change in its concepts, ideas, beliefs, and false doctrines. People's beliefs, ideas and concepts may not be of sound wisdom. How are they changed? The word of God is the wisdom from above: the inspired words which give good doctrine, instruction, rebuke and correction.

Man is given five senses, {knowledge}; but the sense of **seeing** and **hearing** is the seedlings of knowledge that bear substance. Seeing and hearing ranks superior to the other senses. The other three senses alone are limited in advancing man's life. They are dependent on seeing or hearing to define the nature of the things that affect them. For example, the sense of taste judges the flavor of a food by having perceived (seeing) the contrast. It utilizes the knowledge of other flavors known to the taste. The sense of touch perceives the contrast of hot and cold. Hearing brings on understanding, which clarifies to the sense of smell, touch and taste when exercised. Smell, is to discern the word of God. Touch, is to directly communicate with the word. Taste, is to partake of the word of God. **Read:** Romans 10:10-**17**; *Transformed*: Romans 12:2; 1 Peter 1:13-19; 1 John 2:15-17; Ephesians 1:17-23; & 4:21-24;

The Sower was Jesus in the parable; and his work was to do the will of God. Through his death, burial and resurrection, he will bring forth much fruit. The seed is the word of God that Jesus sowed in the earth. Jesus said, *"Except a corn of wheat fall into the ground and die, it abideth alone: but if it dies, it bringeth forth much fruit."* John 12:24 Jesus was speaking of his suffering; his death, burial and resurrection. In the same discourse concerning being born again, Jesus also said, *"And as Moses lifted up the serpent in the wilderness, even so must the Son of man be lifted up: that whosoever believeth in him should not perish, but have eternal life."* **John 3:14-15.** The corn of wheat planted in the earth speaks of the death, burial and resurrection of the Seed.

The apostle Paul taught that the promised seed is Christ. This was the fulfillment of what God swore to Abraham. To understand the mystery of the kingdom of heaven was for the Jews to know the meaning of the message. But their hearts were dull of hearing and perceiving the message. They had set up their own system of doctrines and beliefs. The Jews leaned to their own understanding; not able to perceive and understand the parable of the sower.

13

Faith Pathway

Abraham sojourns to Hebron: Hebron is a place in Palestine. The land that one day the children of Israel were to possess. Abram' moving forward after his separation from Lot brought him into another faith experience. *"By faith Abraham, when he was called to go out into a place which he should after receive for an inheritance, obeyed; and he went out, not knowing whither he went."* **Hebrews 11:8** He followed the hearing of his faith. At this place God allowed him to envision the promised inheritance. Perception makes it easy to associate the voice heard with the thing hoped for. The Lord said to Abram, *"Lift up now thine eyes, and look."* Genesis 13:14 A twofold vision; to lift up the eyes is to accept, and regard what is beheld. To have no vision, is like one whose eyes are closed. Before coming to Hebron, Abraham followed the voice of God: he was not shown the land at the time he began his journey.

Through time, place and the circumstances in his life which later positioned him in Hebron. The land of Ur was not the place of the vision to associate the voice of God with to the land of promise. Abraham had traveled a great distance from Ur to the land of Palestine. The substance of the things he hoped for; the evidence of things not seen, measured the period of time faith guided him. Faith was the place of origin when God spoke to him in the land of Ur. All the events and circumstances Abram under went from Ur to Hebron were trials of his faith. The apostle Paul said, *"And not only so, but we glory in tribulations also: knowing that tribulation worketh patience; and patience, experience; and experience, hope; and hope maketh not ashamed; because the love of God is shed abroad in our hearts by the Holy Ghost which is given unto us."* Romans 5:3-5

The reward of faith satisfies the hope that is in the Believer. Afterward, glory is the praiseworthy recognition of an accomplished course of action. The work that had begun in Abraham's faith walk, resulted in" little space grace" given to him. God grants "little space grace" to assist, because it strengthens us through many trials experienced in a lifetime. In every trial or distress, the Believer will experience a measure of the grace of God. Each trial of faith, God's grace is sufficient for overcoming the trouble. When the apostle Paul sought God for the problem he experienced, *"For this thing I be sought the Lord thrice, that it might depart from me. And he said unto me, <u>my grace is sufficient for thee: for my strength is made perfect in weakness.</u>* "2Corinthians 12: 9. Grace that is sufficient was a measure of the Grace of God given to Paul: "little space grace." Also God's strength enables man's deliverance. In the Lord's Prayer, it is written, *"Deliver* <u>us from evil.</u>" God's deliverance is in his word: and his word is Christ, the Seed of Abraham. *"Therefore being justified by faith, we have peace with God through our Lord Jesus Christ: By whom also we <u>have</u> **access** <u>by faith</u> **into this grace** <u>wherein we stand,</u> and rejoice in hope of the glory of God."*

To God be the glory for the things he hath done for mankind through Jesus Christ our Lord. Peace is a place of victory; after having overcome the conflict, the condition and the circumstance. These blessings come because of faith in God. Everything Abram viewed was the view of the land God 'will give.' The substance of things faith hoped for; manifested because God uttered his command and promise.

Being fashioned in faith, Wisdom directed Abraham to the plain of Mamre, which is Hebron. It is interesting to know that Mamre *means* **"vigor".** And Hebron *means,* **"seat of association"** *a society; a company.* As the trail blazer of faith, Abraham experienced beforehand what the children of Israel would learn or gain from obedient to God. The favor of God is "little space grace" that will assist Believers through their troubles. Trials are not an experience that someone would desire to find pleasure in. But VIGOR, which is "to strengthen by God." And while experiencing trials "little space grace" is desired.

With Abraham, it may be asked how vigor is known in his sojourning to Hebron. Or what occurred in Hebron to strengthen him along the Way? God said unto him, *"For all the land which thou seest, to thee will I give it, and to thy seed forever. And I will make thy seed as the dust of the earth; so that if a man can number the dust of the earth, then shall thy seed also be numbered. Arise; walk through the land in the length of it and in the breath of it; for I will give it unto thee"* Genesis 13:15-16.

First of all, the source of strength is power: and to be strong is degree of power. The previous scripture stated a combination of terms which provides the value of power. Take a look at the words: To Abraham, the land God **"will give"** The land is what God will bestow, award, grant unto Abraham and his seed. The word **"forever"** measures the extent of time for possessing the gift; no specified limitation. The magnitude of the gift is measured by a ratio. In a proportion, **"the dust of the earth"** equals the number of Abraham's seed. But it is humanly impossible to count every grain of dust. Naturally so, to possess a vast amount of land empowers a person. The person would become strong in influence and control; having the capacity to produce as effect. And people equate riches by the quantity of things that they possess.

Next power is the enabler of strength; the force behind what is manifested. "Forever is the durable certainty of power; for we know the Almighty God is omnipotent. Abraham obtained vigor in Mamre: his strength came from the Lord. Given to Abraham was strength; he became the father of many nations. Many are a great number: Abraham's power and strength was because of the great number. God said unto Abraham, *"For the land which thou seest, to thee will I give it, and thy seed forever. And I will make thy seed as the dust of the earth; so that if a man can number the dust of the earth, then shall thy seed be numbered."* Genesis 13:15-16

Hebron is the land Abraham associated the view of the land with the covenant God made with him the land of Ur. With faith, all things are possible because the power of God make it so. Now ask the question, how then could Abraham measure the land? He had no instrument for which to measure the land. When he lifted up his eyes and looked from the place he was standing it became a circumference. The position Abraham was standing in became the center of the earth he stood on. A circle has a center; and all that extends from the center becomes the length and breath of the land. God said unto him, *"lift up thine eyes and look."* north, south, east and westward.

Envision the spiritual image of the Lord's House. The children of Israel were called *"the apple of God's eye."* By definition, the Hebrew wording apple means **pupil**. In other words, man is in the pupil of God's eye. The important fact about the pupil is to have vision. *"And God saw everything that he had made, and behold,* ↔ to look]. *It was very good, And the evening and the morning was the sixth day."* Genesis 1:31. As with Abraham, he viewed the land God would give him. The substance of things hoped for; to be made manifested because God uttered his command and promise.

To **look** meant that Abraham was to advise self; take heed, experience, perceive those things the eyes beheld. Abram's attention was drawn to what God purposed to do. Look is very directional: God told him to look north, south, east and westward. How awesome it was to see the whole scope of what God will give to him and his seed forever. David, said, *"The counsel of the Lord standeth forever, and the thoughts of his heart to all generations. Blessed is the nation whose God is the Lord: and the People whom he hath chosen for his own inheritance. The Lord* **looketh** *from heaven; he* **beholdeth** *ALL the sons of men. From the place of his habitation he looketh upon ALL the inhabitants of the earth. He* *fashioneth their hearts alike; he considereth all their works."* Psalm 33:10-15 in another scripture, David said, *"When the Lord shall build up Zion,* **he shall appear in his glory.** *This shall be written for the generation to come: and the people who shall be created shall praise the Lord.* <u>For he hath looked</u> *down from the height of his sanctuary; from heaven* <u>did the Lord behold the earth</u>*;"* **Psalm 102:16-19**

The sojourner of faith was given vigor from God in the plain of Mamre; there he could also associate the promises of God with his prosperity. The Lord's "Little space grace" was the reward of faith experienced by Abraham. *"Then Abram removed his tent, and came and dwelt in the plain of Mamre, which is in Hebron, and* <u>built there an altar unto the Lord</u>*."* **Genesis 13:18** People of faith never remain in the same place of an experience or a visitation from God. Faith is active; it is in motion. Faith is ready to give sacrifice and to offer up to God. The tent, a temporary dwelling place must be removed. A literal removal of a tent is the labor of a man. Speaking spiritually, *"Faith without works is dead."* Abraham acted upon what he was told to do. His altar speaks of worship: which would involve sacrifice and offerings. In the presence of God, man must build an altar as a place to offer up and sacrifice unto God.

"For thus saith the Lord unto the eunuchs that keep my Sabbaths, and choose the things that please me, and take hold of my covenant: Even unto them will I give in <u>mine</u> *house and within my walls a place and a name better than of sons and of daughters: I will give them an everlasting name, that shall not be cut off. Also the sons of the stranger [Gentiles] that join themselves to the Lord, to serve him, and to love the name of the Lord, to be his servants, every one that keepeth the Sabbath from polluting it, and taketh hold of my covenant; Even them will I bring to my holy mountain, and make them joyful [strengthen] in my house of prayer: their* **burnt offerings** *and* **their sacrifices** *shall be accepted upon mine altar; for mine house shall be called a house of prayer for all people. The Lord God which gathereth the outcasts of Israel saith, yet will I gather others*

[Gentiles] *to him, beside those that are gathered unto him."* **"Little space grace"** Isaiah 56:4-8

God's covenant with Abraham assures man's salvation. It was in the foreknowledge of God from the beginning. *"T he counsel of the Lord standeth forever, the thoughts of his heart to all generations. Blessed is the nation whose God is the Lord: and the people whom he hath chosen for his own inheritance. The Lord looketh from heaven; he beholdeth all the sons of men."* Psalm 33:11-13

In the Book of Genesis the faith of Abraham was in the embryonic stage for man's salvation. His faith came by hearing; and hearing by the word of God. The apostle Paul said, *"For the grace of God that bringeth salvation, hath appeared unto all men."* **Titus 2:11** By faith we have access to the grace of God. Note the word <u>appeared</u>; this also is a beholding or a seeing experience. The Greek word > appeared, **means** to *shine upon: become visible or known; give light.* The grace or gift of God rests upon the soul of Believers who heareth and doeth "these words" of Christ. They are hearing and seeing what is spiritually revealed from God.

That which God showed Abraham was worthy of being beheld: because it added to faith a more excellent nature. The nature of the word bringeth light. The first response in creation to the command of God's word was *"and there was light."* God saw that the light was good; and he divided light from darkness. Good is the virtue that came forth from light. We believe "Jesus is the light of the world;" and everyone that is enlightened by him hath light. Beholding the things of God adds the knowledge of God. For the one who seeth is a wise man; but a foolish man is blind or dim sighted.

The land that God **"will give"** was worthy of being contemplated. To contemplate is to view or consider with continual attention: to meditate on. King David said, "Blessed *is the man that walketh not in the counsel of the ungodly, nor standeth in the way of sinners, nor sitteth* *in the seat of the scornful. But his delight is in the law of the Lord; and in his law doth he meditate day and night."* Psalm 1:1 And God said unto Joshua, "This *book of the law shall not depart out of thy mouth; but thou shalt meditate therein day and night, that thou mayest observe to do according to all that is written therein: for then thou shalt have **good success**."* Joshua 1:3-8

The account of Adam in the garden; he was given the command to "*dress and keep*" the Garden of Eden. The command of God was given which involved the activity of contemplating. Continual attention to the garden is necessary in order to have a good harvest. If there is a continual attending to the things of God; the virtue of temperance, for being stedfast is added to faith. The Hebrew writer said, *"For we are made partakers of Christ, if we hold the beginning of our confidence* [faith] steadfast *unto the end;"* Hebrews 3:14 If Adam had attended to the law of God, he would not have lost the blissfulness of God's presence. Adam was not steadfast in the law of God.

To be steadfast is to hold to; firm in and assured of God's oaths and counsels are immutable. The fall of Adam brought on the need for salvation. Man became destitute in his soulish nature. Man was in need of a Redeemer; one who will reconcile him back in the presence of God. "Little space grace" is the measure of God's love and his gift to man. God's word is sure; his counsels and promises are unchangeable. Therefore let us, "*lay hold upon the hope set before us: Which hope we have as an anchor of the soul, both sure and steadfast, and which entereth into that within the veil; Which the forerunner is for us entered, even Jesus, made a high priest forever after the order of Melchisedec."* Hebrews 6:17-20. The blissful place is in the presence of God: but to neglect or to not consider his word brings separation, evil and death.

Abraham attended to God's word; he received great blessings from above. God gave him a picture of the magnitude of his blessing. By numbering the dust of the earth counted as the number of his seed.

Good success is known by the numeration of the seed: the reward of faith. Abraham as our example of faith; the gift of God is to consider his word. God's word obeyed will bless the Believer to advance in the doctrines of virtue. *"To them that have obtained like precious faith with us through the righteousness of God and our Savior JESUS Christ; Grace and peace be multiplied unto you through the knowledge of God, and Jesus our Lord. According as his divine power hath given unto us exceeding great and precious promises: that by these ye might be partakers of the divine nature, having escaped the corruption that is in the world through lust. And beside this, giving all diligence,* **add to your faith virtue;** *and to virtue knowledge; and to knowledge temperance; and to temperance patience; and to patience godliness. And to godliness brotherly kindness; and to brotherly kindness charity. For if these thins be in you, and abound, they make you that ye shall neither be barren nor unfruitful in the knowledge of the Lord Jesus Christ."* 2Peter 1:1-8.

The apostle Paul taught the increase of the seed sown in the heart of men. The knowledge of Christ multiplies grace and peace in the Believers. To gain knowledge of Christ, it comes by hearing and keeping the word of God. This is what God was saying to Joshua; he must attend to His word. Not only so, in the beginning man was given the blessings of increase. *"And God blessed them, and God said unto them, Be fruitful, multiply, and replenish the earth, and subdue it; and have dominion."* Genesis 1:28

14

TENDING TO

The reward of faith is given because the Believer tends to the word of God. The farmer that plants his crop must tend to the crop with the expectation of a good harvest. It is ludicrous to think that what is expected will sprout and bear fruit "over night." The seeds planted and the land attended to is part of the course of action. But, "In due season ye will reap, if ye faint not." In Christ, a Believer will hold fast to hope by faith with patience. Faith is like the seedling of the word of God that bears fruit. Take notice of this scripture: *"But the fruit of the Spirit is love, joy, peace, <u>longsuffering</u>, gentleness, goodness, <u>faith</u>, meekness, temperance: against such there is no law."* Galatians 5:22. The apostle Paul did not use the term fruit in the plural. But there are nine properties of the spiritual fruit. Three of these are not acquired by the carnal efforts or the works of men. These three are <u>love, joy</u> and <u>peace</u>. Love is the nature and law of God. Joy is not the same as being happy; but it is when God's word is accomplishing his will. God is pleased with his word working in man. And Peace is the banner of victory; because of overcoming the conflict. Therefore the word of God does prosper where unto he sends it. There is the fivefold operation of the seed; <u>longsuffering</u>, <u>gentleness</u>, goodness, meekness and temperance. They operate in unison; attending to faith by keeping the soul from sinning. The word of God is ordained to bringforth of its kind. The spiritual administration and operation of the word of God in man will produce of its kind. For example; the law given to the apple seed does not change. The apple seed always produces the apple fruit. *"And God said let the earth bring forth grass, the herb yielding seed, and the fruit tree yielding fruit after his kind, whose seed is in itself, upon the earth: and it was so. And the earth brought forth grass, and herb <u>yielding seed after</u>*

his kind, and the tree yielding fruit, whose seed was in itself, after his kind: and God saw that it was good," Genesis 1:12

Christian's faith should be established on the principles of Gods' word that changes not. God is the same yesterday, today and forever. In God *"is no variableness neither shadow of turning."* James 1:17. Knowing that seeds are seasonal; there is a time appointed for the bringing forth of the fruit. A spiritual principle for attending and reaping the reward says *"let patience to have her perfect work."* James 1:4. King Solomon said, *"To everything there is a season, and a time to every purpose under the heaven: A time to be born, and a time to die; a time to plant, and a time to pluck up that which is planted."* Ecclesiastes 3: 1-**3**. When the sun, moon and stars were created, God commanded the division of night and day, God said, *"Let them be for signs, and for seasons, and for days, and years."* Genesis 1:14. On the fourth day of creation, the heavenly bodies began the time line of human history. No matter how desirous the farmer may want to see corn shooting forth in December; it's not the right season. What God has established with his word will never change.

Abraham BUILT an ALTAR unto the LORD: When God revealed his word unto Abram, the man of faith bowed himself to worship God. As stated earlier, worship involves sacrifice and offering. In the account of Cain and Abel; man is a worshipper of that which rules over him. The acceptable sacrifices and offerings are always in accord with faith.

What Abram sacrificed and offered to the Lord is not mentioned in Genesis 13:18 during the time he was in the land of Hebron. Therefore let us draw from the mere fact that he *"built there an altar unto the Lord."* Things that constitute worship are prayer, praise, thanksgiving, and communing with the Lord. To see a man in worship; in his physical form, the hands are raised to the heavens, his head bowed, with a sincere facial expression. But a true worshipper will worship the Lord in Spirit and in truth.

The word **"built"** in Hebrew means, *to obtain children; make, repair, set up; to build; Builder.* The word **"altar"** comes from a Hebrew word that means, *to slaughter, i.e. the flesh of an animal (usually) in sacrifice; Kill, offer, (do) sacrifice, slay.* Abraham was a true worshipper of God. He heard the word of God and he obeyed God. These two actions {hear-obey} are what makes a person faithful to God. Illustrated in Abraham's faith; he was securing the salvation of his seed to come. His Faith gave access to the grace of God. In due time, Abraham obtained children. Later faith operated to make, repair, set up and build God's dwelling place. His life foreshadowed the things that were made manifest in the lives of the children of Israel. Keep in mind, the scripture said, *"Wisdom hath built her house."* The word of God that made all things is the word making man in the image and likeness of God. Men are to worship God in Spirit and in Truth: Jesus spoke this to the woman at the well.

There are many prescribed rituals some people follow to say they are worshipping God. Note the contrasting words for **"in spirit," and** the words **"in flesh."** This narrows down the ritual forms of worship. Truth redirects the form of worshipping that some may exhibit. As to the Spirit of God, he is HOLY; therefore clean and pure. The mind, heart and soul of Believers are in submission to the word of God.

John the Baptist came preaching repentance; he prepared the way of the Lord. His message called for a turning from the way in which the people were going to the way of Christ. *"As it is written in the prophets, Behold, I send my messenger before thou face, which shall prepare thy way before thee. The voice of one crying in the wilderness, Prepare ye the way of the Lord, make his paths straight. John did baptize in the wilderness, and preach the baptism of repentance for the remission of sins."* John 1:29 John said unto the people, "Behold the lamb of God, which taketh away the sin of the world."

To illustrate this; Abram left the land of his nativity: he followed the voice of the Lord. Following the voice of God is to be obedient to the words the Lord has spoken. In the Book of Acts, Stephen preached, saying, *"And he said, Men, brethren, and fathers, hearken; The God of glory appeared unto our father Abraham, when he was in Mesopotamia, before he dwelt in Haran, And said unto him, Get thee out of thy country, and from thy kindred, and come into the land which I shall show thee. Then came he out of the land of the Chaldeans, and dwelt in Haran: and from thence, when his father was dead, removed him into this land, wherein ye dwell."* Acts 7:2-4

If a person is traveling southward, and Christ is standing in the north; there must be a turning around in order to behold him. In Hebron, Abram was able to associate the voice spoken to him in the land of Ur. He viewed the land God promised to give him. This is in the sense of "hearing and seeing" as when Jesus told his disciples that it is given unto them to know the mysteries of the kingdom of God. The word of God directs, as like "the rod and staff" spoken of by David. A Shepherd will use the rod and staff to guide the sheep; preventing them from going astray. The gospel of repentance John preached was to turn the mind, heart and soul of men. When there is recognition for the need for salvation; the mind considers. The heart accepts the message and the soul responds by the right action in compliance to the word.

Worship God in Spirit: The Spirit of God is invisible; but it is the agent whereby man can commune with God. Previously it was stated that the Spirit of God is Holy, clean, and pure. The word of God cleanses man from unrighteousness and sin when it is obeyed. There is no reason to think that God accepts sin. To come before the Lord with a petition; desiring out of the lust of the flesh, is unclean. The word of God works on the heart, mind, soul and the strength. One of the great commandments is to love God with all thine heart, mind, soul and strength. To worship God in Spirit is to deny self, take up your cross and follow him; this is true sacrifice. Our lives become a holy and living sacrifice unto God; which is acceptable to him. *"And be not conformed to this world: but be transformed by the renewing of your* *mind that ye may prove what is good, and acceptable and perfect will of God."* Romans 12:1-2

Abraham built an altar unto the Lord: his sacrifice was holy and acceptable. He denied self and followed the call of God. *"By faith Abraham, when he was called to go out into a place which he should after receive for an inheritance, obeyed; and he went out, not knowing whether he went."* Hebrews 11:8 "For we walk by <u>faith,</u> not by sight:" 2 Corinthians 5:7

What make the worship more viable are <u>adoration, supplication, petitioning, thanksgiving, forgiveness,</u> <u>submission and interceding</u> prayers. When these prayers are done in sincerity and lived; then communion and fellowship with the Spirit is the connection. This is what worshipping the Lord in the Spirit means. Prayers are answered: and the blessings of the Lord are in the lives of the Believers. A broken and contrite heart will God hear. The person becomes <u>restored</u>, reconciled, requited, <u>regenerated</u>, <u>redeemed</u>, <u>recovered</u>, <u>reclaimed</u>, <u>remitted</u>, and <u>renewed</u>. Salvation is man's deliverance from the power and effect of sin. Can you envision the seed {word} in good ground? This symbolizes spiritual baptism, which is the death, burial and resurrection life in God. It is the experience of salvation working in man by the word of God.

The above nine words begins with the letter **R** - {which has a numerical value of nine} which speak of *edification.* In things pertaining to man's salvation, they are God's gifts to edify man. Edification improves, builds up, enlightens and establishes the Believer in Christ. The gifts given are, pastors, prophets, evangelists, apostles and teachers. The gifts are for the body of Christ: not to be used in misguided forms of religious practices and works of men. When Jesus ascended on high, Jesus led captivity captive; he gave gifts unto men, *"For the perfecting of the saints, for the work of the ministry, and for the edifying of the body of Christ."* When the church becomes edified, then the church will take on the *"measure of the stature of the fullness of Christ."* Ephesians 4:8.

This measure is for the church to be presented perfected in Christ. Raised up or resurrected; becoming exalted in him. It is written, *"Whosoever shall exalt himself shall be abased; and he that shall humble himself shall be exalted."* Matthew 23:12

Expounding further on the number <u>nine</u>: the nine is the highest digit for counting. Nine is the exalted number; no greater number to advance the single digits onward. There are nine gifts of the Spirit; nine fruit of the Spirit; Abraham was ninety and nine years old when he was circumcised in the flesh of his foreskin. Jesus taught about having left ninety nine sheep in the wilderness, to go after the lost sheep. There are numerous scriptures which call out nine. The spiritual implication of the number nine is to <u>recognize its rank</u>. Nine ranks in a place of administrations and the operations of the Spirit of God. Christ the Exalted One, the Noble One, Esteemed, Royal, and he rules in the Highest. The High ranking positions of Christ are "first fruit", the Resurrection and the Life. The work of edification will cause those that live godly to be raised unto eternal life also. *They "shall be EXALTED."* Matthew 23:12 Also Read: <u>*NINE– the ministry of EDIFICATION:*</u> Genesis 17:27; Luke 15:1; Galatians 5:22; 1Corinthinas 12: 1, 8-10; Deuteronomy 28:8-14;

To worship God in Spirit is a sacrifice, a clean and holy offering unto the Lord. We are to lay aside every weight and sin that so easily beset us. As early as Cain and Abel, worship has been the way of giving homage to God. The practice of worship in the OT was to obtain the blood for sacrifice; an animal was slain. Remember the sacrifice of Abel, *"By faith Abel offered unto God a more excellent sacrifice than Cain, by which he obtained witness that he was righteous, God testifying of his gifts: and by it he being dead yet speaketh."* Hebrews 11:4

Redemption for man came by the shedding of the blood of Christ; he is the Lamb of God. The pattern of worship was taught by Moses and the Levitical priesthood. The Law covenant pointed to Christ; the sacrifice for the sin of mankind. Jesus was the perfect sacrifice: but under the law, animal sacrifices had to be clean, and without blemish. *"For if the blood of bulls and of goats, and the ashes of a heifer sprinkling the unclean, sanctifieth to the purifying of the flesh; How much more shall the blood of Christ, who through the eternal Spirit offered himself without spot to God, purge your conscience from dead works, to serve the living God.?"* Hebrews 9:13-14

Jesus obedience to the Father put in force the Will; he is the mediator of the New Testament. Jesus ate the Passover with his disciples: *"And as they were eating, Jesus took bread, and blessed it, and broke it, and gave it to the disciples, and said, Take, eat; this is my body. And he took the cup, and gave thanks; and gave it to them, saying, Drink ye all of it; For this is my blood of the new testament; which is shed for many for the remission of sins."* He put in force a new covenant; he did away with the old covenant that was practiced under the Law. The old covenant wasn't abolished: it was fulfilled in Christ. Therefore a new covenant because Jesus came to fulfill the law and he prophets. It is written, *"Whereupon neither the first testament was dedicated without blood. For when Moses had spoken every precept of all to the people according to the law, he took the blood of calves and of goats, with water, and scarlet wool, and hyssop, and sprinkled both the book, and all the people, Saying, this is the blood of the testament which God hath enjoined unto you. Moreover he sprinkled with blood both the tabernacle, and all the vessels of the ministry. And almost all things are by the law purged with blood; and without shedding blood is no remission."* Hebrews 9:18-22.

The Believer is a partaker of Christ's blood when they worship God in Spirit and truth. *"Having therefore, brethren, boldness to enter into the holiest by the blood of Jesus, By a new and living way, which he hath consecrated for us, through the veil, that is his flesh; And having a high priest over the house of God; Let us draw near with a true heart in full assurance of faith, having our hearts sprinkled from an evil conscience, and our bodies washed with pure water." Let us hold fast the profession of our faith without wavering; for he is faithful that promised;"* **Hebrews 10:19-23**

True worship is to present "your" body a living sacrifice; holy, acceptable unto God, which is your reasonable service. The promises of God bring restoration, redemption, requital, renewing, returning, recovering, reconciliation, and so on. Abraham received by faith all these blessings and his seed after him. God made the children of Israel the head and not the tail. They were a peculiar treasure unto the Lord above all the people of the earth. The mighty works of God to the children of Israel are examples the church should learn from.

Worship God in TRUTH: Jesus said to the woman at the well that the true worshippers *"shall worship the Father in Spirit and in Truth: for the Father seeketh such to worship him."* Presenting the body a living sacrifice, holy unto to the Lord is worshipping in Spirit. Jesus told the woman, *"Ye worship you know not what:"* This statement was to redirect the woman's form of worship. The woman was holding to the traditions taught her; but she was in need of being enlightened as to a true worshipper. Jesus stated, "in spirit and in truth' as the only <u>form</u> of worship God accepts. Just for a moment, notice the word <u>form</u>. This word defines structure and identity. Believers are to be conformed into the image of Christ by the renewing of the mind. The mind is a reservoir for housing knowledge. The knowledge of God is gained from the proclamation of his word. The knowledge of Christ enlightens us: his light shines in us.

From the scriptures, it is written, *"Grace and **truth** came by Jesus Christ."* To become a true worshipper, one must be a hearer and doer of the word Jesus taught. In doing so, the truth will conform and transform the Believer. The twelve disciples Jesus chose were first taught of him. They adhered to Christ doctrines of truth. By example, it was previously mentioned that Jesus ate the Passover with his disciples. Bread and a cup were given to the disciples to partake of. This represented partaking of his word and suffering. Jesus is the "Bread of Life" that came down from heaven. If man should eat of "this Bread" he will live. Bread is man's natural food; or the substance for sustaining natural life. The Bread that is given by Christ is the **word**: and if thou eat of it, thou shall live.

Also it was important for the disciples to be aware of the leaven of the Pharisees. Jesus spoke concerning false teachings in this manner; *"Then Jesus said unto them, Take heed and <u>beware of the</u> leaven of the Pharisees and of the Sadducees. And they reasoned among themselves, saying, it is because we have taken no bread. Which when Jesus perceived, he said unto them, O ye of little faith, why reason ye among yourselves, because ye have brought no bread? Do ye not yet understand, neither remembers the five loaves of the five thousand, and how many baskets ye took up? Neither the seven loaves of the four thousand, nor how many baskets ye took up? How is it that ye do not understand that I spake it not to you concerning bread, that ye should beware of the leaven of the Pharisees and of the Sadducees?*

*"<u>Then understood they how that he</u> **bade** <u>them not beware of leaven bread</u>, **<u>but of the doctrine of the Pharisees and of the Sadducees</u>.**"* Jesus reminded the disciples that when he gave thanks over the five loaves and two fish, the fragments left filled twelve baskets. Therefore they should not think that having no bread would have been a problem for Jesus. But he wanted them to see the leaven of the Pharisees. The false teachings of the Pharisees and the Sadducees are like unto leaven bread; because it adds to truth, causing defilement to the holy word. When people follow the doctrines of men, they are not worshiping God in Truth. Bowing down to false teachings hinders spiritual growth and can cause spiritual death. *"Jesus saith unto him, I am the Way, the Truth, and the Life: no man cometh unto the Father, but by me."* John 14:6 Jesus teachings and doctrines are truth; why should man establish his own doctrine? If men are to come to the Father, then they must follow the way, the truth and the life God has given. Read: Mark 8: 14-21; Luke 12: 1-3;

The apostles furthered the teachings of Jesus by the preaching the gospel of truth. The apostles suffered trials, afflictions and even death by the hands of those that sought to prevent the message of Christ. But before time, **wisdom** was building her house; a place for God to dwell. The man that enters in by faith is he that, "know my voice." The sheep will not follow a stranger's voice because they KNOW the truth. Jesus is the Truth. Abraham knew the voice of God and he obeyed him. What Abraham placed on the altar that he built is not written in the scripture. Therefore, the inference is that he acted on being a hearer and doer of what God had spoken unto him. The altar Abraham built unto the Lord showed that he was a true worshipper of God. He worshipped in spirit and in truth: which was an acceptable sacrifice unto the Lord. **Read:** John 6:48-58; & 6: 60-64; 12:44-50; 17: 2-3; 1John 2: 21-29; 1John 5: 6-12. The next recorded event in the Old Testament concerning Abram, is the rescue of his nephew Lot. "Wisdom Building Her House" is reflected in the experiences the father of faith lived through. Paraphrasing, "the word of God hath built or established his dwelling place." Continue to read and learn that "little space grace" was effectually operating in the life Abraham.

15

NOT AN OASIS, BUT A MIRAGE

THE HOUSE of GOD: and a Dungeon Place. After Lot separated himself from Abraham; he moved to the plains of Sodom. *"But the men of Sodom were wicked and sinners before the Lord exceedingly."* **Genesis 13:13.** This verse of scripture is only one sentence long, but it states the place he was in, and the sinful nature of the men of Sodom. Also, the word "exceedingly" was used to express the extreme degree of the wicked men lifestyles. "Before the Lord" is said to place emphasis on the fact that the people sins were not hidden from God. Lot lived with Abraham long enough to know the lifestyle of a righteous man. His selfish lust for the things he saw was his own down fall. *"And Lot lifted up his eyes, and beheld all the plain of Jordan, that it was well watered everywhere, before the Lord destroyed Sodom and Gomorrah, even as the garden of the Lord."* **Genesis 13:10** Lot lusted for the rich lifestyle of the people of Sodom. When Abraham had the experience of looking; he heard the voice of God commanding him to look. The words 'lifted up' and 'Lift up' creates a time factor. The 'ed' is past tense; which would mean that Lot already had the desire to have the well watered plains of Sodom. The indication of sin working in his nature started with the lust of the eyes. But Abram's response to the voice of God, gave him a view of greater promises. *"Whereby are given unto us* **exceeding great** *and* **precious promises:** *that by these ye might be partakers of the divine nature,* **having escaped the corruption that is in the world through lust."** 2Peter 1:4 Read: 1John 2:16

Often when people are faced with crossroads in life; seeking to find the solution without acknowledging God. Like as when Lot was faced with a decision to choose. The separation between Lot and Abraham was understandable as to refuting strife among the herdsmen. But Lot's failure was in not regarding the voice of God and his promises. For the scripture says, "*The fear of the Lord, that is wisdom; and to depart from evil is understanding.*" This also resonates the voice of Christ: "he that heareth these sayings of mine, and doeth them, I will liken him unto a wise man, which built his house upon a rock:" The Psalmist said, the *fear of the Lord is the beginning of wisdom: a good understanding have all they that do his commandments.*"

Every man is a builder of his own life: and the wisdom of God protects against disaster and loss. It was most unlikely for Abraham to have chosen the plains of Sodom to dwell in. Abraham didn't venture to make a choice to go forth; nor allowing the lust of the flesh to guide him. He walked by faith, not by sight. Unwise Lot walked by sight; and his experience brought him into captivity. He was given a direction to go: Abraham said unto Lot, "*Is not the whole land before thee?*" What is before thee is the position of something in front of you. "If *thou wilt take the left hand, and then I will go to the right: or if thou depart to the right hand, then I will go to the left.* This verse identifies three directional planes: front, right and left. Read examples of Crossroads/Choices→ Genesis 13:1-4; 13:9; JOB 1:19-21; 2:9-19; Luke 4:1-12; Proverbs 17:2

<u>FRONT</u>: **"before thee"** The land Lot viewed was in appearance the presence opportunity of a desired outcome. In a relationship, there may come a time the crossroad called separation will be eminent. "Before you" is what a person is faced with in life that beckons a confrontational choice. To go right or left is a directional straight path. Right and left creates a straight line between any point and object. Was Abraham showing Lot that a straight path is the choice to follow? The physical layout of the land of Bethel, Hebron, and Sodom will draw the direction Lot went. Earlier Abram left Egypt; he traveled northward, coming from a southward direction: he came to Bethel. After Lot separated himself, Abram went to Hebron. Bethel to the north became the "before thee" direction of Abraham's

view of the land. The place called Hai, which was to the east where he pitched his tent between Hai and Bethel. The plains of Sodom are southeast of Bethel. Learning from geography, south is at the bottom on the world's map. South has the hottest temps; the rain forests, poor natural resources; turbulent weather, earthquakes, and usually the poorest people of the earth.

Figuratively speaking; what is below is a pit, <u>a dungeon</u>, the grave, and hell. These are places of suffering, darkness. A place of separation, and intensely consuming away of spiritual life; which are the effects of transgression. The south therefore reveals the direction Lot went. In a place where new circumstances in his life arose; then eventually the "little space grace" delivered him out of his perils of life.

The reason to infer this is to show the moral message, and spiritual principles that should be received. Jesus taught that it is given for man to know the mysteries of the kingdom of God. In the Old Testament, types and shadows; parables, dark saying of old, similitudes, figure of speech and metaphors are given to enlighten men. The knowledge of good and evil becomes the theme of many biblical accounts, especially when the man of God is the main character. The law of Spirit will always defeat the law of sin and death. It is because God is omnipotent, the omnipresence and omniscience, the Father and Creator who has established his law in all things seen and unseen. Let the spiritual eye be enlightened by the moral message, rather than to see merely a story told. Know that God "*wilt have a desire to the work of his hands.*" **JOB 14:15** He provided in his word all things that pertain to man's salvation. The Bible is the word of God; therefore seek to understand his message and receive his law in the heart.

"Hear attentively the noise of his voice, and the sound that goeth out of his mouth. He diercteth it under the whole heaven, and his lightning unto the ends of the earth..." God thundereth marvelously with his voice; great things doeth he, which we cannot comprehend. He sealeth up the hand of every man; that all men

may know his work. Touching the Almighty, we cannot find him out: he is excellent in power, and in judgment, and in plenty of justice: he will not afflict. Men do therefore fear him; he respecteth not any that are wise of heart." JOB 37:2-8; v. 23.

"O sing unto the Lord a new song; for he hath done marvelous things: his right hand and his holy arm hath gotten him the victory. The Lord hath made known his salvation: his righteousness hath he openly showed in the sight of the heathen. Make a joyful noise unto the Lord, all the earth: make a loud noise, and rejoice, and sing praise. Sing unto the Lord with the harp; and the voice of a psalm. With trumpets and sound of cornets make a joyful noise before the Lord, the King." Psalm 98:1-6

It is apparent that Lot traveled southeast when he separated from Abraham. Sodom was southeast of the location of Bethel and Hai. Having revealed the spiritual significance of South; Lot situated his dwelling in an environment of wickedness. Apparently he did not make a wise choice. He followed the lust of his flesh, the lust of his eyes and the pride of life. Is this not the same entrapment Eve fell into when she was deceived by Satan? It is written, *"And when the woman saw that the tree was good for food,* [lust of the flesh], *and that it was pleasant to the eye,* [lust of the eyes] and a tree to be desired to make one wise. At times the pursue of happiness is lust some people seek for: [pride of life].

She took of the fruit thereof, and did eat, and gave also unto her husband with her; and he did eat." **Genesis 3:6**

Lot lusted after: *"And Lot lifted up his eyes, and beheld all the plains of Jordan,"* The first influence to sin is when a person's attention is drawn towards the thing beheld. Images are like idols in the vision of the man that have not the knowledge of God. They are the gods many men from the beginning of time bowed down to. Why is this so? Because men seek satiety, pleasure and power; being deceived in thinking that images provide those things. Lot did not error because he saw the land; but because he sought for something to appease his flesh. Abraham had already made Lot aware that "the whole land is before thee." The sight of the thing pleasant to the eyes stimulated the passion call **lust**. The lust of the eyes made the heart ready to pursue what was seen. It is written, *"Let no man say when he is tempted, I am tempted of God: for God cannot be tempted with evil, neither tempteth he any man: But every man is tempted, when he is <u>drawn away of his own lust</u>, and <u>enticed</u>. Then when lust hath <u>conceived</u>, it bringeth forth <u>sin</u>, and sin, when it is finished, <u>bringeth forth death</u>."* **James 1:13-15**

Notice the double vision; Lot **saw** and he **beheld** the plains of Jordan. First, Lot "saw" which gave him knowledge of what was before him. Secondly, he "beheld" the things he desired to have. When he beheld, Lot became enticed; and this was his entrapment. Jesus taught, *"The **light** of the body is the eye: if therefore **thine eye be single**, thy whole body shall be full of light. <u>But if thine eye be evil</u>, thy whole body shall be <u>full of darkness, if</u> therefore the light that is in thee be darkness, how great is that darkness!"* Matthew **6: 22-23; Read**: Luke 17:28-30.

Jesus referred to light, which connotes knowledge; is to be single eyed. But if the eye be evil, this implies a wicked vision or knowledge. Explaining further, Jesus said, <u>*"No man can serve two masters: for either he will hate the one, and love the other; or else he will hold to the one, and despise the other. Ye cannot serve God and mammon. Therefore, I say unto you, take no thought for your life, what ye shall eat, or what ye shall drink; nor yet for your body, what ye shall put on. Is not the life more than meat, and the body than raiment?*</u> *"For after these things do the Gentiles seek: for your heavenly Father knoweth that ye have need of all these things."*

Lot's second view, *"he beheld all the plains of Sodom,"* which caused his life to become full of darkness. Those that pursue after riches of this world's goods, sometimes come to realize that those things bring no happiness. Living in the environment of wickedness can influence or affect the moral character of a person. The outcome is known by the conditions the lifestyle creates. The wickedness of mankind becomes degenerate; the practices of lewdness, culpable or criminal behavior, mischief, malicious acts and corruption. Jesus said, "*The whole body shall be full of darkness*" This Jesus said, speaking of the entire domain of a man's life that is effected by a wicked vision.

The "Whole Body" as related to person's judgment, the character and one's interactions in life "*shall be full of darkness.*" These things evolve over a period of time; but the result is the darkness. At first, Lot was rich when he "*pitched his tent*" toward Sodom. But Lot lost all his worldly possessions in the destruction of Sodom and Gomorrah. Therefore, his "whole body" or life became full of darkness. Lot suffered the loss of what he thought was a gain for his life. His sight caused him to partake of the experience of trouble; the double vision had obscured his judgment. Remember, Lot "looked" and he "beheld" all the plains of Jordan. Read: Luke 11: 23-36**; Psalm** 107: 34;

The choice Lot made also foreshadowed the captivity he would experience. A few years after living in Sodom, Lot actually became a captive to the kings of that land. But God is merciful; he sent his word by the angels first before the destruction. Faith comes by hearing the voice of God to give us right judgment. The word of God is the direction to follow. When men experience the loss of their goods, often it is because the voice of human reasoning and logic snares them to act without the command of God. Solomon said, "*Trust in the Lord with all thine heart; and lean not unto thine own understanding. In all thy ways acknowledge him, and he shall direct thy paths. Be not wise in thine own eyes: fear the Lord, and depart from evil. It shall be health to thy navel, and marrow to thy bones.*" **Proverbs 3:5**

Solomon learned from his father these sayings, "*Hear, O my son, and receive my sayings; and the years of thy life shall be many. I have taught thee in the way of wisdom; I have led thee in right paths. When thou goest, thy steps shall not be straitened; and when thou runnest, thou shalt not stumble. Take fast hold of instruction; let her not go: keep her; for she is thy life.*

Enter not into the path of the wicked, and go not in the way of evil men. Avoid it, pass not by it, turn from it, and pass away." **Proverbs 4:10:15**

Lot Beheld: When he saw the land, the lust of the flesh was conceived in his heart. A man can see a lot of things; but everything he sees is not always received in the heart. Emotions and passions proceeds from the heart: some are covered by righteousness. But some passions that proceed forth are unrighteous acts. Jesus said, *"But those things which proceed out of the mouth come forth from the heart; and they defile the man. For out of the heart proceed evil thoughts, murders, adulteries, fornication, thefts, false witness, blasphemies: These are the things which defile a man: but to eat with unwashen hands defileth not a man."* **Matthew 15:18-20**

The Greek word is **stoma,** for mouth. By implication, <u>language</u> fig. an opening; spec. the *front* or *edge* (of a weapon)-face, edge, mouth. In the Book of James, it is written, *"For any man offend not in word, the same is a perfect man, and able also to bridle the <u>whole body.</u> Behold, we put bits in the horses' mouths, that they may obey us; and we turn about their whole body. Behold also the ships, which though they be so great, and are driven about with a very small helm, whithersoever the governor listeth. Even so the tongue is a small member, and boasteth great things, Behold, how great a matter a little fire kindleth! And the tongue is a fire, a world of iniquity; so is the tongue among our members, that is defileth the whole body, and sitteth on fire the course of nature; and it is set on fire of hell."* **James 3:2-5**

The expression, "the whole Body shall be full of darkness" alludes to the entire life experiences of a man. In all his experiences, a man will communicate. Language is the most common means of communicating. If evil communication corrupts good manners; evil issuing forth from the heart defiles a man. What is the heart? The heart is the seat of the intellect; the place of emotions and passions. God commands man to "love God with all thy heart." because the love affection will come from the heart also. The heart is not the physical organ that pumps the blood in the body the scripture refers to. But the heart is <u>the will of man</u>; a desire created out of an acceptance of what is heard and perceived. If things that are heard and perceived enter the heart of man; then the heart will perform it. If lust is in the heart; adultery will issue forth. If hatred is in the heart; killing and murdering will issue out. Also, the 'doctrine of men born with free-choice' is a misguided concept. A man's free choice leads him away from the will of God. Therefore, to Christians, their desire is to do the will of God. This is why the voice from heaven said, *"This is my Beloved Son, and in him I am well pleased."* In Jesus suffering, he prayed to the Father, "If thou be willing, let this cup pass from me, but not my will but thou will be done."

Lot's Heart: When he, *"beheld all the plains of Jordan, that it was well watered everywhere, before the Lord destroyed Sodom and Gomorrah, even as the **garden of the Lord**, like the **land of Egypt**, as thou comest unto Zoar."* That which entered Lot's heart came by way of what he saw, and desired presently. In that moment he recalled, historically what he heard about of the Garden of Eden. Lot experienced time in Egypt when Sarai was in Pharaoh's house. But he had his own perception of life. One thing was heard, which was story about the garden of the Lord {Eden}. Lot's experience in Egypt was seemed by him. This created his reasoning to choose to go to Sodom. The "well watered" plains seemly would provide for Lot, his flocks, herds and tents all the substance for living. Places that are well watered promises growth and development. A man can excel when natural resources are in abundance.

The water represented being enticed to elevate the spirit in Lot. But this became the pulsation for the first sign to the conception of lust. Then the desire of his flesh was materializing. To germinate this conception of lust, Lot compared the plains *"even as the garden of the Lord."* He also compared the plains *"like the land of Egypt, "as thou comest unto Zoar."* He expressed a dual comparison, but with an opposing contrast. He was told of the paradise of God, which was

Eden: a place well contained, peaceful and blessed. But Egypt cannot be compared with the garden of the Lord. Was there something in Lot's heart that made him desire a place like Egypt? His time in Egypt brought him no notoriety, no riches; only flocks, herd and tents. Looking back at Egypt apparently speaks of his lust to have the things of others: this lust is called "to covet." A description of the territory Lot compared to the plains of Jordan was "unto Zoar." This area is a wilderness place. The Hebrew word for Zoar is **Tsoar, from the word tsar,** defined > to *be small*; (fig) ignoble—*be brought low, little one,* be small.

Spiritual so, the children of God will undergo the wilderness experiences in life; purposed to humble and make them lowly in spirit. *"Blessed are the meek: for they shall inherit the earth."* **Matthew 5:5** But what Lot beheld *was what* he coveted; he desired and went after the things he lusted for. Lust was conceived in his heart: and this is "that" which defiled the man. He acted out of the dictates of his heart, [will]. The scripture says, *"And Lot dwelled in the cities of the plain, and pitched his tent toward Sodom."* He took up residency in the cities of the plain. His life began to intermingle with the people of that land. Sodom was in his view: implying that Lot felt comfortable in the land of Sodom.

> *He that hasteth to be rich hath an evil eye, and considereth not that poverty shall come upon him."* **Proverbs 28:22**

Lot acted out of lust: *"Then Lot chose him all the plain of Jordan; and Lot journeyed east: and they separated themselves one from the other."* The conception of lust in his eyes brought on the action to go forth; he followed his vision. Lot chose a vast amount of land: "all the plains of Jordan." This land in today's market of sales would equate to great riches. The land lies at the eastern border to the land of Canaan. Pictured like a crescent of the Arabian Desert; separated by the Salt Sea and the Jordan River. Figuratively, Lot partook of the tree of knowledge of good and evil; in a sense like as did Eve. Only the word of God can give life more abundantly. To see the riches of the plains were not from the planting of God's law. Wicked kings of that time had established cities and laws for them to rule in. Eventually the works of wicked men were destroyed.

Lot learned that the fruit or success of the wicked was not good. "Partake" *means,* to take part in; to participate. Partake is to have some of the qualities or attributes of something. Like Adam and Eve, Lot took part in the things of life that eventually became death. The symbolic tree of the knowledge of good and evil fruit is *experience.* Knowledge is acquired by experience: but good and evil is the experience. The voice Eve heard was that of the devil. So as with Lot: enticed by logical reasoning to the pursue of happiness. His life was greatly affected; which was the results of partaking of that experience. But the measure of God's grace, {"little space grace"} brought to Lot salvation. Lot learned obedience later in his life, by exemplifying the righteousness of Abraham.

Men seek after things to satisfy their natural life, but what they find is vanity or emptiness; not having contentment in the things they possess. This is the travail which God hath given to men to be exercised therein. The reason God allows the travail, is for man to know, *"that there is no good in them, but for a man to rejoice, and to do good in his life. And also that every man should eat and drink, and enjoy the good of his labor, it is the gift of God.* "God doeth it, that men should fear him."* **Ecclesiastes 3: 10-13;** Partaking of this knowledge of God is good. It would have been Lot's right direction to go. *"Better is little with the fear of the Lord than great treasures and trouble therein."* **Proverbs 15:16.** Nevertheless, God will show mercy to the man void of this knowledge. David prayed, *"My heart was hot within me, while I was musing the fire burned: then I spake I with my tongue, Lord, make me to know mine end, and the measure of my days, what it is: that I may know how frail I am."* **Psalm 39:3-4**

To God be the glory for the things he has done! *"The Lord is gracious, and full of compassion; slow to anger, and of great mercy. The Lord is good to all: and his tender mercies are over all his works." "He delighteth not in the strength of the horse: he taketh not pleasure in the legs of a man. The Lord taketh pleasure in them that fear him, in those that hope in his mercy."* Psalm 145:8-10 & 147:10

They Separated, one from the other: After Lot chose the plains of Jordan, he separated himself from his uncle. The scripture reads, *"Abram dwelled in the land of Canaan."* Unwavering faith is to remain in the place of promise. The land of Canaan later was possessed by the children of Israel; the *"land of promise;" Israel* received it because of the covenant God made with Abraham. He walked by faith: the word of the Lord that guided him on the path he sojourned in.

Separation settled the problem of the strife that arose among the herdsmen of Abraham and Lot. Recall the strife of Abraham and Lot's herdsmen. To settle the problem, Abraham said, *"let there be no strife,"* he was showing authority and rule. Then he said, for *we be brethren."* Abraham was teaching the law of love for Lot to adhere to. The greatest law is to love God and thy neighbor as thou self. Abraham presided over the matter as a judge; he gave the law that Lot was to follow. Then Lot separated himself from his uncle; he chose the plains of Jordan.

Separation created a new atmosphere and environment for Lot to "dwell" in; for "he pitched his tent toward Sodom." But *"Abram dwelled in the land of Canaan, and Lot dwelled in the cities of the plain, and pitched his tent toward Sodom."* Genesis 13:12. The underlined words draw attention to the following comments concerning this scripture.

First the **Hebrew word dwelled, is yashab;** a primitive root: probable
> *to sit* (specifically as judge, in ambush, and in quiet) by implication,
> *to dwell, to **remain**: to settle, to marry:* [make to] **abide** *continue,*

ease self, endure, **establish***, habitation, haunt,* [make to] **inhabit***, make to keep* [house]*, seat, set,* (down)*, tarry.*

The words defining **dwelled,** describe Lot's life experiences as he dwelled in the plains of Jordan. The same or similar experiences people gain from separating to a new environment for living. People will set up habitation; they abide in a place; they may marry and establish a new life. Dwelling in the cities of the plain made an impact on the experience of separating. No popular city is without ordinances, statues and laws to govern its citizens. Lot became a citizen of the cities; therefore he had to abide by their laws. Prior to his new submission to the laws of the cities, Lot once followed his uncle Abraham. The man that walked in faith and only the voice of God was the law Abram followed. But Laws instituted by men do not make a man faithful. Nor do laws make him a believer to the cause for which laws are established. There is no mercy in laws; they are given to rule over others to satisfy the purpose they are designed to gain. But the law of God is Love: it gives rather than gain.

Separation from one place and dwelling in the cities changed Lot's position, status and power. He was faced with adapting to traditions, customs and the lifestyles of the people of the plains. Lot learned their economy, the market places, and the schools of learning, the city leaders, areas of resort, and the demographics of the cities. Before God spoke to Abram concerning the *"exceeding great reward" Lot* would have by lineage, inherited Abram's prosperity. In the cities of the plains, Lot had no inheritance there; but as the nephew of Abram, he would have inherited his goods. Being of blood kin, Lot knew the customs and traditions taught by his forefathers. In the plains, Lot wasn't accustomed to the traditions, nor customs of the people. Read: 2Corinthians 6: 14-18; 7:1; 1Corinthians 3:16;

The following passage is from the book, "The Works of Josephus." He was an historian who was highly esteemed in Jewish history. Josephus wrote the following passage. "Abram, having no son of his own, adopted Lot, his brother Haran's son. With his wife Sarai's he left the land of Chaldea when he was seventy-five years old, and at the command of God went into Canaan; therein he dwelt himself, and left it later to his prosperity. He was a person of great sagacity, both for understanding all things and persuading his hearers. Not mistaken in his opinions; for which reason he began to have higher notions of virtue than others had. He determined to renew and change the opinion all men happened at that time to have concerning God. He was the first that ventured to publish this notion that there was but one God, the Creator of the universe; and that, as to other [gods] if they contributed anything to the happiness of men, that each of them afforded it only according to his appointment, and not by their own power. This was his opinion, being derived from the irregular phenomena that were visible both at land and sea, as well as those that happen to the sun and moon, and all the heavenly bodies thus. "If [said he] theses bodies had power of their own, they would certainly take care of their own regular motions; but since they do not preserve such regularity, they make is plain, they are subservient to Him that commands them: to whom alone we ought justly to offer our honour and thanksgiving." Copied from "The Complete Works of Josephus," Flavius Josephus, Translated by Wm. Whiston: P. 33

This excerpt is given to enlighten the reader in realizing that Lot was taught by Abram; and learning from Abram that God is the Creator. Lot was taught that God is the almighty with power to govern the heavens and the earth. That God careth for the universe and for men; upholding everything by the power of his word. Abram taught virtue, and he turned men attention toward God rather than to idol gods. But in the cities of the plains, Lot learned how the people governed their affairs. Read: Psalm 72:11; 97:7; 100:2 Luke 16:13 & 17:8; John 12:26

Living in the new environment, Lot lost his liberty to rule; because he was subject to another man's rule. Being less in power to control or govern made Lot diminished in strength and might. The new environment produced change and uncertainty, because of the unfamiliarity that surrounded him. Not only the new environment effected Lot's life, but his "view" of Sodom had an emotional effect. Everything he viewed while in Sodom did not bring him the pleasure he thought it would be. His soul became vexed after a period of time because the wickedness of the people. He was not exposed to such wickedness when he was with Abraham. Lot was experiencing the contrast between good and evil. He left that which brought him good because he allowed lust to enter his heart. The vanity of life Lot found himself in did not award him with happiness. One day he was delivered from this vanity of life through the mercy of God; when Abraham rescued him. Read in the Second Epistle of Peter: *"According as his divine power hath given unto us all things that pertain unto life and godliness, through the knowledge of him that called us to glory and virtue: Whereby are give unto us exceeding great and precious promises: that by these ye might be partakers of the divine nature,* having escaped *the **corruption** that is **in the world through lust**."* 2Peter 1:4 Lot situated himself in a place that permeated lust and corruption. Later he learned that escape was his saving option in the day God brought destruction upon the cities. Lot "And *pitched his tent toward Sodom.*" The positional word toward, implies that Lot could view Sodom from his tent. The tent was a temporary place Lot physically dwelled in. In the cities of dwelling, Lot became a citizen and adapted to city life. Read: Psalm 37:3-9

Read about the tent Lot dwelled in. Consider the spiritual application for the word **tent**; it is a covering that gives no protection to forceful elements such as storms, high winds, and wild beast and to violent intrusion. Tents will dry, rip and rot after a period of time if the conditions are arid or too moist. Tents are portable; they are used as temporary dwelling places; not meant for long term use. And tents provide no security against thieves, robbers and the intruders that may gain access at any point to enter inside a tent. Tents are not established on foundations; they have neither walls nor windows. Tents are flammable, shifty, and too weak to hold weighty items. No true privacy for those that live in a tent. Even small insects and rodents can enter a tent without difficulty. *"For a day in thy courts is better than a thousand. I had rather be a doorkeeper in the house of my God, than to dwell in the tents of wickedness."* **Psalm 84:10**

The next verse speak of the environment Lot was in. *"But the men of Sodom were wicked and sinners before the Lord exceedingly."* It is believable to think that Lot was aware of the kind of people he lived around. Although the place was new to him; Lot knew that the people of Sodom were wicked and sinners. Did Lot realize what it was to be wicked; which is to be bad? The people of Sodom exhibited a behavior which was morally and ethically unacceptable. Morally, bad behaviors are vile and disgraceful acts of mankind. The scriptures record many instances of the wickedness of men. But Lot acknowledged that the well watered plain "as the garden of the Lord;" Lot was recalling his-story passed on to him by the forefathers. He knew something about what God required of Adam, and the ten generations that came after Adam. In his historical account, there was a cause for the destruction of the world by the flood in Noah's day. *"And God saw that the wickedness of man was great in the earth, and that every imagination of the thoughts of his heart was only evil continually."* Genesis 6:5

Lot recalled his most recent experience with Abraham in Egypt. He saw God's displeasure against Pharaoh's house because of an evil that would have been perpetrated against Abraham. This added to his knowledge and judgment of what was right or wrong by God's standards. His choice to move to the plains of Jordan, situating himself there was a thing of fleshly desire. With his true historical accounts, Lot used them to justify his reason to move; a choice undeniably inexcusable to God. Remember, Adam was not deceived; he was told by God what not to partake of. Neither was Lot deceived: Lot knew, but he became enticed by what he beheld. Lot knew what was right; and neither was there any problem or flaw in memory. Both his long and short term memory was intact. His long term memory was what he spoke of concerning "the garden of the Lord," which was

Eden. His short term memory was his statement about Egypt. He could not say truthfully, I didn't know: neither could he say no one ever told me better. Ignorantly, people often disrespect the wisdom of God, when they make the excuse, "God knew I was going to do this." *For the wrath of God is revealed from heaven against all ungodliness and unrighteousness of men, who hold the truth in unrighteousness; Because that which may be known of God is manifest in them; for God hath showed it unto them."* **Romans 1:18**-19 Lot had the free will to do otherwise, but he took that freedom for an occasion to his flesh. Read: Galatians 5:13

Note the word "sinners" from the **Hebrew, ahatta; a** *criminal,* or one accounted *guilty*— offender, sinful, sinner. The Bible records many instances of God's disapproval of wickedness. With making his decision, Abram said to him, that the land is before thee. Clearly he was at liberty to go forward; right or left to encompass the land of promise. Remember, Lot left Haran and traveled with Abraham to Canaan. This land was chosen by God: and Lot apparently knew the reason why Abraham came to Canaan.

Wickedness: Something important to be said about this immoral behavior. In the Book of Galatians 5:19-21 there are seventeen works of the flesh named. They are adultery, fornication, uncleanness, lasciviousness, idolatry, witchcraft, emulations, hatred, variance, wrath, strife, seditions, heresies, envying, murders, drunkenness and reveling. These acts are contrary to the Spirit of God: for the law and nature of God is love. To do an in-depth study of each of these works of the flesh will expand knowledge to the learner of truth. If all the works and the spirits that operate in them were known, they would be called collectively "Legion" for they are many. For an example; the work of the flesh called, 'adultery' evolved out of lust, covetousness, falsehood, evil concupiscence, evil surmising, deceit, and other ungodly spirits that may be known. The work of the flesh called 'variance' and the spirits that operate are strife, division, making differences, separating or making asunder, bitterness, unforgiving, blaming, contention, opposing, debating and other spirits that do not manifest the nature of God. The demons of Satan work to kill steal and destroy the temple of God. In the gospels, Jesus said, *"When the unclean spirit is gone out of a man, he walketh through dry places, seeking rest, and findeth none. Then he saith, I will return into my house from whence I came out: and when he is come, he findeth it empty, swept, and garnished. Then goeth he, and taketh with himself seven other spirits more wicked than himself, and they enter in and dwell there: and the last state of that man is worse than the first. Even so shall it be also unto this wicked generation."* Matthew 12:43-45 Jesus was speaking concerning a wicked generation in this scripture: rebuking those who sought after a sign. The Christian walk is by faith; not by sight. The choice Lot made was by sight. Read: Galatians 5: 19-21; Romans 7: 8; Colossians 3: 5; 1Thessilonians 4:5; Mark 7: 22; Proverbs 12: 5 & 20; Jeremiah 14: 14

Unethical behavior is considered to be criminal activity against society. Wicked behaviors develop over a period of time when men follow after the lusts of their own flesh. Take a look at the lawless practices of today; they are greater than crimes committed forty years ago. A news report may televise fifty violent crimes committed the first month of the year. Then they may compare this to fifty crimes committed over a period of the first six months of the previous year. Behavior not governed by laws and behavior not penalized will become behaviors not corrected. God destroyed the old world in Noah's day because men continually practiced wickedness. After only a few hundred years between Adam to Noah, the soul of men became more degenerate. In the beginning God established laws in the earth. But God will also rebuke, reprove, chastise and punish those that offend or disobey his laws.

History teaches that the Assyrians people were dominant in rule and power in that land. When Lot first moved near Sodom, the plains were flourishing both with people and riches. Perhaps like one of the mega cities of America; New York, Houston or L.A. Any city that flourishes with people and riches would seem to have laws that govern the affairs of that city. The question that comes to mind is how did they become wicked? Remember the flood of Noah's day cleaned the earth of corruption, making it habitual without the wicked. At the time, there were no morally bad behaviors being practiced. But wickedness once again happened in the earth.

With Adam, all people born after him had his sinful nature. From Adam to Noah there were ten generations of the sin nature in all men. *"Wherefore, as by one man sin entered into the world, and death by sin; and so death passed upon all men, for that all have sinned." For as by one man's disobedience many were made sinners, so by one shall many be made righteous."* Romans 5:12, 19 Sin entered into the world because Adam transgressed the command of God. Adam is father of all humans: therefore his sin nature is in all who are born. Although the flood removed the wicked from the earth, it had no effect on the nature of sin in man. It is said, that "laws cannot govern human nature:" laws are made to govern human behaviors. News reports are daily on the increase concerning crime in the world. Such crimes are greater than known in the beginning of time. This is why the message goes forth that the Lord is soon to return to earth. Wickedness is prevalent in the world. The imaginations of the hearts of men are continually wicked.

According to the scripture, it was a period of years before Lot was mentioned again. It wasn't until the kings who ruled in the land were attacked by other kings when Lot was mentioned again. But before Abram came to Canaan, king Chedorlaomer had extended his power westward to the borders of Egypt. Five kings near the Dead Sea served him in tributes. They later rebelled after king Chedorlaomer fourteenth year of ruling. This king, along with three of his allies came to put an end to the rebellion of the other five kings. He was successful in defeating the cities along the trade route of the plains of Jordan, and also south of the Dead Sea. Among Chedorlaomer's captives was Abraham's nephew Lot. It was a period of fourteen years of living among the wicked and sinners, and then Lot became a captive. His perils were soon known to Abraham. Lot was in great turmoil along with the citizens of the cities. The five kings of the plains could not provide safety for their citizens. The cities of the plains of Jordan were overthrown and Lot was taken captive. Two of the rulers fled to safety for their own selves. *"And the Vale of Siddim was full of slime pits; and the kings of Sodom and Gomorrah fled, and fell there; and they that remained fled to the mountain."* Genesis 14:10 Lot learned by experienced the words of Solomon, *"By the blessing of the upright the city is exalted: but it is overthrown by the mouth of the wicked."* Proverbs 11:11

16

IN THE PIT

CAPTIVITY: A condition or circumstance brought about by someone or something more dominate. The person is carried away; taken or transported from one place to another. The person is a prisoner, being confined, restrained and prevented from escaping. Heavy chains or bars were fastened on to the captive, making it difficult to escape. The chambers for housing prisoners earlier in Lot's time were called dungeons. They were usually underground, cold and dark. Read: Isaiah 54: 17; 2Corinthians 10: 4-6; Ephesians 6:13; 1Thessalonians 5:8-9; 1Timothy 1:8-11.

The rebellion and warfare of the kings created captivity in the lives of those they had rule over. Most warfare's are with collateral damage, captives and carrying away of the booty. These are the perils Lot experienced. Before the foundation of the world, the word of God, which is wisdom, was establishing his will. If loving one another is the will of God; then warfare is God's displeasure. He has power and authority over the conditions of men. Lot learned that "no weapon formed against thee shall prosper." The word of God actively accomplishes his will: his word prospers where unto it is sent. Wisdom said, *"The Lord possessed me in the beginning of his way, or ever the earth was. "When he gave the sea his decree, that the waters should not pass his commandment: when he appointed the foundations of the earth: Then I was by him: and I was daily his delight, rejoicing always before him: Rejoicing in the habitable part of his earth; and my delights were with the sons of men. Now therefore hearken unto me, O ye children: for blessed are they that keep my ways."* Proverbs 8:22, 30-32

In the beginning of creation, God said, "let there be" wherefore instituting his law in all things created. With man, *"God having predestinated us unto the <u>adoption of children</u> by Jesus Christ to himself, according to the good pleasure of his will."* Ephesians 1:5 Adoption is a legal process for obtaining children. That which is legal pertains to a law that orders the process. Adoption is the placing of a "son" or to be a "kin". Why would there be a need for a son other than to enter into a relationship with. Lot was Abraham's nephew; he was adopted by Abraham once he left Haran. His adoption was not to be a son; because Jesus Christ, {the Word} had legal rights to that relationship. The scripture said, "And *when Abram heard that* **<u>his brother</u>** *was taken captive, he armed his trained servants."* Genesis 14:12. This was the relationship Lot had with Abraham: as a brother. All men that obey the heavenly Father are brethrens; a relationship entered in by Jesus Christ.

God has prepared deliverance for men, out of their perils of life. Solomon said, *"There was a little city, and few men within it; and there came a great king against it, and besieged it, and built great bulwarks against it. Now there was found in it a poor wise man, and he by his wisdom delivered the city; yet no man remembered that same poor man. Then said I, Wisdom is better than strength: nevertheless the poor man's wisdom is despised, and his words are not heard. The words of wise men are heard in quiet more that the cry of him that ruleth among fools. Wisdom is better than weapons of war: but one sinner destroyeth much good."* Ecclesiastes 9:14-18

The Hebrew word b<u>uilded is</u> *banah,* and defined > to build (lit or fig): begin to build, *obtain children,* make, *repair,* set (up); Now we see Abraham as the elder brother with authority, who took charge in the rescue of Lot. A brother to brother relationship is stronger than a nephew to uncle relationship. Brothers have a moral obligation to bear one another's burden; when it is in their power to do so. But the brothers' ethical obligation is to have charity. *"Beloved, let us love one another: for love is of God: and every one that loveth is born of God, and knoweth God."* 1John 4:7

It's interesting to note Lot's reason for separating from Abraham; which was the strife between the herdsmen. In similarity, his experiences of conflict and strife reoccurred with the kings of Sodom against the Assyrian kings. After fourteen years of living in Sodom, Lot saw strife again; and this strife eventually leads to warfare. When Abraham resolved the strife between the herdsmen, he stood on the principle of God's word. Abraham said, *"Let there be no strife, I pray thee, between me and thee, and between my herdsmen and thy herdsmen; for we be brethren."* The Beatitudes' as they are often called; Jesus said, *"Blessed are the peacemakers: for they shall be called the children of God."* Matthew 5:9. The children of God are to trust in his word in spiritual warfare; the assured victory over the enemy. The word of God believed will create faith in the heart. Without faith it is not possible to please God. The word is the keeper of the soul; a present help in the time of need. By it all things are possible to them that believe. And in the case of being a captivity in the land of the wicked, Lot needed a deliverer. *"For though we walk in the flesh, we do not war after the flesh: For the weapons of our warfare are not carnal, but mighty through God to the pulling down of strong holds; Casting down imaginations, and every high thing that exalteth itself against the knowledge of God, and bringing into captivity every thought to the obedience of Christ: And having in a readiness to revenge all disobedience, when your obedience is fulfilled."* 2Corinthians *10:3-6*

The strife between the herdsmen was resolved by Abraham ruling in his own house. The spoken wisdom of Abram solved the strife of the herdsmen. The choice to separate was for the purpose of needing more room for their cattle. Lot knew that the disagreement was a private dispute between a few men. He did not hesitate to spread out in the land for the sake of the herdsmen. Lot favored the well watered land; he moved there. He saw what may have been the pleasures that this area would afford him. But strife broke out among five kings against four kings. The kings of Sodom engaged other kings to be their allies. Thousands of men were sent into the battle to fight for their king. They were a large number of rebellious people having strife ready for warfare. The disagreement started with the problem of one king refusing to continue to pay tribute to the other king. The root of conflict was covetousness, a spirit driven to have what another person possess. To covet and to have envy, usually escalates into strife when this emotion is not governed. Division often follows behind strife when it is not resolved. Warfare is the results, causing destruction and death; loss of property, loss of goods and the life of a people affected by warfare.

Lot was captured and brought into captivity after the kings of Sodom and Gomorrah fled and fell in the Vale of Siddim. These two kings sought refuge in the slime pits of the Vale of Siddim. They escaped being killed in the battle; but they showed no courage in protecting the people of their cities. Their fall allowed the people of the cities to be victimized, pillaged over and overtaken by the enemy. The kings fled and fell; this dual action gained no deliverance for the people. To flee, as in hiding, escaping chased away or put to flight. They 'fell' which means that the kings were over thrown. They became inferior to, and fugitives; separated from their cities. Recall, Lot became separated because of strife also. Experiencing this situation, the kings were in distress, afraid and at a loss of their control and power. The cities of the plains suffered lost: the scripture records, *"And they took all the goods of Sodom and Gomorrah, and all their victuals, and went their way. And they took Lot, Abram's brother's son, who dwelt in Sodom, and his goods, and departed."* Genesis 14:11

The situation of Lot becoming a captive is the Dungeon Place he became victim to. Lot was in need of a deliverer to rescue him from what may have been his eminent death. Abraham was his redeemer; the one who found grace with God. Abram literally acted upon the message Elihu spoke unto Job when he was in distress. It is written: *"Then he openeth the ears of men, and sealeth their instruction, that he may* *withdraw man from his purpose, and hide pride from man. He keepeth back his soul from **the pit** {grave}, and his life from perishing by the sword. He is chastened also with pain upon his bed, and the multitude of his bones with strong pain: So that his life abhorreth bread, and his soul dainty meat, His flesh is consumed away, that it cannot be seen; and his bones that were not seen stick out. Yea, his soul draweth near unto the grave and his life to the destroyers. If there be a messenger {Abram} with him {Lot}, an interpreter, one among a thousand, to show unto man his uprightness: Then he is gracious unto him, and saith, <u>Deliver him from going down **to the pit**: **I have found a ransom.**"* JOB 33:16-24*

Abram was the interpreter of the word of God because he heard his voice and obeyed the word. He found grace in the sight of the Lord; therefore he became Lot's Deliverer. Lot was rescued from going down in the pit. **This pit** or dungeon is death; but his life was saved. This is an illustration and type of the redemption of Christ to those in captivity or bondage. Christ's life was the ransom given for man to receive eternal life. Read: John 3:16

Abraham was the interpreter of the message and he sought redemption for the captives. Like the words of Elihu, *"Deliver him from going down into the pit: for I have found a ransom."* Redemption is the mercy of God. JOB 33:24

Lot and some of the people of Sodom experienced the "Dungeon Place:" The place wisdom foreknew and wisdom predestined man's deliverance from. God has ordained man to be spiritually ransomed by the grace of God, Jesus Christ. *"The Spirit of the Lord is upon me, because he hath anointed me to preach the gospel to the poor; he hath sent me to heal the brokenhearted, to preach deliverance to the captives, and recovering of sight to the blind, to set at liberty them that are bruised."* Luke 4:18 Isaiah 61:1 But this deliverance speaks universally to all those in captivity to be set free. Jesus entered into the dungeon place in death. He preached deliverance to the souls in hell or the pit. *"For Christ also, hath once suffered for sins, the just for the unjust, that he might bring us to God, being put to death in the flesh, but quickened by the Spirit: By which also he went and preached unto the spirits in prison."* 1Peter 3: 18-19

*"Jesus, when he had cried again with a loud voice, yielded up the ghost. And, behold the veil of the temple was rent in twain from top to bottom; and the earth did quake, and the rocks rent; And the graves were opened; and many bodies of the saints which slept arose, And came **out of the graves after his resurrection, and went into the holy city, and appeared unto many.**"* Matthew 27: 50-53

Grace is the measure of God's mercy shown the people who were rescued because of Abram's faith; "little space grace." If Lot had not moved to Sodom, Abraham probably would not have fought with the Assyrian kings. He fought them with his three hundred and eighteen trained servants of his own household. Apparently, he was a leader who had great influence over the trained men.

When Abram came out of Egypt, the scripture said, *"And Abram went up out of Egypt, he, and his wife, and all that he had, and Lot with him into the south."* Genesis 13:1; Less than twenty years, Abram's household had enlarged; he had servants, cattle, silver and gold. The blessings of God were in his life because he walked by faith. God had promised Abram: *"I will make thy name great."* He had influence, control, authority, material possessions and favor with men. His faith made those things possible unto him, because he believed God.

Good Success: the reward of Faith The law of success as spoken in the Beginning of Creation is, *"" So God created man in his own image, in the image of God created he him: male and female created he them. And God blessed them, and God said unto them, Be Fruitful, and Multiply, and Replenish the earth, and Subdue it: and have Dominion over the fish of the sea, and over the fowl of the air, and over every living thing that moveth upon the earth."* Genesis 1: 27-28; This scripture spoke of man before he was formed from the dust of the earth. This implies the true image of the god-man is spiritual. And out of the spiritual nature

147

of God, male and female were given his law. They were ordained to be fruitful, multiply, replenish, subdue and have dominion upon the earth. There are no Blessings a man can acquire that are without increase. Material wealth does not grant to man the blessings of life and good that God's word promises to give.

But we see Abram as a man blessed of God. It wasn't his servants, cattle, silver nor gold that gave him good success. Abraham had the law of God working in him that blessed him. By comparison, the two kings of Sodom and Gomorrah ruled over their cities. They were rich and armed with a military; but they had no good success. They fled and fell because of other kings more powerful than they. God's favor upon Abraham caused redemption for Lot and others. What would three hundred trained servants be to five military forces of the kings? It's wasn't by might, nor by human power that made Abraham the victor; but by the Spirit of God. For Abram to have an armed military force that numbered like the five kings may have given the praise to man; but the glory was for God.

Everything that will be known of the faith walk with Abraham, teaches wisdom establishing faith as the path in which the seed of Abraham would follow. In a passage of scripture; Abraham chased the kings toward Dan and Damascus. This same territory was the area his grandson Dan was given as an inheritance. Later Moses spoke of Blessings of obedience to the children of Israel in the following verses. *"And I will give peace in the land, and ye shall lie down, and none shall make you afraid: and I will rid evil beasts out of the land, neither shall the sword go through the land. And ye shall chase your enemies, and they shall fall before you by the sword. And five of you shall chase an hundred, and a hundred of you shall put ten thousand to flight: and your enemies shall fall before you by the sword."* Leviticus 26:6

17

SUBDUING THE ENEMIES

Abram pursued them unto Dan: The area mentioned was where Abram pursued the enemies. He *"pursued them unto Dan"* Genesis 14: 15. The area was the northern top part of the land of promise. In Abraham's day, this territory may seem coincidental, because it was later possessed by Dan. The reason is because the tribe of Dan, who is the son of Jacob, received this land when Joshua divided the children of Israel their lot. But God promised Abram the land; and the chasing out the enemies was a prelude to what Israel would do. God told the children of Israel to drive out the inhabitants of the land of Canaan. They obtained the land through overcoming battles against their enemies. Realize that the father of faith trail-blazed all things that his seed would experience. You can see Wisdom establishing the plan of God before it became manifested.

Dan was the 5th son of Jacob; and he was the firstborn son of his mother Bilhah, the maidservant of Rachel. It was Rachel that named the son Dan, saying, *"God has acted as my judge.* She said, *"So that he gave me a son."* **Genesis 30:6** When Jacob was dying, he called all his sons before him to bless them. To Dan he said, *"Dan will judge his people as one of the tribes of Israel.* <u>*Dan shall be a serpent*</u> *by the way, an adder in the path, that biteth the horse heels so that his rider shall fall backward. I have waited for thy salvation, O Lord."* Genesis 49: 16-18

There are several things to give attention to concerning Dan. His name means "judge" in **Hebrew, diyn** *deen; to rule;* by impl. *To judge* (as umpire); also to **strive**, (as at law): contend, execute (judgment), minister judgment, plead (the cause), at strife. Jacob said to his son that he would be as a serpent. **Dan as a Serpent**; generally so, a serpent is a snake. One that hiss, whisper a (magic) spell; to prognosticate {foretell} or predict; learn by experience and to diligently observe. This is the nature of a serpent; wise but deadly. Jacob also called him to be an Adder. **Dan as an Adder**: a kind of serpent known (as snapping). Quick!! Alert!! Sudden!! Then Jacob spoke to Dan as his manner of conduct to his enemies. **Dan Biteth:** this action is used against the enemy. The power of the serpent is in his mouth; the effect of his bite is deadly. Numbers 2: 25-31; & 10: 25; Genesis 46:23;

HORSES are mentioned in scripture usually represents the forces of war or warfare. Envy leads to Strife; strife leads to Division, and division brings on conflict and warfare. Dan would attack the enemy; his bite was indicated in warfare. His bite of the horse' heel, made the rider to fall backward. A metaphor of the power Dan would have over the enemy. Horse HEELS: **Hebrew aqeb,** a heel as protuberant: hence a track; fig. The rear (of an army); A sense of tripping up or restraining: to supplant. These things are singled out for the reader to understand Abram's pursuant of the kings to Dan was not coincidental. This action of Abram foreshadowed the prophecy and blessing Jacob would give Dan. Next, Abram "divided *himself against them, he and his servants, by night, and smote them, and pursued them unto Hobah, which is on the left hand of Damascus."* Genesis 14:15. Abram dividing the servants; this equalized their strength and power to attack. They were able to cover more territory to effect greater damage on their enemies. The night time gave them the benefit of the attack being made unaware. Preparations come with forethought; but to be caught off guard placed the enemies in confusion.

Abraham pursued them unto Hobah: This is the second area mentioned to where Abram pursued the enemies. Not much is known about Hobah; but it was north of Damascus. The location of Hobah is associated with Hoba, a large spring on the road between Palmyra and Damascus. The activity of Abraham in his day can be seen as a shadow of what the children of Israel would experience later after leaving Egypt. The history behind Damascus, which is in Syria, had to do with trade, commerce and warfare. Abraham defeated these kings in Damascus; and later this road over which the armies of Egypt, Assyria, Babylon, and Persia, became a prominent route. This road was commonly called "The Kings Highway." Much travel was made on this road. The children of Israel asked for passage through that land. Abraham defeated the kings and rescued Lot out of captivity. Moses was the Deliverer of the children of Egypt: they also were in captivity under Pharaoh. There came the time when Israel needed to pass through the land of the Amorites. Rear: Joshua 19: 40-48; *THE KING'S HIGHWAY:* Numbers 20:15-21; Deuteronomy 2: 16-37;

"And Israel sent messengers unto Sihon king of the Amorites, saying, Let me pass through thy land: we will not turn into the fields, or into the vineyards; we will not drink of the waters of the well: but we will go along by THE KING'S HIGHWAY, until we be past thy borders. And Sihon would not suffer Israel to pass through his border: but Sihon gathered all his people together, and went out against Israel into the wilderness: and he came to Jahaz, and fought against Israel. And Israel smote him with the edge of the sword, and possessed his land from Amon unto Jabbok," Numbers 21:21-31

Abraham's victory: "And *he brought back all the goods, and also brought again his brother Lot, and his goods, and the women also, and the people."* **Genesis 14:16** *Abraham* achieved success over the struggle and difficulty he sought to overcome. He gained rule; he had compassion and influence over those who were taken. As a type of Christ, Abraham rescued, reclaimed, and restored. With faith, Abram had access to the grace of God. There will be times in life when some will experience captivity; and in need of someone to rescue. "Little Space Grace" through Jesus Christ is given, to do away with the bondage. Jesus led captivity captive. *"And I will cause the captivity of Judah and the captivity of Israel to return, and will build them as at first." The voice of joy, and the voice of gladness, the voice of the bridegroom, and the voice of the bride, the voice of them that shall say, Praise the Lord of Hosts: for the Lord is good; for his mercy endureth forever: and them that shall* *bring the sacrifice of praise into the house of the Lord: For I will cause <u>to</u> <u>return the captivity of the land, as at the first, saith the Lord.</u>"* Jeremiah 3:7 Ephesians 4:8 Abraham brought back Lot from his captivity. This account shows that God is faithful to His word; he sent His Grace and delivered man. His work was in the hands of Abram, like as with the disciples. His gifts are given unto men that the body of Christ may be edified. A true minister of God preaches his gospel and walk by faith, aiding to man's rescue.

Lot was freed from his captivity. After being freed, it would have been wise to adhere to a new direction in reforming his life. The cities were no longer in conflict; and the people could regain their livelihood. Abraham had defeated the enemies and restored the people. The right course of action would have been for the people to follow the teaching of Abraham. But instead, the people continued their wicked and sinful life styles. Those who paid tribute to other kings, and captured in the warfare apparently did not accept a new way.

Following the laws of God, and walking in a new direction is life changing. *"And be not conformed to this world; but be ye transformed by the renewing of your mind, that ye may prove what is good and acceptable, and perfect will of God."* Romans 12:2. *"Wherefore gird up the loins of your mind, and be sober, and hope to the end for the grace that is to be brought unto you at the revelation of Jesus Christ; As obedient children, not fashioning yourselves according to the former lusts in your ignorance:* 1Peter 1: 14 *"And we know that all things* work *together for good to them that love God, to them who are called according to his purpose. For whom he did* foreknow, *he also did predestinate to be conformed to the image of his Son, that he might be the firstborn among many brethren."* Romans 8:28 *"Dearly beloved, I beseech you as strangers and pilgrims, abstain from fleshly lusts, which war against the soul. "That he no longer should live the rest of his time in the flesh to the lusts of men, but to the will of God. For the time past of our life may suffice us to have wrought the will of the Gentiles, when we walked in lasciviousness, lust, excess of wine, revellings, banqueting, and abominable idolatries."* 1 Peter 2:11

Lot and the others experienced lost because of the things that were taken from them. Abraham, the man of faith brought restoration: "*he brought back all the goods.*" This act foreshadows Christ; "*he restoreth my soul,*" Psalm 23:3 "all the goods" collectively, all material goods a man possess. These goods may become lost or stolen. A person may lose their goods because of neglect or that the person haven't kept watch over them. The goods may have been stolen because the act of a thief, or robber coming in unaware taking them away. Restoration is a measure of God's grace; a work to make whole, repair and heal the injury. The restoration brought by Christ assures men that "all things are possible to them that believe." What could have been impossible in the eyes of Lot was possible with God; because Abram believed God.

Not only did Abraham bring back all the goods of Lot, but the goods of the people as well. Before men would see the manifestation of the promise God made to Abraham, God's wisdom was establishing the promise. During that time, Abraham was not yet the father of many nations; but this act of rescuing Lot and the people signified a claim on the promise. "*Know ye therefore that they which are of faith, the same are the children of Abraham. And the Scripture, foreseeing, that God would justify the heathen through faith, preached before the gospel unto Abraham, saying, in thee shall all nations be blessed.*"

The word of God promised redemption and salvation for all people. The people of Sodom were heathen people; the other nations God included in the plan of salvation. The other nations among them were rescued by Abram defeating their enemies. Recount the beginning of time with Adam to Abraham. The scripture do not record a time when God delivered the unjust out of their troubles. Lot and the women and children were rescued by Abraham. But to show his word is sure, God blessed the heathens because of his promise with Abraham. Their rescue foreshadowed the salvation will be given to the Gentiles also. God determined their salvation before the gospel of Christ was preached. "*That the blessing of Abraham might come on the Gentiles through Jesus Christ; that we might receive the promise of the Spirit through faith.*" Galatians 3: 7-8; and v. 14

18

VICTORY GAINED

Abram met 2-kings after the slaughter: Abraham became victor after the slaughter of the kings. First the king of Sodom came out to meet him. Then Melchizedek king of Salem also came to meet Abraham. One king came empty handed and asking for something in returns. But king Melchizedek *"brought forth bread and wine: and he was the priest of the most high God."* **Genesis 14:17**

The ungrateful king: The kings of Sodom fled and fell in the slime pits of the Vale of Siddim, when the battle was in array. They had lost control over the city and the people. The king of Sodom should have shown gratitude to Abraham for his help. Instead the king asked, *"Give me the persons, and take the goods to thou self."* Genesis 14:21. What the king asked for revealed something about his character. He was selfish, greedy, he gave no honor to Abram, and he had no compassion for the people. He was a wicked leader to the people. This king was oppressed by another king to pay tributes; but delivered from that oppression by Abram. What kind of power, authority, and influence did this king have in his country? How could he allow his house to be broken into and the people taken? Apparently he wasn't a true leader to the people: having no laws established to govern the wicked behaviors of the people of Sodom. The king of Sodom was unthankful: without appreciation for the benefits that afforded pleasure to his life. But Abram acted on the principles of Jesus teaching. *"But love you your enemies, and do good, and lend, hoping for nothing again; and your reward shall be great, and ye shall be the children of the Highest: for he is kind unto the unthankful and to the*

evil. Be ye therefore merciful, as your Father also is merciful." Luke 6: 35-56;
Matthew 5: 43-48; Genesis 14:22

What can be learned from this unthankful king? To be thankful is an acknowledgment, and recognition for favor given. The people know that the circumstance or condition became favorable and pleasing because of the merciful. The merciful act should have revealed to the king the righteousness, compassion, strength and power of Abram. When mercy is given to anyone, there is a sense of being indebted too; a desire to give back in returns and a respect to the person who showed mercy. None of these things were known to be the case with the king of Sodom. Ungratefulness can lead to a more distant relationship. It may predetermine the actions of the merciful the next time mercy is needed. And the ungrateful sometimes belittle the motive and action of the one that offers mercy. But Abram was merciful; therefore he obtained the mercy of God. Peacemakers are called the children of God.

Abram, a merciful man: But Abraham answered the king, *"I have lifted up mine hand unto the Lord, the most high God, the possessor of heaven and earth, That I will not take from a thread even to a shoe latchet, and that I will not take any thing that is thine, lest thou shouldest say, that I made Abram rich: Save only that which the young men have eaten, and the portion of men which went with me, Aner, Eschol, and Mamre; let them take their portion."* Genesis 14:22

Abram's merciful act was not with the expectation of a reward in return. His motive was to rescue Lot; but in doing so, Abram helped others that needed to be rescued. It was already in his heart, which he purposed not to take "from a thread even to a shoe latchet" anything that belonged to the king. His reasoning was in knowing God prospered his way; not the king. Abram also was just in his acts: he allowed the men with him to have their portion. The state of blessedness Jesus taught in Matthew 5:3-12 was known in the life of Abraham.

Blessed of God: Melchizedek, King of Salem came to meet Abraham after the battle was won. He brought forth bread and wine when Abraham returned from the slaughter of the kings. It is written that Melchizedek was also a priest. There are three titles that identified Melchizedek: he is <u>King of Righteousness</u>, <u>king of Salem,</u> which is <u>king of Peace</u>. Melchizedek had no natural blood line; no father, no mother and without an ancestral line. *"But made like unto the Son of God; abideth a priest continually."* **Hebrews 7:3** *The "Bread and Wine"* given by Melchizedek expressed a <u>hand of fellowship.</u> The wisdom of God was establishing the fellowship of man and God; for the children of Abraham will partake of Christ Bread and Wine. As a priest, Melchizedek's Bread and Wine are the Manna from heaven and the shed blood of Christ. Abram received the bread and wine as a type of the body and blood of Christ that is given for redemption. God has called man unto the fellowship of his Son Jesus Christ. *"And as they were eating, Jesus took bread, and blessed it, and broke it, and gave it to the disciples, and said, Take, eat; this is my body. And he took the cup, and gave thanks, and gave it to them. Saying, Drink ye all of it; for this is my blood of the new testament, which is shed for many for the remission of sins. But I say unto you, I will not <u>drink this fruit of the vine, until that day when I drink it new with you in my Father's kingdom."* {Vine wine} Matthew 26:26-30. In a king's house, bread and wine are given for the feast; therefore communion is the act of partaking at the king's table. *"That which we have seen and heard declare we unto you that ye also may have **fellowship** with us and truly our **fellowship** is with the Father, and with his Son Jesus Christ."* 1John 1:3 1Corinthians 1: 9

Melchizedek was more than a king; he was the priest of the Most High God. He was preeminent over the fleshly priesthood served for an appointed time. Melchizedek was made like unto the Son of God. *"For it is evident that our Lord sprang out of Juda: of which tribe Moses spake nothing concerning priesthood. And it is yet far more evident: for that after the similitude of Melchizedek there ariseth another priest, who is made, not after the law of a carnal commandment, but after the power of an endless life."* Hebrews 7: 14-16 The Levitical priesthood instituted by Moses was four hundred years after Abram; the priesthood was to remain until Christ. But Abraham was blessed of Melchizedek before his grandson Levi was born. The tribe of Levi was those that served as priests to the nation of Israel. This reveals another spiritual etching out of wisdom establishing the plan of God. The father of faith lived as the substance of what the word of God had determined. The experiences of Abraham's life of faith are the evidence and witness of what was to be made manifested in the fullness of times.

BLESSED

Melchizedek Blessed Abram: "and *said, Blessed be Abram of the most high God*," Blessed defined; Hebrew word is, **Barak,** to kneel; by impl. To bless God (as an act of adoration), and (vice-versa) [as a benefit]; praise, salute, thank. (An euphemism, meaning to curse). The salutation of Melchizedek to Abram marks the early beginning of the messianic prophecy. The statement that made this greeting prophetic is, *"possessor of heaven and earth."*

The apostle Paul wrote, *"Now to Abraham and his seed were the promise made, He saith not, And to seeds, as of many; but as of one, And **to thy seed, which is Christ**."* Galatians 3: 16. To become a possessor of heaven and earth is to be Lord over all. Jesus is Lord of Lords; he said *"all power is given unto me."* David said of him, *"The Lord said unto my Lord, Sit thou at my right hand until I make thine enemies thy footstool. The Lord shall send* [prophetic utterance] *the rod of thy strength out of Zion: rule thou in the midst of thine enemies, Thy people shall be willing in the day of thy power, in the beauties of holiness from the womb of the morning: thou hast the dew of thy youth. The Lord hath sworn, and will not repent; **Thou art a priest forever after the order of Melchizedek.**"* Psalm 110:1

POSSESSOR: The Hebrew word **qanah, a** prim, root; to *erect* i.e. *Create;* to procure. Especially by *purchase; (*caus. Sell); *To own;- attain,* buy (-er), *teach to keep cattle,* get, provoke to jealousy, possess (-or), *purchase, recover, redeem,* x surely, verily. Each word that define possessor, points to the person who has control and authority. Jesus is "Lord of Lords" Read: Matthew 10:24; Luke 6: 40; John 13: 16; & 15: 20;

The expression *"the Lord" means* the self-Existent or Eternal; Jehovah, The Jewish national name of God. He is the Creator of heaven and earth; God is the everlasting Father, possessor of all things. Throughout the OT, the children of Israel ascribed greatness unto the Lord. His name is great in all the earth. They saw his works, experienced his power, guided by his counsels and taught to worship him in righteousness. In the NT, Jesus was called "Emmanuel" being interpreted is, God with us. When Jesus was tempted of the devil in the wilderness, he said, "Get *thee hence, Satan; for it is written, Thou shalt worship the Lord thy God, and him only shalt thou serve."* Matthew 4:10 Jesus said unto his disciples, *"Verily, verily, I say unto you, the servant is not greater than his lord; neither he that is sent greater than he that sent him."* . . *"The disciple is not above his master: but every one that is perfect shall be as his master."* Matthew 10:24; Luke 6:40

The expression "my Lord" means to rule; sovereign, i.e. *controller*–lord, *master, Jesus* is Lord, and he fulfilled the words spoken by David concerning himself. When John the Baptist was born, his father prophesied, and said, *"The oath which he sware to our father Abraham, That he would grant unto us, that we being delivered out of the hand of our enemies might serve him without fear, In holiness and righteousness before him, all the days of our life. "And thou, child, shalt be called the prophet of the Highest: for thou shalt go before the face of the Lord to prepare his ways*; Luke 1 73-77; Matt. 4:10. It was revealed unto him that John was the forerunner of "the Lord."

Melchizedek was described as, *"made like unto the Son of God:"* Melchizedek in the likeness of Christ; he received gifts and offerings; he ministered to offer sacrifice for sin. And Melchizedek received a tenth (tithes) from Abraham. Melchizedek ruled in the city of Salem. Melchizedek is none other than Christ. Jerusalem was not yet; but Melchizedek was king there. The laws of sacrifices and offerings were not yet instituted. Jesus priestly order is the order of Melchizedek; which continues. He is king and priest, ruling in the midst of men. Jesus is the son of David by an earthly lineage; and the Son of God by the will and power of God.

"David's LORD"

"And he said unto them, how say they that Christ is David's son? And David himself saith in the book of Psalms, the Lord said unto my Lord, Sit thou on my right hand, till I make thine enemies thy footstool. David therefore calleth him Lord, how is he them his son?" **Psalm 110:1** Read also; Luke 20:41-44' Mark 12:35-37; Matthew 22: 41-46; The scribes and Jewish leaders of Christ' day on earth knew their lineage. In Matthews 1:1 it is recorded, *"The book of the generation of Jesus Christ, the Son of David, the son of Abraham, "*and in verse 17, *"So all the generations from Abraham to David are fourteen generations; and from David until the carrying away into Babylon are fourteen generations; and from the carrying away into Babylon unto Christ are fourteen generations."*

Christ is Possessor: of God's house. The word ERECT can be used also to describe the word possessor. Many scriptures are given concerning Christ establishing, building, causing his word to fitly frame together his dwelling place. Melchizedek Blessed Abram, saying *"Blessed be Abram of the Most High God, possessor of heaven and earth:" The* blessing upon his seed, who is Christ; will bless all nations. Years later God spoke to Abraham's grandson, Jacob in a dream. *"And he dreamed, and behold a ladder set up on the earth and the top of it reached to heaven: and behold the angels of God ascending and descending on it. And, behold the Lord stood above it, and said, I am the Lord God of Abraham thy father; and the God of Isaac: the land whereon thou liest, to thee will I give it, and to thy seed; And thy seed shall be as the dust of the earth, and thou shalt spread abroad to the west, and to the east, and to the north, and to the south: and in thee and in thy seed shall all the families of the earth be blessed. And behold, I am with thee, and will bring thee, and will keep thee in all places whither thou goest, and will bring thee again* *into this land: for I will not leave thee, until I have done that which I have spoken to thee of."* **Genesis 28: 12-15** Read carefully, and see the plan of God: wisdom built her house. The dream refers to something that is to be established, controlled, spread or increase, protected and blessed by the Designer. Then we are directed to behold the One that will accomplish this work on earth. **"The Lord stood above it."** The Anointed One is Christ who pleased the Father and fulfilled all that was prophesied in the word. Jesus ministry began in the NT; and when he chose his disciples it is written, *"Jesus saw Nathanael coming to him, and saith of him, Behold and Israelite indeed, in whom is no guile! Nathanael saith unto him, whence knowest thou me? Jesus answered and said unto him, before that Philip called thee, when thou was under the fig tree, I saw thee. Nathanael answered and saith unto him,* **Rabbi, thou art the Son of God; thou art the King of Israel.** *Jesus answered and said unto him, because I said unto thee, I saw thee under the fig tree, Believest thou? Thou shalt see greater things than these. And he saith unto him, Verily, verily, I say unto you,* **hereafter ye shall see heaven open, and the angels of God ascending and descending upon the Son of man."** John 1:35-51; Matthew 1:1, 17, 23;

Jacob awakens from his dream and said, *"Surely the Lord is in this place: and I knew it not."* Jacob arose up early that morning and built an altar, and he called the name of that place, *"**Bethel**"* the name means, *House of God:* God's dwelling place. In Abraham time, he was lead out to a place that afterwards his seed would inherit. Melchizedek said unto Abram that he was blessed of the Most High God; for God is possessor of heaven and earth. Genesis 14: 19

This salutation gave Abram assurance, protection, comfort; it secured the plan of salvation for all people. God used the occasion of Abram defeating the enemies in his day as an illustrative way for Abram to understand the prophecy of the Christ who was to come. Abram experienced lordship; therefore he learned, **"my Lord"** the master and ruler of all. Jesus is "my Lord" whom David spoke of in the Psalms. Next Abram learned of **"the Lord"** the Eternal God that

Melchizedek represented. For he was a man *"Without father, Without mother, without descent, having neither beginning of days, nor end of life, BUT made like unto the Son of God; abideth a priest continually."* Hebrews 7:3 through the lineage of Abraham, Isaac and Jacob, Christ came. Judah the son of Jacob; was the kingly tribe, in whom also came King David. The Jews of Christ day called him the son of David. And the son of any king is called a prince. Jesus is the Prince of Peace: as son of King David he is a prince. But more than a prince, we see Jesus, "a priest forever after the order of Melchisedec." Hebrews 7:11

What is Melchizedek's order? As with Melchizedek, so is the same with Christ:

1. Jesus is king of Salem.

2. Jesus is the Prince of Peace.

3. Jesus is the priest of the Most High God.

SALEM: In the ancient Jewish tradition, Salem is identified with Jerusalem. The word Salem is incorporated in the name "Jerusalem" and King David parallel Salem with Zion; Referred to as the city of God. *"Great is the Lord, and greatly to be praised, in the city of our God, in the mountain of his holiness. Beautiful for situation, the joy of the whole earth, is mount Zion, on the sides of the north, the city f the great King." "The mighty God, even the Lord, hath spoken, and called the earth from the rising of the sun unto the going down thereof, Out of Zion, the perfection of beauty, God hath shined."* **Psalm 48: 1-2; Psalm 50: 1-2 *David*** called Jerusalem, Mt. Zion the city of God: in this city, God placed his name and established his dwelling place.

The name Solomon means peace: his kingdom rule was of peace. There are similarities between the reign of Solomon and that of Christ. Solomon rule was on a small scale a pattern of the Messianic rule of Christ. Christ is called the "Prince of Peace." In the time of Solomon's reign, there was no warfare. The Pharisees accused Jesus of casting out devils, "by *Beelzebub the prince of the devils.*" It is written, *"And Jesus knew their thoughts, and said unto them, every kingdom divided against it is brought to desolation. And if Satan cast out Satan, he is divided against himself; how shall then his kingdom stand? . .But if I by Beelzebub* <u>*cast out devils by the Spirit of God,*</u> *then the* <u>*kingdom of God is come unto you.*</u>" Matthew 12: 24-32 Next Jesus spoke about Solomon and his wisdom. Jesus said, *"The queen of the south shall rise up in judgment with the men of this generation, and condemn them; she came from the utmost parts of the earth to hear the wisdom of Solomon; and behold, a greater than Solomon is here."* 1Kings 10: 1-9; Matthew 12:38-**42.** Jesus proclaimed the kingdom of God was at hand. He is the Son of David, ruling over his own house. His rule is with justice and judgment; this was prophesied of him in Isaiah and in the NT. Luke 1:32-33 The queen of the south acknowledged Solomon's wisdom, the house he had built, the meat of his table, the attendance of his ministers, their apparel, his cupbearers, and his ascent up unto the house of the Lord. The queen of the South said, *"Happy are thy men, happy are these servants, which stand continually before thee, and that hear thy wisdom. Blessed be the Lord thy God, which delighted in thee, to set thee on the throne of Israel: because the Lord loved Israel forever, therefore made the king,* <u>*to do judgment and justice*</u>*."* Luke 11: 31

Some may only take knowledge of Solomon's Adamic sin nature: but humans are all born in sin. The temple Solomon built, illustrated wisdom hewing out God's house. Sin cannot nullify the nature and character of Christ when a man is walking in righteousness. Every man of God in scripture was a part that added to the etching out of the Temple of God. Abraham was called out by God; his life was used to define faith. If he is the father of faith; then the origin of faith is known in the life he lived. Moses' was a type of Christ, for his life as man's Deliver or Savior. Joshua served to survey the land of promise; and he won all the battles of the enemies of Israel. All these men of God; their works were exemplifying the wisdom, judgment and passion of Christ.

Solomon name means peace; and he was great, but Jesus is the Prince of Peace. The prophet Isaiah wrote, *"For unto us a child is born, unto us a son is given: and the government shall be upon his shoulder; and his name shall be called **Wonderful, Counselor, The mighty God, The everlasting Father, The Prince of Peace**. Of the increase of his government and peace there shall be no end, upon the throne of David, and upon his kingdom, to order it, and to establish it <u>with judgment</u> and <u>with justice</u> from henceforth even forever. The zeal of the Lord of hosts will perform this."* Isaiah 9:7

The time Jesus walked upon the earth, Solomon's kingdom no longer existed. There was no increase of Solomon's government, especially because of the goddess religion he allowed. His heart was turned to foreign women and he disregarded God's law. Jesus is greater than Solomon; his government and throne has no end. He did the will of the Father: for God said "this is my beloved Son, in whom I am well pleased." John 1: 29

Christ is Possessor: he purchased and he recovered. Not only does the Possessor build, create or establish; he maintained his possession through redemption. The work of Christ was to redeem or become a ransom for man. Man's bondage is sin; and to be set free is to have a deliverer. By the transgression of Adam, sin entered into the world. The apostle Paul said, *"For we know that the law is spiritual: but I am carnal, sold under sin."* To sell is the exchange of merchandise; in this case Adam traded off what was rightfully his by disobeying God. He was no longer a free man to enjoy the pleasure of paradise. Adam was separated from the presence of God and driven out of Eden. God sent his only begotten Son to redeem man from under the law. That law is the law of sin and death; for the wages of sin is death. Christ shed his blood for the remission for our sins. Sins are remitted {forgiven} because Christ was made sin for us. His death is the condemnation that was upon all men, but he made the sacrifice for our sins. Hebrews 9: 22 Isaiah said, *"All we like sheep have gone astray; we have turned everyone to his own way; and the Lord hath laid on him the iniquity of us all." "And he made his grave with the wicked and with* *the rich in his death; because he had done no violence, neither was any deceit in his mouth. Yet it pleased the Lord to bruise him; he hath put him to grief: when thou shalt make his soul an offering for sin, he shall see his seed, he shall prolong his days, and the pleasure of the Lord shall prosper in his hand. He shall see of the travail of his soul, and shall be satisfied: by his knowledge shall my righteous servant justify many; for he shall bear their iniquities."* Isaiah 53:6; & 9-11

The Blessings Melchizedek spoke of included all people. Paul wrote in his epistle, *"And the Scripture, foreseeing that God would justify the heathen through faith, preached before the gospel unto Abraham, saying, in thee shall all nations be blessed."* **Galatians 3: 8** Paul also said, *"Christ hath redeemed us from the curse of the law, being made a curse for us: for it is written, Cursed is every one that hangeth on a tree. That the Blessing of Abraham might come on the Gentiles through Jesus Christ; that we might receive the promise of the Spirit through faith."* Galatians 3:13-16 Melchizedek proclaimed this blessing to Abraham in the day he returned from the slaughter of the kings. Melchizedek blessed the Most High God who delivered Abram's enemies into his hand. Genesis 14:19. The father of faith served to illustrate the power of God over the enemies. With faith, God favor is upon the believer: by faith, he overcomes the conflict. To have power over the kings of the land showed the extent of victory given to Abram, because he believed God. Naturally, when a man becomes a ruler, he would have dominion over others. Abraham acquired the ability to rule when he fought the five kings; rescued Lot, the people and brought them back. Genesis 14: 9-12. He was a faithful man of character, who withstood danger, fear and defeat. Unlike the two kings that fled and fell in the Vale of Siddim. These kings left their cities, the people and their goods because of fear, danger and defeat. Abraham's faith moved mountains; another experience of being justified by faith. The spiritual implication for 'mountains 'symbolizes governments {kingdoms}. The rules of the kings were of their government. Faith is like the spiritual vision; it looks far ahead of the natural sight.

God's word is prophecy. The kings were driven out literally by Abraham. Isaiah spoke this prophecy which ties in with the blessing Melchizedek spoke to Abraham: as to how God will help Israel. "Who *raised up the righteous man from the east* [Abram], *called him to his foot, gave the nations* [the kings] *before him, and made him rule over kings? He gave them as the dust of his sword and as driven stubble to his bow. He pursued them, and passed safely; even by the way that he had not gone with his feet.* "Isaiah 41: 2-4. Recall, Abram chased the kings to Damascus: the way was called the kings highway; {read Numbers 21:22} "*Who hath wrought and done it, calling the generations from the beginning?* [the plan of God]. *I the Lord, the first, and with the last; I am he.*" . . . "But *thou, Israel, art my servant, Jacob whom I have chosen, the seed of <u>Abraham my friend.</u> "Thou whom I have taken from the ends of the earth, and called thee from the chief men thereof, and said unto thee, Thou art my servant; I have chosen thee, and not cast thee away. Fear thou not; for I am with thee: be not dismayed; for I am thy God: I will strengthen thee; yea; I will help thee; yea, I will uphold thee with the right hand of my righteousness.* "Behold, *I will make thee a new sharp threshing instrument having teeth: thou shalt thresh the mountains, and beat them small, and shalt make the hills as chaff.*" Isaiah 41:4, 9-*15* Abram's battle with the kings was a prelude to the time when this prophecy will fulfill. V. 20 "*That they may see, and know, and consider, and understand together, that the hand of the Lord hath done this, and the Holy One of Israel hath created it.*" Isaiah 41:20

God decreed from the beginning of the creation of man, "Let us make man in our image, after our likeness." Genesis 1:26. The entire process and working of the Holy Spirit is forming men to become what God commanded. Now you may ask, how is God performing his word? Solomon spoke of the wisdom of God fashioning his temple. "*Wisdom hath builded her house.*" Proverbs 9:1. All things created were made by the Word: and man is the crown of his creation. Before the foundation of the world, man was chosen to be holy and without blame before God in love. God's word in earth performs his will.

God established faith with Abraham as one of the seven pillars of the house Wisdom hath built. Large buildings are supported by pillars to bear the weight of the structure. The dwelling place of God, which is man; and his temple, is supported by faith. Without faith it is not possible to please God. There are 7-pillars or supports that wisdom hewn out in building God's house. Wisdom established God's dwelling place with faith, **his judgments**, **his name**, his **prophecy**, **his promises, his commandments** and **the horn of salvation** which is Jesus Christ. {Read Proverbs 9:1} Ephesians 2:19-22; 1Corinthians 3:16; 6:19; 1Peter 2: 5

Blessed is the redemptive work of Christ; for we are "helped." Those that are of faith are the children of Abraham; and inheritors to the same promises. We are strengthened by God's help because we are his temple, his dwelling place. Man is blessed because, *"Christ is faithful over his own house."* Hebrews 3:6. The scriptures records God's plan of salvation from the beginning of creation: for he is the author and finisher of our faith. All history and the events in scripture etch out God's plan and purpose for mankind.

God's desire for man is to know him. Men should not follow the course of action Adam chose which caused his paradise loss. Adam's choosing to partake of the fruit of knowledge of good and evil was deadly. Adam lost fellowship with God. Now this sin is in the flesh nature of all men; experiencing good and evil. The by this knowledge men experience evil and death. They may also know healing; good and life. Through death men know life; through suffering men learn obedience; through sadness, men know merriment; through being a base, men know exaltation. The tree of knowledge provides many contrasts in life. And the contrast of good and evil is the fruit thereof. Good and evil is totally opposite; but when one is known the other is known also. The God, by his mercy gave us his love, "Little Space Grace" that we may overcome the troubles of our day. This coincide with the apostle Paul saying, *"Where sin abound, grace did much more abound."* Romans 5: 20; 1Timothy 1: 14; I Corinthians 15:10

19

...And He Blessed Him

ABRAHAM GAVE "tithes of all: In Abram's presence, there were two kings; the king of Sodom and the King of Salem. Melchizedek did not ask for anything that Abram brought back from the battle. But the king of Sodom asked for the people. Abram shared nothing with the king of Sodom; neither did he take from the battle anything that belonged to the king of Sodom. Genesis 14: 16; Numbers 18:19-32. There are godly principles learned from Abram dealing with the king of Sodom. God's word never fails: and men are not forsaken by God, when they follow it. Faith is rewarding and grants success in warfare. Men should not fear the face of a king, when God is with him. Abram's faith held to the knowledge that God gave him good success over the enemies. When Lot and Abram had separated, God showed Abram all the land that his seed would inherit. The battles in that land were an example of defeat and conquer. Abram did not go out in his own strength to take the land. At that time he had neither son nor children to inherit the promise. Furthermore, to acquire the land with no children or people would have only been wasteland. Abram felt no obligation to enrich the hand of the king of Sodom. To give the king the people would have placed them in the hands of a ruler that showed no compassion for them. The people found security and mercy; being rescued by Abram.

The king of Sodom asked for the people because he knew that without people, the city would be desolate. Without the people, the king had no one to preside over. Without the people, the laws of the king would be null and void. Abram refused to give the king of Sodom the people. Read: Genesis 14:22-24. Because of his righteousness and faith, he honored the law of God that had not yet been instituted. [Hebrews 7:4-6] Abram was worshipping God in Spirit by faith. He had no legal statues written on the law of giving. There were no restrictions on what to give or how much to give. To obey by the law does not demonstrate faith; usually, this is out of human sentiments. It was four hundred years after Abram when Moses instituted the law of giving tithes in worship. Ephesians 2:15-22

Abram gave tithes of all to the king of Salem. Melchizedek priestly ministry was a spiritual type of the ministry of Christ. The offering that he received from Abram was for the purpose of, "the *storehouse, that there may be meat in mine house.*" Abram's act of faith proved God, because he believed, *"God will open you the windows of heaven, and pour you out a blessing, that there shall not be room enough to receive it. And will rebuke the devourer for your sakes, and he shall not destroy the fruits of your ground; neither shall your vine cast her fruit before time in the field, saith the Lord of hosts."* **Malachi 3:10-11; Read:** Ephesians 3: 11-12; Hebrews 4:16

Now the questions that can be asked are what did Abram give Melchizedek? Were the goods of a monetary value? Did Abram give Melchizedek the people also? One thing is certain; Abram gave a tenth of all. The scripture clearly said of Abram, *"And he brought back all the goods, and also brought again his brother Lot, and his goods, and the women also, and the people."* **Genesis 14: 20**

Abraham gave tithes of all the goods he brought back from the battle. GOODS as they relate to something that is valuable, useful and enriching to the person that possesses them. Melchizedek, the priest of the Most High God received these goods long before Moses gave the law concerning tithes. Tithes given to the Levitical priesthood is mentioned in Numbers 18:20. The priests shared no inheritance with land ownership in Israel. God told the priest, *"I am thy part and thine inheritance among the children of Israel. And, Behold, I have given the children of Levi all the tenth in Israel for an inheritance, for their service which they serve, even the service of the tabernacle of the congregation."* **Numbers 18:20-32**

The use of tithes for many people of today does not honor this law of God. Many preachers lay claim on being a minister of God, but they are not doing the works the law signified. For the same cause, Jesus rebuked the Pharisee, *"But if ye had known what this meaneth, I will have mercy, and not sacrifice, ye would not have condemned the guiltless."* **Matthew 12:7** Paul spoke of Christ our High Priest; his ministry superseded that of the Levitical priesthood: Christ example is what ministers are to follow. It is written, *"Now of the things which we have spoken this is the sum: We have such a high priest, who is set on the right hand of the throne of the Majesty in the heavens; A minister of the sanctuary and of the true tabernacle, which the Lord pitched, and not man. For every high priest is ordained to offer gifts and sacrifices: wherefore it is of necessity that this man has somewhat also to offer. For if he were on earth, he should not be a priest, seeing that there are priests that offer gifts according to the law. Who serve unto the example and shadow of heavenly things, as Moses was admonished of God when he was about to make the tabernacle: for, See, saith he, that thou make all things according to the pattern showed thee in the mount. But now hath he obtained a more excellent ministry, by how much also he is a mediator of a better covenant, which was established upon better promises."* **Hebrews 8: 1-6**

The children of Israel gave tithes unto the Levitical priests; and the priests were required to offer unto God a tenth part of their tithes. *"Thus ye also shall offer an heave offering unto the Lord of all the tithes, which ye receive of "* **Numbers 18:28** In the Book of Malachi, the prophet message was to the unfaithful priesthood. Malachi said, *"For the priest's lips should keep knowledge, and they should seek the law at his mouth: for he is the messenger of the Lord of hosts. But ye have caused many to stumble at the law; ye have corrupted the covenant of Levi, saith the Lord "of Hosts."* **Malachi 2:7** Read all of > Malachi chapters 1, 2, & 3 Abram gave tithes to Melchizedek, which typified the offering Christ the Great High Priest will offer up to God. If the burning of the incense on the altar in Moses time are prayers offered to God; therefore, the great high priest, is mediating for us before God. The priests offered up offerings and sacrifices unto God on the altar, now we see even greater ministry with Christ.

As an act of faith, Abram was giving God his tenth before the 10-tribes became the lost Israel. Spiritually, he was securing Israel's recovery; like as with the rescue of Lot. All victors return with a booty, or spoils and goods from the battle; even so with Abram. Jesus is the One who Rescues the lost or captive out of the hands of the enemy. He is the Redeemer, who came to seek and save those that are lost. Mary the mother of Jesus sung this praise, *"He hath helped his servant Israel In remembrance of his mercy, as he spake to our fathers. To Abraham and to his seed forever."* **Luke 1:50-56.** After the birth of John the Baptist, John's father prophesied, and said, *"As he spake by the mouth of his holy prophets, which have been since the world began: That we should be saved from our enemies, and from the hand of all that hate us; To perform the mercy promised to our fathers, and to remember his holy covenant; The oath which he sware to our father Abraham, That he would grant unto us, that we being delivered out of the hand of our enemies might serve him without fear, In holiness and righteousness before him, all the days of our life."* **Luke 1: 69-80** Only faith can provide this kind of spiritual vision: and by Abram's faith he pleased God. Jesus first advent was not for the purpose of setting up an earthly kingdom at the time. The scripture said, *"For if he were on earth, he should not be a priest, seeing that there are priests that offer gifts according to the law."* **Hebrews 8:4** Christ came as the Redeemer; he was the priest of the Most High God. *"But when the fullness of the time was come, God sent forth his Son, made of a woman, made under the law, To redeem them that were under the law, that we might receive the adoption of sons."* **Galatians 4: 5**

"For the grace of God that bringeth salvation hath appeared to all men, Teaching us that, denying ungodliness and worldly lusts, we should live soberly, righteously, and godly, in this present world; Looking for that

blessed hope, and the glorious appearing of the great God and our Savior Jesus Christ. Who gave himself for us, that he might redeem us from all iniquity, and purify unto himself a peculiar people, zealous of good works." **Titus 2:11-14**

Spiritually so, God's tenth is his Israel; the lost sheep. Jesus spoke in parables concerning the ten tribes to illustrate those he came to seek and to save. While on earth, Jesus dealt with adversity from those who were noted as rulers of the Jews. The Pharisees and scribes began to murmur, saying, *"This man receiveth sinners, and eateth with them."* Then Jesus spoke the parable of a man having a hundred sheep and lost one. He leaves the ninety and nine in the wilderness, and goes after the sheep that is lost, until he finds it. The audience that was before Jesus were *"all the publicans and sinners,"* also there were Pharisees and scribes. Jesus spoke this parable knowing the fashion each person's life. With the publicans, Jesus knew that they understood fractions and numerical problems. Publicans were tax collectors; skilled with counting. The sinners were those having missed the mark, as if in a race; in other words, <u>off course</u>. The Pharisees; their name was acquired from having been the remnant ones of Judah after the Babylonian captivity. The name Pharisee is defined as, *"<u>the separated ones.</u>"* **Luke 15: 1-3**

Sometimes a self-righteous or a false person is called a Pharisee, because of hypocrisy. And the scribes were those that copied the Torah or the Law and other scriptures. It was known that the scribes were men who carefully examined the written scriptures. They copied the scriptures being careful not to miss one jot or tittle of the law. If an error was made, the Scribes would start over and recopy again. The rulers of the people of God were the Jews; they were entrusted to shepherd over the sheep. If 1/10 of the hundred sheep goes astray, it was the responsibility of the shepherd to go seek for the lost sheep. The scribes knew the history of the 10-tribes that went astray. Jacob was told in his dream that his seed will spread north, south, east and west. Therefore, the audience that stood to hear Jesus parable of the lost could understand the meaning.

God also promised a return of the seed; those who were dispersed into all the land. Jacob heard the voice of God saying, *"And, behold, I am with thee, and will keep thee in all places whither thou goest, and will bring thee again into this land; for I will not leave thee, until I have done that which I have spoke to thee of."* **Genesis 28: 15**; Deuteronomy 30: 1-4. The plan of salvation for man was already preordained. Jacob, whose name was later changed to Israel, became the father of the 12-tribes. At the time of his dream, he had no seed or children. Therefore, his dream was a word of prophecy from the Lord. Jacob was assured of the covenant God made with Abraham would come to pass. It foreshadowed the history of his seed being scattered and later returning. Read about, *GOD LOVES UNFAITHFUL ISRAEL:* Hosea 2: 14-23; Hosea 1: 10-11; Hosea 11: 1-12; *ISRAEL TO RETURN:* Hosea 6: 1-11; Moses prophesied unto the children: *"And the Lord shall scatter thee among the people, from one end of the earth even unto the other; and there thou shalt serve other gods, which neither thou nor thy fathers have known, even wood and stone. And among these nations shalt thou find no ease, neither shall the sole of thy foot have rest: but the Lord shall give thee there a trembling heart, and failing of eyes, and sorrow of mind; And thy life shall hang in doubt before thee; and thou shalt fear day and night, and shalt have none assurance of thy life."* **Deuteronomy 28:64-67** Also Moses spoke of the promise of Israel's returning. *"And it shall come to pass, when all these things are come upon thee, the blessing and the curse, which I have set before thee, and thou shalt call them to mind among all the nations, whither the Lord thy God hath driven thee, And shalt return unto the Lord thy God, and shall obey his voice according to all that I command thee this day, thou and thy children, with all thine heart, and with all thy soul;"* **Deuteronomy 30:2**

The holy prophets prophesied to Israel concerning her separation and the promise Abram **Tithes "of all" were valuable:** To be of value meant that Abram's goods were worthy of a price; goods having esteemed and desirable characteristics or qualities. In the scripture, the word GOODS described the quality of the things Abram brought back; by which he gave a tenth to Melchizedek. In the law, taught by the Levitical priesthood, all offerings were to be clean or holy unto the Lord. *"And all the tithes of the land, whether of the seed of the land, or of the fruit of the land, or of the fruit of the tree, is the Lord's: it is holy unto the Lord."* **Leviticus 27: 30**; Peter 1: 6. This law was instituted in Moses day, but Abram gave tithes four centuries before Moses. The principle given in the above scripture is, "it is HOLY unto the Lord." And the understanding that GOODS given to the Lord are to be clean, pure and of the right virtue; these three constitute what is **holy**.

To Be Clean: The Believers are cleansed by the word Christ hath spoken. Cleanliness involves sanctification or separation from the unclean things of the flesh. All that is contrary to the nature and likeness of Christ is unclean. *"For I am the Lord your God: ye shall therefore sanctify yourselves, and ye shall be holy; for I am holy: neither shall ye defile yourselves with any manner of creeping thing that creepeth upon the earth."* **Leviticus 11: 44**; John 15: 3; & 17: 17. Note the word creeping thing. This would mean anything that moves, swarm, bring forth increase, to wiggle or breed. An example of this is looking at today's fads, fashions and folly. Getting tattoos are more wide spread than they were a century ago. Many people desire to live a life of vanity, greed, lasciviousness, and all kinds of sensual pleasures of the flesh. What you are witnessing today, are the creeping things that creepeth {actively moving} upon the land. In other words, widespread wickedness is on the increase, spurning out more ungodliness. The apostle Peter wrote to exhort the people to Holiness; teaching them not to fashion themselves according to their former lusts. *"But as he who called you is holy, so be ye holy in all manner of conversation."* **1 Peter 1:15** The word for conversation in the Greek means, behavior. This would cover all the activities in life: man's conversation is to be holy. To be holy does not limit behavior to going to church on Sunday: but to conduct oneself right in every aspect of living. To sanctify you works on the soulish nature; the character, personality, behavior and conduct of the individual. To be Clean is to obey the word of God. Jesus said, *"Now ye are clean through the word which I have spoken unto you."*

To Be Pure: When something is pure, it is not only clean but it is unmixed with any other matter or material. Pure means the best in quality, sheer, spotless, free from moral fault and chase. This is the nature of the gifts and offerings that God accepts. It is holy unto the Lord. Abram gave an acceptable offering to Melchizedek, because it was holy unto the Lord. He said to the king of Sodom, *"I have lifted up mine hand unto the Lord, the Most High God, the possessor of heaven and earth. That I will not take from thee a thread even to a shoe latchet, and that I will not take any thing that is thine, lest thou shouldest say, I have made Abram rich."* **Genesis 14:22** If Abram had taken anything of the king's, and offered it as a tenth to Melchizedek would have been unholy unto the Lord. That would have meant that he acquired those goods by misconduct or by thievery. But Abram's offering was holy. During the time Moses was establishing the tabernacle of the Lord; he followed what God had commanded. God spoke in specific details to Moses of the things that were to be pure of. God spoke to Hosea and illustrated his love, his judgment and his redemption for Israel by his marriage to Gomer. The seed was scattered; God put them away by dispersing the seed throughout all the earth. The scattering of the seed brought in other nations blessed of Abraham. Now Jesus came to seek and to save those that are lost. The Pharisees and the scribes knew what was written in the law and the prophets. But they were not true shepherds. Why would Israel be sought after as the lost sheep, if those shepherds were attending to the flock of God?

The prophet Ezekiel said, *"As a shepherd seeketh out his flock in the day that he is among his sheep that are scattered; so will I seek out my sheep, and will deliver them out of all places where they have been scattered in the cloudy and dark day. And I will bring them out from the people, and gather them from the countries, and I will bring them to their own land, and feed them upon the mountains of Israel by the rivers and in the inhabited places of the country." I will seek that which was lost, and bring again that which was driven away, and will bind up that which was broken, and will strengthen that which was sick: but I will destroy the fat and the strong; I will feed them with judgment." I will set up one shepherd over them, and he shall feed them, even my servant David: he shall feed them, and he shall be their shepherd."* READ: The Good Shepherd: Ezekiel **34: 11-16 v. 23; John 10:1-14.**

The furnishings, the vessels, the decorations and the altar were to be pure or overlaid with pure gold. Those things were types and shadows of the temple God desire to dwell in. The message spoken is that true worship must be pure, chaste, undefiled to God. He is holy, therefore man must be holy. God purposed to make man in his image and after his likeness. It is written, *"Every word of God is pure: he is a shield unto them that put their trust in him."* Proverbs 30:5 God's laws do not change: and there's no excuse to neither do wrong nor change God's word. The Palmist said, *"The law of the Lord is perfect, converting the soul: the testimony of the Lord is sure, making wise the simple. The statutes of the Lord are right, rejoicing the heart: the commandment of the Lord is PURE, enlightening the eyes.* **Psalm 19:7-8.** The apostle Paul wrote to Timothy, saying, *"Therefore I endure all things for the elect's sakes, that they may also obtain the salvation which is in Christ Jesus with eternal glory. It is a faithful saying: For if we be dead with him, we shall also live with him. If we suffer, we shall also reign with him: if we deny him, he also shall deny us; If we believe not, yet he abideth faithful: he cannot deny himself."* **2Timothy 2:10-13**

Of the right Virtue: Worshipping God is to be clean, pure and of the right virtue: this becomes the holy offering unto the Lord. In the Bible is given a number of virtues that are righteous toward worship. Virtue means it is of an excellent nature or quality which ascribes to the character of a person. Virtue is recognizable in a person's character: The person may be righteous, just, faithful, kind, humble, a peacemaker and honest. These virtues are noteworthy, but CHARITY is the greatest of all virtues. The entire chapter of

1Corinthians 13, the apostle Paul taught and defined love. Charity is longsuffering, does not envy, is not of a proud look, and is not puffed up. Charity is not selfish, always with the right behavior, is not easily provoked and does not contemplate to do wrong. Charity rejoices in the truth; and not in iniquity. Charity beareth, believeth, hopeth and endureth all things. There is no load too heavy; no belief so profound; no desire so craving nor circumstance so lingering that charity cannot rule over. Charity never faileth, but abideth beyond prophecies, tongues and knowledge. **1 Corinthians 13: 1-13; John** 3:16; 1John 3: 11-17; 1John 4: 7-14;

Abram tithes were of the right virtue; he gave a holy offering unto the Lord. The things Paul wrote about which defines charity, are the things that were exemplified in Abram's life. To some, the preaching of tithes appeals to carnal understanding; avoiding the spiritual message that should be gained. Man is not redeemed with corruptible things as silver and gold. Redemption is by the blood of Christ given for salvation. Abram as a man of faith gave God his tenth, his lost ones {Israel} before his seed was born. Therefore charity excelled the prophecy of promise; it moved beyond language barriers and the knowledge of men.

Remember, the lost in whom Jesus spoke parables about were the 10-lost tribes of Israel. Then Jesus gave a parable of the woman that had ten pieces of silver. His message was to show that he came to seek and to save the lost. "*Either what woman having ten pieces of silver, if she lose one piece, doth not light a candle, and sweep the house, and seek diligently till she find it? And when she hath found it, she calleth her friends and her neighbors together, saying, rejoice with me; for I have found the piece which I had lost.*" **Luke 15: 8-10 Luke 15: 4; and** Luke 15: 11-32. The woman's love for the lost coin made her search for it until she found it.

The tenth Abram gave through an act of faith to God is Israel. Whatever is given to Christ must be holy unto him. When the lost is found, this brings rejoicing and joy in heaven. Every time tithes are given, tithes should be given for the purpose of the ministers as overseers of the church to bring back the lost. Some preachers preach "plant a seed faith" but this is to lure people to give to enrich themselves. It is unjust and unfaithful to give like as if gaming in a lottery. Melchizedek did not tell Abram that God will double the pot or return his goods in a hundred fold portion. The tithes the priests received were to maintain them as they ministered the things of God. They did not own real estate, land or acquire great material riches from the tithes. The "storehouse" was a store of supply to feed Israel. The focus is not on meat that will perish, but on the word of God that perish not. This is a picture of the church that should provide substance for the lost. The implication is that the teaching or the word of God is the meat in God's storehouse. But like as Cain, many will bring an offering of the earth. Many will do alms in the church, but yet unrighteous towards their brethrens; sometimes with iniquity in the heart. A form of godliness is what many church practices are all about. But to know what is the most chased of all attributes pleasing unto the Lord is to know charity. Abram's faith teaches us charity; the most excellent way to love and to give. Faith can be viewed like pure gold; it overlay everything that we offer to God. True worship, which is of the right value: the price most excellent is love.

It is important to know the value of Abram's goods: and why they are highly esteemed and desirable. The value of the goods has a great price: it is because the price became the ransom for man. God chose Israel as His peculiar treasure: *"For the Lord hath chosen Jacob unto himself and Israel for his peculiar treasure."* **Deuteronomy 7:7-9; & 10: 15-22** Moses said to the people, *"For thou art an holy people unto the Lord thy God: the Lord thy God hath chosen thee to be a special people unto himself, above all people that are upon the face of the earth. The Lord did not set his love upon you, nor choose you, because ye were more in number than any people; for ye were the fewest of all people: But because the Lord loved you, and because **he would keep the oath** which he had sworn unto your fathers,* [the fathers >Abraham, Isaac and Jacob] *hath the Lord brought you out* *with a mighty hand, and **redeemed you** out of the house of bondmen, from the hand of Pharaoh king of Egypt..*" Psalm 135: 4; Exodus 19:5.

The great price, the gift of God is eternal life through Jesus Christ our Lord. His blood is the ransom price that redeemed man. Like as with Abram in the natural, he rescued Lot; and he gave tithes of all the goods. In the fullness of times, God sent his only begotten Son into the world to redeem man. He did not forfeit his promise to Abraham: but through Christ, {the promised SEED} Abraham became the father of many nations. All who are of faith are the children of Abraham. In the New Testament, Zacharias said *"From the hand of all that hate us; to perform the mercy promised to our fathers, and to remember his holy covenant; the oath which he sware to our father Abraham." That he would grant unto us, that we being delivered out of the hand of our enemies might serve him without fear, In holiness and righteousness before him, all the days of our life."* **Luke 1: 70-80**

Not only was Abram's goods valuable, but he gained them; having gone out to seek for that which was lost. He found his nephew Lot and rescued Lot and the people. This is in like manner, a type of Jesus, who came to seek and save that which was lost. Jesus spoke this parable: *"Again, the kingdom of heaven is like unto treasure hid in a field; the which when a man hath found, he hideth, and for joy thereof goeth and selleth all that he hath, and buyeth that field.* Matthew 13: 44. First of all, the Lord saw Israel, his treasure not yet discovered in the earth. This was a visionary time when the plan of God was not yet known to men. But when he *"hath found"* speaking in a tense of already done; because man's redemption was preordained before the foundation to the world. *"He hideth"* which is to say, God secured his treasure in the earth. Jesus prayed concerning this for his disciples: *"I pray not that thou shouldest take them out of the world, but that thou shouldest keep them from the evil."* **John 17: 15** Christ rescued man.

A person who follows the teachings of Jesus is his disciple; therefore his prayer covers all believers. To take his treasure out of the earth would have been premature, because all prophecy haven't yet fulfilled. But man's hope is made alive because he ascended on high and led captivity captive. He is the only firstborn of the dead: no one else has yet resurrected to eternal life. His treasure is yet in the world, awaiting the first resurrection. *"But ye are a chosen generation, a royal priesthood, a holy nation, a peculiar people; that ye should show forth the praises of him who hath called you out of darkness into marvelous light: Which in time past were not a people, but are now the people of God: which had not obtained mercy, but now have obtained mercy."* 1Peter 2:9. *"For joy"* God is pleased with his Beloved Son. Jesus did the will of the Father; and Joy is evidence that the Spirit of God was working in him. His life is the ransom for man's redemption: for he rescued his own. It was *"for joy" that* Christ gave his life for his treasure. A manifested fruit of the Spirit: the first fruit from the dead. But Joy *"comes in the morning"* an awaking of a new day; the time of the eternal reign of Christ. This joy is not a sensual pleasure of human passion. As concerning Jesus baptism by John, it is written, *"And Jesus, when he was baptized, went up straightway out of the water: and, lo, the heavens were opened unto him, and he saw the Spirit of God descending like a dove, and lighting upon him: And lo a voice from heaven, saying, **This is my beloved Son, in whom I am well pleased.**"* Matthew 3:16-17

Little Space Grace appeared in every episode of Abraham's life because his faith gained access to God's grace. God's word never failed Abram because he trusted in it. Faith comes by hearing the word of God and it anchors hope for that which will be manifested. As a spiritual type, the value of the tithes given by Abram was the price of redemption. The value of Abram's goods pertained to a ransom that was greater than the natural goods Melchizedek received. The acts of Abram defined his walk of faith. Whatever was the situation of his life, Abram acted beyond natural perception. He allowed the word of God to be the substance of the things hoped for. And the exceeding great reward was the magnitude of the blessings received.

Wisdom established Faith as the pillar that supported Abram as the temple of God. In the same instance the promises of God were given to Abraham. For his promises are to support his temple.

Wisdom establishing God's Promises: The next phase of the faith walk of Abram was when the word of God came to him in a vision. This was not the first time God spoke with Abram. Recall the time he was in the land of Ur, among his relatives, God spoke with him. When Abram left Ur and went to Haran, God spoke with him. Then in the plains of Mamre, Abram viewed the land God showed him of his seed's inheritance. Now after the return of the slaughter of the kings, God spoke his word to Abram in a vision. His natural view of the land was not prophetic; but to have a vision presents a prophecy. This prophecy established another pillar called the promise of God that wisdom hewed out. The word hewn is used in masonry work. It is the activity of engraving, cutting away; to dig, split, square, divide and mason. This is the activity of a builder: and the Builder is the wisdom of God.

20

WISDOM REVEALS THE PLAN

*"After these things the word of the Lord came to Abram in a vision, saying, Fear not, Abram: I am thy shield, and thy exceeding **great reward**."* Genesis 15:1 Abram gave tithes to Melchizedek prior to this vision from the Lord. His act was strictly of faith because he had no bases for giving with the expectation of receiving a reward. Now prophecy will support his cause for the actions that went forth in his life. Abram would rely on the promise and prophecy from the word of God that was spoken unto him.

In the above scripture, the communication of God to Abram was in a vision. How awesome, to experience a vision with a voice that speaks. God said, "Fear not" Abram. The humanity of Abram was capable of being affright, alarmed, and brought into reverence. But the comforting words from God were, "I am thy shield." Was God referring to a natural shield? NO: the shield is a symbol of faith. The Hebrew word for faith means door. And a door is an entrance way, which is purposed to safeguard or prevent uninvited access.

To Communicate: This is the way by which people convey knowledge of or gain information about. Communicate is to connect or transmit thought or a desire to be satisfactorily understood. The word of God in a vision was something Abram had not previously experienced. He taught others to believe in the Almighty God. He now had a spiritual encounter with the presence of God. Abram heard the voice, saw the vision and understood the message communicated to him. Men are to hear and understand the word of Jesus taught in the gospels.

"FEAR NOT"

Affright: This is one of the first emotional experiences from sudden horror, terror or something strange to the senses. Then, the first line of defense for the person that is frightened is to protect self. But followed by the words "fear not," God said to Abram, "<u>I am thy shield</u>." In warfare, Abram understood the purpose for the shield. He could associate and dispel the emotion to fear, because he knew how to use the shield. Prior to his vision, Abram had fought five kings in battle. He overcame fear, danger and defeat in his warfare. Abram was faithful, skillful, precise, patient, tactful, forceful, commanding, charging, strengthen, courageous, encouraging, neglecting, sacrificing, articulating and merciful in his warfare activity. Armed with these virtues, the shield of faith gained him victory. In the battle with the kings, Abraham lost not one man. He was confident in the rescue Lot; although he had few men in comparison to the armies of the kings. Wisdom was engraving the right nature and character in Abraham.

Alarmed: A person that is alarmed by a voice and by a sign is a person mystified. But something is being communicated. *"Wherein he hath abounded toward us in all wisdom and prudence; Having made known unto us the mystery of his will, according to his good pleasure which he hath purposed in himself: That in the dispensation of the fullness of times he might gather in one all things in Christ, both which are in heaven, and which are on earth; even in him."* Ephesians 1:9

Reverence: Sometimes to revere is of the emotion of fear; it is when a transitioning away from the alarmed and frightened is the response. A person who reverence is one who submits; which leads to humility and obedience. Fear of itself is just the emotion; but fear needs a directive. The word **"not"** is the authority used along with the word fear. Whether it is in front of the word fear or after the word fear, "not" commands a course of action. Fear is to be done away with in order for reverence to rule the heart. **"Not"** reverses the fear, and bring it to naught. Abram was able to "fear not" because he reverenced the voice and vision of God. His human fear of the things that caused fear was gone. The wisdom of the word created the Godly fear Abram received, because he reverenced God. It is written, *"Whence then cometh wisdom? And where is the place of understanding? 'And unto man he said, Behold the fear of the Lord, that is wisdom; and to depart from evil is understanding."* Job 28:28

"I AM..."

God Proclaims: The self-existent God of all creation made himself known in the words, "I am." The "I" is a letter and word of consciousness. The word "I" is understood as the existing being, or the self. '**I**' is not without knowing that there is an 'I.' but what did '**I**' mean to Abram the Hebrew? The tenth letter of the Hebrew alphabets is the letter "Y" which is' yod' In language, there are many words which can carry the same pronunciation as the letter 'I' For an example, words like mynd-mind; key-kei; bye-bi; and so on. The letter "I" is the ninth letter of the Greek alphabets, which is 'iota'. The word and vision of the Lord came to Abram as an iota (jot or tittle) from the vastness of God's word. God said, "I am" the word declaring God exist and he is the beginning and the end. The word "AM" is of two alphabets; when separated '**A**' becomes the Greek word <u>Alpha,</u> meaning **first**. The letter "**M**" is the last of the Greek alphabet; <u>Omega,</u> meaning **last**. Read: **Genesis 15: 1; Exodus 3:14;** *"Verily, verily, I say unto you, The hour is coming, and now is, when the dead shall hear the voice of the Son of/God: and they that hear shall live. For as the Father hath life in himself; so hath he given to the son to have life in himself; and hath given him authority to execute judgment also, because he is the Son of man."* John 4:25–27. The Lord said, *"I am Alpha' and Omega, the beginning and the ending, saith the Lord, which is, and which was, and which is to come, the Almighty."* **Revelation 1:8** God spoke in full authority of the beginning and the ending of the course Abraham followed.

Abram was intelligence, and he understood this proclamation of God. He interpreted out of the words he heard in the vision that God exist. Not only does God exist, but God is the author and finisher of Abram's faith. The knowledge of God and his divinity established God's name, "I Am" to Abram. What Abram heard in the vision introduced him to the name of God. The words of God gave him knowledge of God; but the voice of God gave Abram recognition to identify God with. Abram derived knowledge from three Hebrew alphabets, **I-A-M,** These words identify God.

I, iota, infinitesimal, {*from infinite*} meaning endless; or immeasurable

and incalculable.

A, aleph, FIRST, Beginning; Before in time, position, place, and order.

God is Omnipresence! God Exist everywhere.

God is Omniscience! All Knowing God. **He is Wisdom.**

M, omega, LAST; continual in time, enduring;

God is Omnipotent!!! God is all power and eternal.

Abram was Hebrew, therefore he defined the 13th Hebrew letter '**m**'; he gained understanding of the word of God. He was able to correlate the God that spoke to him of his yesterday; by saying "in the land of Ur." God also spoke to him in his present day; in the plains of Mamre. And the God of his tomorrow; was pointing to the Promised Land. *"Fear not; I am the first and the last: I am he that liveth, and was dead; and behold, I am alive forevermore, Amen; and have the keys of hell and of death."* Revelation 1:17-18

Now the letter **M** or **mem.** The 'mem' is abbreviate for the words member, memoir and memorial. As MEMBER: God's word in the iota form is a part of the whole. As MEMIOR: God's word is a record of noteworthy accounts. As MEMORIAL: God's word is the keepsake; His name is kept as a memorial that preserves in memory his works. Galatians 4:4-6 *"Forever, O Lord, thy word is settled in heaven Thy faithfulness is unto all generations: thou hast established the earth, and it abideth. They continue this day according to thine ordinances: for all are thy servants. I have seen an end of all perfection: but thy commandment is exceeding broad."* Psalm 119: 89-91

". . Thy SHIELD,"

"Thy" is a word that relates to 'thee or thyself' as possessor, or relating to an object. Abram possessed the shield; but God presented himself as Abram's shield. The shield, as a symbol of God's protection and defense is under the authority of God. For the man of faith, God is protection. No man subdued God's authority in Abram's life. The shield is a defensive armor; used mainly in close range conflict. It can also safeguard against fiery darts, spears and arrows thrown or shot from a distance. *"Finally, my brethren, be strong in the Lord, and in the power of his might, "For we wrestle not against flesh and blood, but against principalities, against powers, against the rulers of the darkness of this world, against spiritual wickedness in high places. Wherefore take unto you the whole armor of God, that ye may be able to withstand in the evil day, having done all, to stand."* Ephesians 6:10-12

Little Space Grace was given in measures of mercy God showed to Abram. The Palmist said, *"His mercy endureth to all generations."* His protection was another measure of his grace to Abram. And "all things are possible unto him that believe" which was the extent of Abram's faith. Psalm 107: 1-8; Psalm 18: 1-6; & 46-50. When Abraham's seed became a nation of people, God protected them through many conflicts and perils of life. Knowing God was the Protector; Abram found love and peace in God. Protection by God demonstrated God's love; and for this cause, Abram experienced and gained knowledge of God's love. A faith relationship develops the love relationship. Abram love toward God was known in that he loved his brethrens: rescued his nephew Lot and the people. *"Beloved, let us love one another: for love is of God; and every one that loveth is born of God, and knoweth God."* Abram performed the law of God. *"And this is love that we walk after his commandments. This is the commandment, that, as ye have heard from the beginning, ye should walk in it."* 1 John 4:7; 2 John 1:5; John 14:15-20 *"If ye keep my commandments, ye shall abide in my love; even as I have kept my Father's commandments, and abide in his love."* John 15:10

". . Thy Exceeding Great Reward,"

Having faith, the HOPE is the desire with expectation. Hope will keep alive the vision; and hope suffers long for the reward to manifest. This hope is the trust and reliance on the word of God. As a trail blazer of faith, Abraham walked in the commandment of God. He pleased God and was called the Friend of God. Faith made things possible in his walk of obedience with God. Abram believed on the word of God: not wavering in faith was his hope. Those that waver are entertaining doubt and unbelief. The expression, "I'll believe it when I see it." This is a kind of belief that is dependent upon a sign. Jesus said, *"An evil and adulterous generation seeketh after a sign; and there shall no sign be given to it, but the sign of the prophet Jonah: For as Jonah was three days and nights in the whale's belly; so shall the Son of man be three days and three nights in the heart of the earth. The men of Nineveh shall rise in judgment with this generation, and shall condemn it: because they repented at the preaching of Jonah; and behold, a greater than Jonah is here."* Jesus spoke about a wicked generation seeks for a sign; this is like the kind of unbelief in Noah's day. *"By faith, Noah, being warned of God of things not seen as yet, moved with fear, prepared an ark to the saving of his house; by the which he condemned the world, and became heir of the righteousness which is by faith."* The sign given is the death, burial and resurrection of Jesus Christ. Through him men are rewarded eternal life if they believe on him as the scripture has said. Matthew 12: 39-41; Genesis 6:13, & 22; Romans 3:19-26; & 10: 9-13; Matthew 28:19; Mark 16:15; Hebrews 3:7-19; & 11:7.

Faith signifies that the Believer love God, because they keep his commandments. What God has promised in his word is his reward to the Believer. We can have confidence in his word because God is the same yesterday, today and forever: his oath and counsels changes not. His works are known and written, so that men may obtain faith to overcome like as Abraham. Through Jesus is the access to the grace of God by faith. Christ is the Door, the Way, the Truth and the Life; follow him and receive the exceeding great reward promised.

Earlier the word **"thy"** was defined as a possessor of something. God said to Abram, *"I am thy shield and thy exceeding great reward."* God spoke in terms of that which already is; not something to expect he will become. All things were established by Him before the foundation of the world. Melchizedek had said unto Abram, "Blessed be Abram of the Most High God, possessor of heaven and earth." Genesis 14:19 Before Abram obtained the blessings; Melchizedek spoke of them to Abram. The New Testament reveals the blessings: *"Blessed be the God and Father of our Lord Jesus Christ, who hath blessed us with all spiritual blessings in heavenly places in Christ: According as he hath chosen us in him before the foundation of the world, that we should be holy and without blame before him in love." Having predestinated us unto the adoption of children by Jesus Christ to himself, according to the good pleasure of his will."* Ephesians 1:3-5; Genesis 12:7; 15: 1

<u>**God is the Exceeding Great Reward:**</u> The word exceeding is a word often used with other words to express an intensive or superlative amount, quality or degree. Exceeding is from the root word EXCEED, and defined: *to extend outside of; to be greater than or superior to; to go beyond a limit set: <u>predominate.</u>* The superlative to the word *great* is greater or greatest; but with God he did not measure himself to any other thing. He didn't say to Abram, I am thy greater or greatest reward; but he used the term <u>exceeding</u>. This word expressed God's vehemence: He is powerful, and mighty with an intensive force. God taught Abram that he alone is powerful and mighty. The word <u>great</u> distinguished his **reward**. The great reward is remarkable in

magnitude or notably large in size. REWARD, in Hebrew is **sakar,** meaning, *payment of contract; salary, fare, maintenance; by* implication, *Compensation, benefit: hire, price, wages, worth.* Jesus blood was the great price of the covenant. ***"Blessed be the Lord, who daily loadeth us with* Benefits, *even the God of our salvation."*** Psalm 68:10

To paraphrase; with Abram, God is powerful, almighty, and with a notable benefit. Many generations have passed on, but the power of God and his blessings promised to Abraham remains. His blessings are superior and beyond all the limitations of men. Abram understood the vision from God, therefore he replied, *"What wilt thou give me, seeing I go childless, and the steward of my house is this Eliezer of Damascus?* Genesis 15:2

The Desire of Abram's Heart: Abram was rich in cattle silver and gold: all the things a man would care to possess. But his reply to God in the vision alluded to his heart's desire; which was for a son of his own bowels. What was in his heart pertained to the promise God gave him in the land of UR. Abram reference God's word that he kept in his heart concerning a son. The word God spoke to him in Canaan was, *"And the Lord appeared unto Abram, and said, unto thy seed will I give this land: and there builded he an altar unto the Lord, who appeared unto him."* Genesis 13:15-17. Abram was 75 years old at that time. After he spent time in Canaan, Egypt and Mamre, Abram came to be about eighty-five years old. He held to the promise of a seed. Ordinarily it was past the age of siring a seed. The covenant God made with Abram was years before the slaughter of the kings. The word of God in the heart of Abram became the desire of his heart. The transforming work of God's word received in the heart renews the mind; therefore it gives new perspectives in life. The wisdom of God, His word was establishing his plan and purpose in the heart of Abram. ***WISDOM said:*** **"I love them that love me; and those that seek me early shall find me. Riches and honor are with me: yea, durable riches and righteousness. My fruit is better than gold, yea, than fine gold; and my revenue than choice silver. I lead**

in the way of righteousness, in the midst of the paths of judgment. That I may cause those that love me to inherit substance; and I will fill their treasures." **Proverbs 8: 16-21** Recall, Abram possessed gold and silver; but God filled his heart (treasure) with inherit substance.

In Abram's heart was *"what wilt thy give me, seeing I go childless,"* Genesis 15:2. This statement show that Abram was in a <u>place of expectation</u>. He had material riches; therefore he did not pursue worldly substances. But what was lacked in his life, was the promised son. Note how wisdom answered the question that Abram asked, **"what." Wisdom said,** *"I may cause those that love me to inherit substance; and I will fill their treasures."* Proverbs 8:21

<u>**WHAT:**</u> Abram spoke this word, inquiring about the <u>identity</u>, <u>nature</u> and <u>value</u> of the gift God will give. God answered Abram, saying, *"But he that shall come forth out of thine own bowels shall be thine heir."* **Genesis 15:3** God identified the gift Abram would receive; and the nature of the gift would be of his own bowels. God answered to Abram was in terms of the value of the gift. He expressed it in a numerical quantity, and making the gift equivalent to the stars of heaven. The value of the gift God appraised with a degree of Excellency, highly rated, and esteemed. *"For thou art a holy people unto the Lord thy God: the Lord thy God hath chosen thee to be a special people unto himself, above all the people that are upon the face of the earth."* Deuteronomy 7:6. Moses said, *"Remember the days of old, consider the years of many generations: ask thy father, and he will shew thee; thy elders, and they will tell thee. "When the Most High divided to the nations their inheritance, when he separated the sons of Adam, he set the bounds of the people according to the number of the children of Israel. For the Lord's portion is his people; Jacob is the lot of his inheritance. He found him in a desert land, and in the waste howling wilderness; he led him about, he instructed him, he kept him as the apple of his eye."* Deuteronomy 32: 7-10.

Take notice of Abram's faith; God gave him to inherit substance, {the Promised Land}. In Abram's words "what wilt thy" alluded to "things hoped for." The promise of God spoken by Wisdom is *"I will fill their treasures."* Jesus taught that where the heart is, there also will be a man's treasure. Abram's heart, his desire or treasure was filled with what God promised. Read: JOB 14:15; Hebrews 6:17; 11:1;

WILT THOU: There are three main usages for the word **will.** (1) "I will" Is an intent or desire declared to be performed; it is in the planning stage. (2) "Thou will" expresses an acknowledgment of the one who will perform the plan or promise. This is an expression of submitting to that person's desire. For an example, Jesus prayed to the Father in the place called Gethsemane. *"Saying, O my Father, if it be possible, let this cup pass from me: nevertheless not as I will, **but as thou wilt.***" Matthews 26:39. "Thou will" is being obedient to the Father's will. (3) "Wilt thou "The words questions the person who will perform the promise. Assurance is in the heart when the believers know God is all powerful, and he is faithful to his promise. In other words, Abram was asking God to perform his word. "Wilt thou" made it God's choice to do as he promised. "I will is my choice. "Thou will" is your choice" but "wilt Thou" is in the hand of God to perform. In the Book of Job, it is written, *"Thou shalt call, and I will answer thee: **thou wilt have** a desire to the work of thine hands."* JOB 14:15 Job realized the power and authority of God; that God will perform that which he desires. God ordained man to be in His image and after His likeness. Abram continued to receive a measure of God's Little Space Grace.

GIVE ME: At this point in the scripture the love of God was made known to Abram. In keeping God's word a fellowship was made. The love relationship was viable by the work of charity, which God showed to Abram. Love always extends out to the other: and love is made known by giving. Remember, Abram gave "a tenth of all" to Melchizedek, the king of Salem and priest of the Most High God. The windows of heaven opened and poured out a blessing: and his gift to man is eternal life, *"For God so loved the world that he gave his only begotten Son, that whosoever believeth in him should not perish, but* *have everlasting life."* John 3:16 Abram did not set his affection on the things of the earth; he knew they were temporal. Apostle Paul wrote, *"While we look not at the things which are seem, but at the things which are not seen; for the things which are seen are temporal; but the things which are not seen are eternal."* Colossians 3: 2-10. Eternal life is the exceeding great reward of faith.

People seek after the material things of this life, often becoming vain in their manner of conduct. They might exhibit behaviors of greed, covetousness, anger, deceit, falsehood and the like. Many will lose their lives by crimes, mental diseases, health problems and distresses. What does it profit to gain material things and lose out with God? For an example to us; the children of Israel were warned by Moses to not follow after the practices of the ungodly. They were to obey the same commandments of God that we should obey today. God never changes; he is the same today, yesterday and tomorrow. *"See, I have set before thee this day life and good, and death and evil; In that I command thee this day to love the Lord thy God, to walk in his ways, and to keep his commandments and his statutes and his judgments, that thou mayest live and multiply: and the Lord thy God shall bless thee in the land whither thou goest to possess it. But if thine heart turn away, so that thou wilt not hear, but shalt be drawn away, and worship other gods, and serve them; I denounce unto you this day that ye shall surely perish, and that ye shall not prolong your days upon the land, whither thou passest over Jordan to go to possess it."* Deuteronomy 30:15; Genesis 15:5.

The children of Israel became wicked; stiffnecked and they tempted God with their unbelief. Wickedness was in the heart of people during the time of Christ; he spoke against seeking for a sign. The sign given to this generation was the Son of God coming down from above. By his death, burial and resurrection much fruit would be brought into the kingdom of God. Jesus made mention of the prophet Jonah. The story recorded Jonah was in the belly of the fish; this typified the death burial and resurrection of Christ. When Jonah obeyed God, the people in the city of Nineveh were saved from the wrath of God. In another scripture, Jesus said to Nicodemus, *"And no man hath ascended up to heaven, but he that came down from heaven, even the son of man which is in heaven. And as Moses lifted up the serpent in the wilderness, even so must the Son of man be lifted up: That whosoever believeth in him should not perish, but have eternal life."* John 8: 37-40; John 3:13-15. What will a man give for his life? God has given to the world his only begotten Son, that whosoever believeth on him should not perish, but should have eternal life. In a figure of speech, Jesus said, *Verily, verily I say unto you, except a corn of wheat fall into the ground and die, it abideth alone, but if it die, it bringeth forth much fruit.* A few verses that followed this saying, Jesus said, *And, I, if I be lifted up from the earth, will draw all men unto me. This he said, signifying what death he should die."* John 12: 24, & 34; Romans 6:5-14; Ephesians 2:4-7 Resurrection is life from the dead; Jesus is the seed that went into the earth. Now he is risen and sitting on the right hand of the Father in heaven, making intercession for us. A seed cannot produce the fruit, unless the seed is first planted in the earth. Christ is the promised Seed of Abraham; he was planted in the earth, and his resurrection paved the way to eternal life for all men.

Abram was promised the greatest gift to be given; and that gift is eternal life. With men, life would cease to be if no child is born. The seed is vital for life to continue in the natural; and definitely so in the spiritual realm. Faithful Abraham became the father of many nations because God kept his promise to Abraham. *"Even as Abraham believed God, and it was accounted to him for righteousness. Know you therefore that they which are of faith, the same are the children of Abraham."* Galatians 3: 7; Colossians 2:9-14.

God brought Abram abroad and told him to look toward heaven and *"tell the stars, if thou be able to number them:* and he said, *"so shall thy seed be."* Genesis 13:16; Genesis 24: 58-61; Genesis 22: 16-18; Deuteronomy 1:8-11; Jeremiah 33: 22;

From the time of Abraham until this day, no one is able to number the many people who became children of Abraham by faith? This is the exceeding great reward of faith promised to Abram. *"Hearken to me, ye that follow after righteousness, ye that seek the Lord: look unto the rock whence ye are hewn, and to the hole of the pit whence ye are digged. Look unto Abraham your father, and unto Sarah that bare you: for I called him alone, and blessed him, and increased him."* Isaiah 51:1-2.

ABRAM's RIGHTEOUSNESS: The scripture said, *"And he believed in the Lord; and he counted it to him for righteousness."* Genesis 15: 6; Romans 4:8-12 & 16. Some people may say, "I believe in God" but their lifestyles are contradictory to the words they speak. Abram not only acknowledged that he believed the word of God; his righteousness declared him justified. Faith developed in his character the virtue of being just. To be just is a virtue which faith brings about. Abram was justified by faith in God. Paul said, *"But that no man is justified by the law in the sight of God, it is evident: for the JUST shall live by faith."* **Genesis 15: 6; Romans 5:1; Galatians 3:11.**

Abram was a Just Man: His character exemplified being righteous, and truthful. *"And he believed in the Lord; and he counted it to him for righteousness."* The word **Believed** takes faith to the level of works. Abram was more than a hearer of the word; he was a doer of the word of God as well. Jesus taught the people to be a hearer and doer of his sayings. The Hebrew word believed is, **aman,** defined > to *build up or support; to foster* as a parent or nurse. Fig. to *render (*or be) firm or *faithful; to be true or believe; to trust; to go to the right hand*—hence assurance, believe, bring up, establish; *long* continuance, stedfast, turn to the right. The definition clearly shows Abram was just; he turned to what was right to do. To be a doer of the word was the **work**; he believed God. Any labor or the activity of doing something is considered as working. A Doer is the person at work; governed by the desire to make something effective or brought forth. For instance: a man may go out to plant corn. His labor helps assure a harvest, which is the expected outcome.

James wrote, *"But wilt thou know, O vain man, that faith without works is dead? Was not Abraham our father justified by works, when he had offered Isaac his son upon the altar? Seest thou how faith wrought with his works and by works was faith made perfect? And the Scripture was fulfilled which saith, Abraham believed God, and it was imputed unto him for righteousness: and he was called the Friend of God. Ye see then how that by works a man is justified, and not by faith only."* James 2:20-24. As children of God, works affirms and justifies the faith the believer holds fast too. The faith of a person is known by their works. Some works do not produce good results. The reason why works produce bad results is because the works are not in accord with God's word. Foremost, wisdom, knowledge and understanding of the word of God authorize the work. Having these in place, it is most likely the outcome will be good fruit. Nobody should say "I believe" and think this is faith. This might be the practice and concept of some people. But faith in God comes by His word enlightening us and revealing His will. Then when the word is heard (understood) we must make an agreement with the truth and act upon this truth. Learning from the life of Abram, keep in mind that he heard the voice of God. Next, Abram made an altar which illustrated him agreeing to the covenant God made with him.

To bow down in worship to God is a form of submitting to His will. Abram obeyed the word he heard. To neglect to hear, submit and do what God has commanded, is the reason prayers are not answered. God will only perform his word. He does not change his word to fit the fleshly passions of men. *"Wherefore, my beloved brethren, let every man be swift to **hear**, slow to speak, slow to wrath: For the wrath of man worketh not the righteousness of God. "But be ye doers of the word, and not hearers only, deceiving your own selves. For if any be a hearer of the word, and not a doer, he is like unto a man beholding his natural face in a glass: For he beholdeth himself, and goeth his way, and straightway forgetteth what manner of man he was. But whoso looketh into the perfect law of liberty, and continueth therein, he being not a forgetful hearer, but a **doer of the work**, this man shall be blessed in his deed."* James 1: 20-25

Abram's righteous<u>ness</u> can further be understood by defining the suffix, **"ness."** This speaks of the condition, degree and quality of Abram's faith. The thing attached to Abram just character was spiritual increase: he was growing in the knowledge of God. Abram received faith and virtue by keeping the word of God. Each time there was a dilemma; little space grace delivered him out of the situation. The apostle Peter wrote in his epistle, "to *them that have obtained like precious faith with us through the righteousness of God and our savior Jesus Christ; Grace and peace be multiplied unto you through the knowledge of God, and of Jesus Christ our Lord."* 2Petr 1:1

Abram condition of faith: The condition or terms of God's covenant with Abram were:

1. God will make Abram a nation.

2. God will bless Abram.

3. God will make his name great.

4. And Abram will be a blessing.

5. God will bless them that bless Abram.

6. God will curse them that curse Abram.

7. In Abram all families of the earth shall be blessed.

The promises of God pointed ultimately to the redemption of the world. Through Abram's seed God channeled his blessing to all men. *"Christ hath redeemed us from the curse of the law, being made a curse for us; for it is written, Curse is every one that hangeth on a tree: That the Blessing of Abraham might come on the Gentiles through Jesus Christ; that we might receive the promise of the Spirit through faith."* Galatians 3: 13-15. Abram was called a Hebrew; and his seed became a nation of people called Hebrews. But the promise given to him to be a father of many nations includes all people. *"Now therefore, if ye will obey my voice indeed, and keep my covenant, then ye shall be a peculiar treasure unto me above all the people: for all the earth is mine. And ye shall be unto me a kingdom of priests, and a holy nation. These are the words which thou shalt speak unto the children of Israel."* Genesis 14:13; & 12: 2, 3

God invoked His divine love upon Abram. Through many centuries of history, Abraham's name was great. Abram was a blessing to the people in his day, and throughout all history. To <u>bless</u> is to praise, to thank, to congratulate; it is an act of adoration. God extended blessings to those who regarded Abraham's faith. The Jews of Christ day made reference to Abraham in their manner of conduct, their teachings and their honor to the Hebrew nation.

At times the Jewish leaders would try to glory in Abraham's name and his righteous character. Abraham was a model and an emblem of all which the Jewish leaders showed others as God's special people. He was like a reference book for guidance, teaching and practices the Jews referred to in their way of expelling any opposition coming from others.

The terms given in the contract were righteous: for God's righteousness was Abram faith. This is what is meant by God "counted" (imputed) it (Abram faith) for righteousness. In other words, God regarded Abram's faith; God considered and qualified Abram's faith as righteousness. *"Even as Abraham believed God, and it was accounted to him for righteousness. Know you therefore that they which are of faith, the same are the children of Abraham. 'So then they which be of faith are Blessed with faithful Abraham."* Galatians 3: 7-9

Abram degree of faith: The steps or stages that Abraham progressed in are known in his life activity. He left his father's house, his country and his kindred. God spoke unto Abram the direction in which he should go. *"So Abram departed, as the Lord had spoken unto him; and*

Lot went with him: and Abram was seventy and five years old when he departed out of Haran." Genesis 12: 4; Hebrews 11:8.

To mark a beginning of his sojourning, first take note of his age at the time he was in the land of Ur. Whatever happened beyond that mark, created a time line: and there afterward measured Abram's stages of faith. *"And these are the days of the years of Abraham's life which he lived, a hundred threescore and fifteen years. Then Abraham gave up the ghost, and died in a good old age, an old man, and full of years."* Genesis 25:7. Abraham lived to be 175 years old. He was 75 years old when God made his covenant with him. The time of one hundred years later, his faith remained unwavering. *"By faith Abraham, when he was called to go out into a place which he should after receive for an inheritance, obeyed; and he went out, not knowing whither he went. By faith he sojourned in the land of promise, as in a strange country, dwelling in tabernacles with Isaac* {his son} *and Jacob* {his grandson}, *the heirs with him of the same promise: For he looked for a city which hath foundations, whose builder and maker is God."* Hebrews 11:8-9. Every event and experience Abram encountered added to his faith. The events of Abram life illustrates and defines the doctrine of faith. *"Giving all diligence, add to your faith virtue; and to virtue knowledge; and to knowledge temperance; and to temperance patience; and to patience godliness; and to godliness brotherly kindness; and to brotherly kindness charity. For if these things be in you, and abound, they make you that ye shall neither be barren nor unfruitful in the knowledge of our Lord Jesus Christ."* 2Peter 1:5. These virtues were known in the life of Abraham, because he was faithful to God's word.

Abraham became an old man full of years; he allowed faith to perfect God's work in him. His years were of growth, maturity, steadfastness, sound in faith, and not barren in his life with God. His name was great because God exalted him. *"Righteousness exalts a nation"* Proverbs 14:34. Righteousness was the advancement in the walk of faith given him. Abram's knowledge of God increased; his knowledge multiplied because of God's grace and peace with him. In the land of Haran he heard the voice of God speak unto him. When he obeyed and left his father's house, the Lord appeared unto him in the land of Canaan. There in Canaan, God said to him *"Unto thy seed will I give this land."* Abram knowledge of God was growing each time he experienced God's voice.

After a period of years experiencing the word of God spoken, his knowledge multiplied. Abram added to his faith virtue; and to virtue knowledge, temperance, patience, godliness, brotherly kindness, and charity. Spiritual increase is the fruit of being faithful to God. Abram obtained precious faith through the righteousness of God. As the father of faith, he is the example or pattern for all who are following the word. Let it be, *"According as his divine power hath given unto us all things that pertain unto life and godliness, through the knowledge of him that called us to glory and virtue."* 2Peter 1:3

Abram quality of faith: Previously stated, Abram obtained precious faith through the knowledge of God. The distinguished attribute of Abram's character was faith. The rank given to his faith was God "justified" him. An accomplishment of his faith, because God *"counted it to him for righteousness,"* God considered and esteemed Abram' faith as righteousness. Therefore, God justified him because he believed. To believe in God is the essential nature of faith. Like as when the nature of a man is identified; there is also known the law that rules the man. That law is in force; whether it is the law of the spirit or the law of sin and death. We are servants to whom we obey. *"Know ye not, that to whom ye yield yourselves servants to obey, his servants ye are to whom ye obey; whether of sin unto death, or of obedience unto righteousness? But God be thanked, that ye were the servants of sin, but ye have obeyed from the **heart** that form of doctrine which was delivered you. Being made free from sin, ye became the servants of righteousness."* For when ye were the servants of sin, ye were free from righteousness. *"But now being made free from sin, and become servants to God, ye have your fruit unto holiness, and the end everlasting life. For the wages of sin is death; but the gift of God is eternal life through Jesus Christ our Lord."* Romans 6: 16-23.

The conditions or the terms of God's covenant with Abram are his promises. The promises were established and fulfilled in Christ. God's word directed Abram to look north, south, east and west to envision the magnitude of the land promised. Land has the potential to produce and bringforth everything for human survival. What about the spiritual land of promise? Through faith men access the "all things are possible" kind of grace. Abram sojourned in the land of promise; looking for a city, whose builder and maker is God. Has there been a time when God built a material city of brick and mortar? Are the material things that are created eternal or temporal? Therefore, the Promised Land is a view of all things possible with God. Healings, miracles, deliverance from captivity and oppressions of any kind, are possible to them that believe.

The measure of Abram's faith started with the knowledge of God; and it began to grow as he experienced God's grace. The word of God was accomplishing his will in Abram. The word of God prospered the life of Abraham. The word of God declared him righteous; therefore he was justified by faith in God. The word of the Lord in the vision, said unto Abram, I *am the Lord that brought thee out of Ur of the Chaldees, to give thee this land to inherit it."* Genesis 15:7. God made himself known to Abram in the vision as "**I am** thy shield and thy exceeding great reward." These words set in place a spiritual revelation of God to Abram. He learned God by his name; I AM; revealing himself as Abram's protection and his love. Abram heard the God of his history; the same God of his day and of his tomorrow. But the new day was on the horizon; old things are passed away. To man who remains in the past produces no growth or life to exceed in. It was God's WILL that he offered Abram and his seed after him. The past is a place that holds dead things; memories, unforgiveness, bitterness, darkness, pain, anger, and whatever is in the spirit of men that brings the death. God brought Abram out of that place to give him a land **"to inherit it"** God gave a gift: the gift was the land of promise. But "to inherit it" is a legal expression of the Testator's will. Therefore, there must be first a death in order for the heirs to inherit the promise. It was God's

WILL he offered Abram and his seed after him. The contract is of God; but to fulfill a Will, there must come the death of the property holder. Jesus fulfilled the will. *"How much more shall the blood of Christ, who through the eternal Spirit offered himself without spot to God, purge your conscience from dead works to serve the living God? And for this cause he is the mediator of the New Testament that **by means of death**, for the redemption of the transgressions that were under the first testament, they which are called might receive the promise of **eternal inheritance**. For where a testament is there must also of necessity be the death of the testator. For a testament is of force after men are dead: otherwise it is of no strength at all while the testator liveth."* Hebrews 9:14-**17**. By the death of Christ, the will of God came in force: he that believeth shall inherit the promise of eternal life. This is the promise God gave to Abram and it came into effect by the death of Christ.

God brought Abram out of Ur of Chaldees to establish his plan of salvation in Abram. We know that our Faith will be exercised in a life of events, situations, circumstances and unfamiliar places. All these were also the happenings in Abram's life. Each experience was to advance Abram onward; and being strengthened by the virtues he acquired through faith "to inherit it."

"Whereby shall I know that I will inherit it? This was the question Abram asked God. Interestingly, Abram didn't ask when, where, why, or what he will inherit. The word **whereby** highlighted the question. He sought to what accord or through what means would he inherit the land. Abram was seeking the mind of God. He wanted to know the plan of God which would grant the purpose of God. Abram knew that the will or testament from the property owner comes with a plan and purpose. The plan of God was his word establishing his ordained will. The purpose of God was to reveal his good pleasure. Wisdom was working out the will of God: which is to make man in his image and likeness. What we see of God choosing Abraham, is the early fashioning of God's house being established. In Eden, God promised that the seed of the woman will bruise the head of the serpent. The seed of promise is Christ. He came and gained power over all the works of the devil. So with Abraham, the covenant was the contract, and sealed because God swore by himself to carry out the agreement. To understand this, recall what Abram said to God at the beginning of the vision. He said, *"To me thou hast given no seed: and, lo, one born in my house is mine heir."* Genesis 15:2. Abram understood that the will of a testator speak in specifics the plan of the testator. The one born in Abram's house would have known by what accord he would inherit the promise. Eliezer of Damascus was the steward in Abram's house. Abram knew that his present situation of being childless, Eliezer would be the inheritor of his goods after death. But with God, The Testator is Christ: it was by his shed blood that became the <u>whereby</u> fulfilling the promise. Jesus said, *"Take, eat; this is my body. And he took the cup, and gave thanks, and gave to them, saying, Drink you all of it: For this is my blood of the new testament, which is shed for many for the remission of sins."* Matthew 26:26-30. The inheritance was obtained through Jesus death.

This was the **whereby** or the manner by which Abram would inherit the promise. The apostle Paul said, *"In whom we have redemption through his blood, the forgiveness of sins, according to the riches of his grace; Wherein he hath abounded toward us in all wisdom and prudence; Having made known unto us the mystery of <u>his will,</u> according to his good pleasure which <u>he hath purposed in himself</u>: That in the dispensation of the fullness of times he might gather together in one all things in Christ, both which are in heaven, and which are on earth, even in him: To whom also **we have obtained an inheritance**, being predestinated <u>according to the purpose of him who worketh all things after the counsel of his own will.</u>"* Genesis 15:8; Ephesians 1: 8-11.

Faith connects us to the grace of God; faith was first fashioned in Abram's life. He is the father or origin of faith; whereas all who believeth becomes the children of Abraham. His seed by multitude are numbered like as the stars of heaven, the sand of the sea and the dust of the earth. God spoke this numerical figure of Abram's seed.

They are the number which no man can number, as it is written in the Book of Revelation, John said, *"After this I beheld, and, lo, a great multitude, which no man could number, of all nations and kindreds, and people, and tongues, stood before the Lamb, clothed with white robes, and palms in their hands."* . . .*"These are they which came out of great tribulation, and have washed their robes, and made them white in the blood of the Lamb."* Revelation 7: 9-14.

The Ordinances of Sacrifice: a preview of "whereby:" Before God commanded Moses to institute the Ordinances of Sacrifice, God revealed to Abram the way by which his promises are inherited. God answered Abram's desire to know the" whereby." God said unto him, *"Take me a heifer of three years old. And a she goat of three years old, and a ram of three years old, and a turtledove, and a young pigeon."* Genesis 15:9. There are five animals of sacrifice mentioned: three of the animals had to be three years old. In contrast with Christ ministry, it was three years before he became the sacrifice for sin. Abraham was given to know the whereby the inheritance would be given. He was blessed to know that through his seed will be the remission of sins. He understood that animal sacrifice represented an offering unto God for remittal of an offense.

Four hundred years before Moses taught the commandments of God concerning sacrifices, God showed unto Abram redemption. With Moses, the offerings of sacrifice were prescribed. The priests were to minister the offerings at the altar. The purpose was to have a substitute for taking away the sins of the priests they may have committed and also the sins of the people. The five animals used in sacrifices covered any sin committed; whether the sin was a sin of rebellion, omission, a sin of guilt, unintentional sins, or practicing sin. Without the shedding of blood there is no remission for sin. As early as with Cain and Abel, animal sacrifice and offering were practiced. God accepted Abel's sacrifice because it was the bloodshed that covered his sin. It symbolized the shedding of Christ's blood to take away the sin of the world. *"By faith Abel offered unto God a more excellent sacrifice than Cain, by which he obtained witness that he was righteous, God testifying of his gifts: and by it he being dead yet speaketh."*... *"So Christ was once offered to bear the sins of many, and unto them that look for him shall he appear the second time without sin unto salvation."* Hebrews 11: 4; 9: 28; Genesis 4:3-11

The offerings and the animals for sacrifice: The animals named in Genesis 15:9; were selected as to the kind of offense or sin. Note something about these animals.

<u>*The HEIFER:*</u> A female cow; but not considered a cow until she begin calving. The heifer replaces older cows because they are young, and for the continuation of providing milk. Once the heifer calves, she is no longer a heifer; but now becomes a cow. Usually a heifer doesn't begin to produce calf until she is 2-3 years old. In the Bible, heifers were used in Burnt offerings, Sin offerings and Guilt offerings. When a bullock was sacrificed, the entire sacrifice was presented to God. This constituted an appeal to God to accept it as given wholly or fully unto him. This signified Christ, who gave himself fully for the sins of man. *"And this is the thing that thou shalt do unto them to hallow them, to minister unto me in the priest's office: Take one young bullock, and two rams without, "And thou shalt take of the blood of the bullock, and put it upon the horns of the altar with thy finger, and pour all the blood beside the bottom of the altar. And thou shalt take all the fat that covereth the inwards, and the caul that is above the liver, and the two kidneys, and the fat that is upon them, and burn them upon the altar. But the flesh of the bullock, and his skin, and his dung, shalt thou burn with fire without the camp: it is a SIN offering."* Exodus 29:14; Leviticus 4:11; 8:17; 16:27; Num.19:5. The bull with all its parts was burned as a sacrifice for sin.

<u>*The She GOAT:*</u> The Hebrew word for she-goat is the same used for the male goat; it means, "strength" As an offering of sacrifice, one goat would be slain and another set free, as the scapegoat. *"And he shall take the two goats, and present them before the Lord at the door of the tabernacle of the congregation. And Aaron shall cast lots upon the two*

goats; one lot for the Lord, and the other lot for the scapegoat. And Aaron shall bring the goat upon which the Lord's lot fell, and offer him for a sin offering. But the goat, on which the lot fell to be the scapegoat, shall be presented alive before the Lord, to make atonement with him, and to let him go for a scapegoat into the wilderness." Read: Leviticus 16:5-10; Isaiah 53:4; Mathew 8:16-17; 1Peter 2:24. The slain goat blood was shed to atone for sin; the scapegoat carried away the sin of the people. This was symbolized with the priest laying his hand on the head of the scapegoat, and then the scapegoat was sent into the wilderness. Christ was the blood sacrifice for redemption; but the transfer of sin upon the scapegoat represented Christ carrying away sin. Isaiah said, "Surely he hath borne our griefs, and carried our sorrows: yet we did esteem him stricken, smitten of God and afflicted." Isaiah 53:4 "When even was come, they brought unto him many that were possessed with devils: and he cast out the spirits with his word, and healed all that were sick: That it might be fulfilled which was spoken by Isaiah the prophet, saying, Himself took our infirmities, and bare our sicknesses." Mathew 8 16-17. "Who his own self bare our sins in his own body on the tree, that we, being dead to sins, should live unto righteousness: by whose stripes ye were healed." 1Peter 2:24.

The RAM: The ram is a big-horn sheep; often living at high elevations, or mountainous areas. Rams are not strong enough to produce sheep until they are three years old. The outstanding thing about a rams is, the ability to balance themselves on clefts; even at the end of a ledge of only two inches of footage. They are strong swift mountain climbers. Another distinct feature of the ram is the large curled horns. The ram's horn was used as a musical instrument, a vessel for oil and to drink from. The ram's horn was blown to signal the congregation for an assembly, or to alarm for warfare and at festivals.

Although a blood sacrifice was for remission of sins; the ram was also used for "guilt {trespass} offerings" This sacrifice would cover guilt of any sort of sin. The individual may have sinned unwittingly, thoughtlessly, or carelessly. When the sin was brought before the priest; desiring to right the matter, a ram was the guilt offering. "And *if a soul sin, and commit any of these things which are forbidden to be done, by the commandments of the Lord; though he wist {to know} it not, yet he is guilty, and shall bear his iniquity. And he shall bring a ram without blemish out of the flock, with thy estimation, for a trespass offering, unto the priest: and the priest shall make an atonement for him concerning his ignorance wherein he erred and wist it not, and it shall be forgiven him. It is a trespass offering: he hath certainly trespassed against the Lord."* Leviticus 5: 17-19. Today people use the statement, "I made a mistake' to cover a sin of not knowing the act was wrong. But it is a sin of guilt.

A TURTLEDOVE: The turtle dove is a small wild pigeon. The Hebrew name for turtledove imitates cry-sound made by the bird. "tur-r-r tur-r- In Palestine there are varieties of turtledoves found. An abundance of the birds made it easy provisional for the children of Israel to obtain for their sacrifices. Some turtledoves migrates; but the ones most common in Palestine, remained year round. The turtledove is shy and gentle; the bird relies on speedy flights as a means of escaping its enemy. Under the Mosaic Law, turtledoves were used in certain sacrifices and purification rites. *"And if he be not able to bring a lamb, then he shall bring for his trespass, which he hath committed, two turtledoves, or two young pigeons, unto the Lord; one for a sin offering, and the other for a burnt offering."* Leviticus 5:7. Turtledoves and pigeons were also used for women after childbirth. *"And when the days of her purification are fulfilled, for a son, or for a daughter, she shall bring a lamb of the first year for a burnt offering, and a young pigeon, or a turtledove, for a sin offering, unto the door of the tabernacle of the congregation unto the priest: "And if she be not able to bring a lamb, then she shall bring two turtledoves, or two young pigeons; one for the burnt offering, and the other for a sin offering: and the priest shall make an atonement for her, and she shall be clean."* Leviticus 12:6-8. After the birth of Jesus, his mother Mary offered either the turtledoves or the young pigeons at the temple. The act was, *"And to offer a sacrifice according to that which is said in the law of the Lord, A pair of turtledoves, or two young pigeons."* Matthew 2: 22-24.

<u>YOUNG PIGEONS</u>: pigeon means, "Fledgling" which is to *furnish with feathers; to rear until ready for flight or independent active; to acquire the feathers necessary for flight.* The Hebrew term, yoh-*nah*, **gohzai** {young pigeon} is used for DOVE; applying to both a young pigeon and dove as the same word. Usually only in Hebrew texts involving sacrifice, pigeons are regularly mentioned. Young pigeons or turtledoves were acceptable for sacrifice if the person was too poor to afford a female lamb or kid for guilt offerings. The priests were to bring the birds to the altar; wring off the head and burn it on the altar. The blood of the bird was wrung out at the side of the altar. *"And he shall pluck away his crop with his feathers, and cast it beside the altar, "And he shall cleave it with the wings thereof, but shall not divide it asunder: and the priest shall burn it upon the altar, "it is a burnt sacrifice, an offering made by fire, of a sweet savor unto the Lord."* The offerings sacrificed were carried out by the priests; those things foreshowed what Christ would do in his redemptive work. In fulfilling this law, Jesus sent his disciples out into the highways and hedges to compel man to come. He told them to seek the **poor,** the halt, the blind and the maimed. No human condition of any kind was left out of the promise of redemption. The pigeons were provisional for the **poor;** the poor were to receive atonement for sin by the sacrifice at the altar officiated by the priests.

Preparing the pigeons for sacrifice; the priest wrung off the head of the bird and burned it in the fire. The blood was wrung out on the side of the altar. This symbolizes the kind of sacrifice God accepts. The head is the governing part of the body; guided by judgment, concepts, logical thinking and decisions. To offer unto the Lord, the sacrifice must yield up the ideas, beliefs, traditions that we carry. We are to submit to the Lord's ways, judgments, statues and commandments. To burn a thing will change the form or image of the thing. The old man and his ways are done away with, and we become a new man in Christ. Not only the sacrifice is to change the carnal mind, but also there is a disrobing of the garment or covering we protect ourselves by. The priest plucked away the feathers of the birds. Feathers covered the body of the birds for protection; and feathers provided warmth. How useful are the feathers to lift the bird in flight to transport itself from one place to another. Birds have a remarkable sense of direction; somehow sensing the earth's magnetic field and the position of the sun. They automatically follow the movement of the sun across the sky, so that the angle of their flight does not err. God created man to be more intelligent than the birds. But it is the law in birds which reflect this distinct nature in them. If men would consider the word of God given them, they would greatly excel in the direction God has given them.

The five animals which Abraham placed on the altar signified that a Burnt offering for sin was ordained for the redemption of man. His vision foretold the Ordinances of Sacrifices which were to come. Every ordinance for a sin offering was established to cover all the sins of the children of Israel. God gave Moses the command to make the Ark of the Covenant, he said, *"And thou shalt make two cherubims of gold, of beaten work shalt thou make them, in the two ends of the mercy seat. "And the cherubims shall stretch forth their wings on high, covering the mercy seat with their wings "David* said, *"How excellent is thy lovingkindness, O God! Therefore the children of men put their trust under the shadow of thy wings."* Psalm 36: 7. The Old Testament types and shadows signify and point to Christ. Notice the words, "under the shadow of thy wings" A figure of speech, expressing being in the presence of God; and that man's covering for protection and comfort is God. The shadows were the laws and ordinances Moses set forth for the children of Israel. **References:** Romans 12; 1-3; Galatians 3:1-6; Acts 10: 44-48; Romans 4:13-17; Ephesians 4: 17-32; and 5: 1-12; Exodus 25: 18-20;

Remember, God was showing Abram the **"whereby"** to receiving the inheritance. Abram desired to know, and God gave him the answer. God's word to Abram in a vision first introduced God by his name "I am." The word assured Abram that God was his covering and exceeding great reward of faith. Next, Abram learned of the love and the gift of God. Abram gained God's approval by believing in his word: God counted it to him as righteousness.

Then Abram put the animals upon the altar; which gave him on hand experience of blood sacrifice. This illustrated to Abram that death must happen first, in order for the heir to become an inheritor. It also taught that the animals served as a substitute to take away sin. Abram believed that through his seed, all nations of the earth would be blessed. The blood of animal sacrifice served to foreshadow redemption through the blood of Christ {the promised seed}. *"For when Moses had spoken every precept to all the people according to the law, he took the blood of calves and of goats, with water, and scarlet wool, and hyssop and sprinkled both the book, and all the people, Saying, This is the blood of the testament which God hath enjoined unto you. And almost all things are by the law purged with blood: and without shedding of blood is no remission."* Hebrew 9:19-22

Wisdom was materializing the plan of God. Wisdom first instituted the pillar of faith to support God's dwelling place. Abraham's faith made him a sojourner: looking for a city who's builder and maker is God. Have faith in the word of God, because it reveals the will of God. The Faith walk seeks out the dwelling place of God. If Moses had established the laws of sacrifice before God revealed it beforehand to Abram; then Moses labor would have been only works. But this wasn't the case. Abram's life teaches what faith is. Faith is the unseen plan of God; it is the substance of things hoped for, and the evidence of things not seen. First by the Spirit, the word of God is revealed, which anchors hope until the word make manifest the will of God. God's answer to Abram revealed his plan of redemption. Abram saw in the spirit, what God would bring to pass in the future with the promised seed. But this vision extended out to all people; for God included all nations in the blessings of Abraham.

<u>Abram's Seed would be Divided:</u> *"And he took unto him all these, and divided them in the midst, and laid each piece one against another:* ***but the***

birds divided he not.*"* Genesis 15:10. The act of placing the animals on the altar, Abram divided the heifer, goat and ram into; but was not to divide the birds. Furthermore, the vision showed what would become of the children of Israel. God was revealing the future of Abram's children: they would be scattered throughout the land because of disobedience. A few hundred years after their exodus from Egypt; the dispersing of Israel happened after the reign of Solomon. God was angry with Solomon, because his heart had turned from God; he went after other gods. Wherefore God said to Solomon, *"And the Lord was angry with Solomon, because his heart was turned from the Lord God of Israel, which had appeared unto him twice. And had commanded him concerning this thing that he should not go after other gods: but he kept not that which the Lord commanded. Wherefore the Lord said unto Solomon, For as much as this is done of thee, and thou hast not kept my covenant, and my statutes, which I have commanded thee, I will surely* **rend** *the kingdom from thee, and will give it to thy servant. Notwithstanding in thy days I will not do it for David thy father's sake: but I will rend it out of the hand of thy son. Howbeit I will not rend away the entire kingdom; but will give one tribe to thy son for David my servant's sake, and for Jerusalem's sake which I have chosen."* 1Kings 11:9-13. The kingdom was made of the 12 tribes of Israel. Two tribes were left after God rend the kingdom; the tribe of Juda, for David's sake, and tribe of Levi {the priestly tribe} for Jerusalem {the place for temple worship}. The ten tribes of Israel were left and "plucked off" from the land when the Assyrians took them captive. *"Therefore the Lord was very angry with Israel, and removed them out of his sight: there was none left but the tribe of Judah only. And the Lord rejected all the seed of Israel, and afflicted them, and delivered them into the hands of the spoilers, until he had cast them out of his sight."* 2Kings 17:18. The birds that weren't divided represented the two tribes God did not rend from the kingdom: they were Judah and Levi.

Israel transgressed the laws of God; falling into wickedness and the abominations of the heathen people. Abram was instructed by God to not divide the birds. The birds represented the Jews who went into Babylonian captivity. The other tribes, which were ten tribes of Israel were scattered throughout the world. God revealed this scattering to Jacob in a dream. *"And thy seed shall be as the dust of the earth, and thou shalt spread abroad to the west, and to the east, and to the north, and to the south: and in thee and in thy seed shall all the families of the earth be blessed."* **Genesis 28:14.** Later, Moses prophesied to the children of their becoming scattered. *"And it shall come to pass, that as the Lord rejoiced over you to do you good and to multiply you; so the Lord will rejoice over you to destroy you and to bring you*

To naught; <u>and ye shall be plucked from off the land whither thou goest to possess it.</u> And the Lord **shall scatter thee** *among all the people, from one end of the earth even unto the other; and there thou shalt serve other gods, which neither thou nor thy fathers have known, even wood and stone."* Deuteronomy 28: 63-64.

The fowls in Abram's vision represented the other nations that came and devoured the children of Israel. God allowed them to be taken into the hands of the spoilers. They were warned by Moses, Isaiah and other prophets of God, their falling into the hands of their enemies. Abram saw the punishment of his seed; and the wrath of God that would come upon the children of Israel. Moses prophesied: *"And it shall come to pass, that as the Lord rejoiced over you to do you good, and to multiply you; as the Lord will rejoice over you to destroy you, and to bring you to naught; and ye shall be plucked from off the land whither thou goest to possess it. And the Lord shall scatter thee among the people, from the one end of the earth unto the other; and there thou shalt serve other gods, which neither thou nor thy fathers have known, even wood and stone. And among these nations shalt thou find no ease, neither shall the sole of thy foot have rest, but the Lord shall give thee there a trembling heart, and failing of eyes, and sorrow of mind."* Deuteronomy 28:63-65.

Isaiah prophecy: *"The Lord spake unto me again, saying, Forasmuch as this people refuseth the waters of Shiloah that go softly, and rejoice in Rezin and Remaliah's son; Now therefore, behold the Lord bringeth up upon them the waters of the river, strong and many, even the king of Assyria, and all his glory: and he shall come up over all his channels, and go over all his banks: And he shall pass through Judah; he shall overflow and go over, he* <u>*shall reach even the neck; and the stretching out of his wings shall fill the*</u> <u>*breath of thy land,*</u> *O Immanuel. Associate yourselves, O ye people, and **ye*** ***shall be broken in pieces**; and give ear, all ye shall be **broken in pieces**; gird yourselves, and **ye shall be broken in** pieces."* Isaiah 8:5-9. Notice the words <u>*broken in pieces*</u> was repeated several times. The emphasis is on the children of Israel being divided. The prophecy pointed to the imminent destruction of the ten tribes. Understanding the land areas mentioned in the prophecy aid in interpreting the message. The waters of Shiloah that go gently, represents real salvation and security in Jerusalem. There was a time when king Rezin reigned in Damascus; he captured many Jews and took them to Damascus. **(2Chron. 28:5)** King Ahaz was greatly frightened by this; although the prophet Isaiah assured him that Rezin and Pekah of Israel were not to be feared. But Ahaz turned to Assyria for help. Tighlath-pileser III was bribed by Ahaz to make the attack on Syria. Rezin was put to death and Syria was taken over by Assyrian domination. 2Kings 17:7-9 Remaliah's son is the father of Israelite King Pekah. Read: 2Kings 15:25; 2Chronicles. 28:6; Isaiah 7:4-5. The same people that helped Judah were the enemies of the children of Israel. The ten tribes were scattered and taken to Assyria, which fulfilled the prophecy of Moses. Deuteronomy 28:48-53. The children of Israel were not to seek help from the heathen kings; this was a dishonor to God. Only by the power of God would they find deliverance. Abram saw **"the fowls"** coming down upon the carcasses; but he drove them away. Isaiah expressed this as, *"the stretching out of his wings shall fill the breath of thy land,"* A figure of speech to say that the Assyrians will attack and take over "thy" land of promise. To go over "all his banks" is the picture of the enemy attack causing trouble; not peace and security. Shiloah, the water canal that channeled softly would be disturbed. O **Immanuel**, the name means, "with us is God" this phrase gave the children of Israel a word of comfort and hope. The scripture said concerning Abram that he *drove them* (fowls) *away.* Abram driving away the fowls, was a sign of God' comforting Israel.

Assyria was used as an instrument of punishment by the hand of God; but later God drove Assyria away. *"O Assyrian, the rod of mine anger, and the staff in their hand is mine indignation. And I will send him against a hypocritical nation, and against the people of my wrath will I give him a charge, to take the spoil, and to take the prey, and to tread down like the mire in the streets."* Isaiah 10:5. God drove the fowls, the enemies of his people Israel away. *"Wherefore it shall come to pass, that when the Lord hath performed his whole work upon mount Zion and on Jerusalem, I will punish the fruit of the stout heart of the king of Assyria, and the glory of his high looks."* Isaiah 10:12.

Notice the metaphor, *"the fruit of the stout heart of the king of Assyria"* The question might be asked, what was the fruit of the king of Assyria stout heart? Isaiah said, *"But it is in his heart to destroy and cut off nations not a few. For he saith, are not my princes altogether kings? Is not Calno as Carchemish? Is not Hamath as Arpal? Is not Samaria as Damascus? As my hand hath found the kingdoms of idols, and whose graven images did excel them of Jerusalem and of Samaria; Shall I not as I have done unto Samaria and her idols, so do I to Jerusalem and her idols? For he saith, By my strength of my hand I have done it, and by my wisdom; for I am prudent : and I have removed the bounds of the people, and have robbed their treasures, and I have put down the inhabitants like a valiant man. And my hand hath found as a nest the riches of the people: and as one gathereth all the earth; and there was none that moved, or peeped."* Isaiah 10: 12-14. The king of Assyria boasted in his heart to destroy Israel. But God said through Isaiah, *"Shall the axe boast itself against him that heweth therewith? Or shall the saw magnify itself against him that shaketh it? As if the rod should shake itself against them that lift it up, or as if the staff should lift up itself, as if it were no wood."* For Samaria, the Israelites were led into exile; but God told Israel to "be not of afraid of the Assyrian: God said, *"For a little while, and the indignation shall cease, and mine anger in their (Israel) destruction."* Their exile was the scattering of the seed of the Israel. Also the prophet Hosea's marriage to Gomer was illustrated the sign of Samaria becoming the lost tribes. Hosea 1:4; **5:8-9;** Hosea 7:11; Ezekiel 23:4-10.

God showed Abram Israel's vexations for disobedience to his commandments. Abram did not divide the birds; this foretold of the remnant tribes. Ten tribes went into exile and the other two tribes, {the birds} Judah and Levi were the remnant of Israel. The Jews were there in Jerusalem when Jesus came to do the will of God. Jesus said *"But he answered and said, **I am not sent but unto the lost sheep of the house of Israel.**"* Matthew 15:24.

After these things were revealed to Abram; *"when the sun was going down, a deep sleep fell upon Abram; and, lo, a horror of great darkness fell on him."* Genesis 15:12. The 'deep sleep' was a period of rest. There will be many years of rest before Abram will inherit the promise. From the time the children of Israel were scattered in the year of 722 B.C. until today, the ingathering has not come to fulfillment. Moses prophesied, and said, *"And it shall come to pass, when all these things are come upon thee, the blessing and the curse, which I have set before thee, and thou shalt call them to mind among all the nations, whither the Lord thy God hath driven thee, And thy shalt return unto the Lord thy God, and shalt obey his voice according to all that I command thee this day, thou and thy children, with all thine heart, and with all thy soul; that then the Lord thy God will turn thy captivity, and have compassion upon thee, and will return and gather thee from all the nations, whither the Lord thy God hath scattered thee."* Deuteronomy 30:1-3.

"And when the sun was going down," After the sunset, then come darkness. Sunset is the time when men retire from their day of labor: it preludes the beginning of a new day. Note the time element, from sunset till sunrise. This prophetic language revealed to Abram the time of Israel's fall until Christ. God instilled hope in Abram in the manner of saying, *"though the vision tarry, wait for it."* The longsuffering and patience of God is the period of time Israel is lost, until God graft them back in the olive tree. The Gentiles have nothing to boast in, because they are the wild olive branch grafted in as partakers of the root and the fatness of the olive tree. → {Read; Romans 11:13 -22} Abram was given the answer to **"whereby"** shall he know that he will inherit it? Abram's faith in the promises of God added to him <u>patience</u> and <u>hope</u>. Men should realize the power of faith in God's word. The word of God in the vision that Abram saw also revealed something about the attributes of God. God is patience, He is love, He is all knowing, He is just, He is faithful, and He is righteous. These are the virtues Abram acquired through faith in the word of God.

The apostle Paul wrote concerning Israel. *"I say then, hath God cast away his people? God forbid.* Paul said, *"For I also am an Israelite of the seed of Abraham, of the tribe of Benjamin. "According as it is written, God hath given them the spirit of slumber, eyes that they should not see, and ears that they should not see, and ears that they should not hear; unto this day."* **Romans 11:1, and v. 8;** This scripture speaks of the "deep sleep" that fell on Abram. In a natural deep sleep; a person doesn't see nor hear at the time of sleep. Abram's deep sleep foretold of years into the future. During his life on earth those things in his vision had not been fulfilled. God forbid that Israel should stumble; but by their fall salvation came unto the Gentiles. Jesus *said* to the chief priests and the elders in the temple, *"The stone which the builders rejected, the same is become the head of the corner: this is the Lord's doing, and it is marvelous in our eyes."* **Matthew 32:42** The Jews of Christ day were blind: they rejected the Lord from heaven. The deep sleep is the long period of slumber which happened to Israel.

Not only did Abram fall into a deep sleep, but also *"**a horror of darkness fell on him."*** Why would darkness be terrifying when a man is in a deep sleep? In the period of rest, which was the time Israel would be scattered; there will be a period of darkness upon the people. Darkness connotes being without light, knowledge, guidance, direction, and understanding. Darkness brings terror, fear, doubt, uncertainty, confusion, vexation, and anxiety. Abram was seeing beforetime the spiritual condition of people through the centuries until Christ. Today many are speaking of the second coming of the Lord because they are seeing the spiritual condition of the world.

God revealed to Abram the darkness that would come upon the children of Israel.

People experience spiritual darkness, because the light or knowledge of Christ is not revealed. Israel became sinful and wicked; they disregarded the commandments and ways of the Lord. The light of God is his word; which will guide and lead men in all truth. Solomon said, *"The light of the righteous rejoiceth: but the lamp of the wicked shall be put out."* **Proverbs 13:9** It is written, *"Yea, the light of the wicked shall be put out, and the spark of his fire shall not shine. The light shall be dark in his tabernacle, and his candle shall not shine."* **Job 18:5-6.** Jesus said, *"I am the Light of the world. He that followeth me shall not walk in darkness, but shall have the light of life."* **John 8:12**

Today, gross darkness is upon the land because of wickedness, transgressions and the disobedience of men. God will again gather in Israel and favor her again. Paul said, *"For I would not, brethren, that ye should be ignorant of this mystery, lest ye should be wise in your own conceits that blindness in part is happened to Israel, until the fullness of the Gentile be come in. And so all Israel shall be saved: as it is written, there shall come out of Zion the Deliverer, and shall turn away ungodliness from Jacob."* **Romans 11:25-26**

Abram' seed would suffer servitude: While in his lethargic state of sleep, God said to Abram, *"Know of a surety that thy seed shall be a stranger in a land that is not theirs, and shall serve them; and they shall afflict (Israel) four hundred years: "*Genesis **15:13**. The word <u>**surety**</u> sounds out a great variety of knowing. The word of God gave Abram certainty that the things spoken will come to pass. Surety expresses positivity and truth. God cannot lie, for his word is truth: therefore reliable. Abram received confidence through the word God spoke. The full impact of knowing the future of his seed is expressed in this word, "surety." Abram ascertained his knowing by seeing, observation, caring, recognition, instruction, acknowledging, being advised, being aware, comprehending, considering, declaring, being diligent, discerning, discovering, being familiar with kinsfolk, kinsman, feeling, taking in knowledge, regarding, having respect, skillful, showing, and understanding. "Surety" answered any question Abram could have asked concerning his seed being a stranger and in servitude for four hundred years. God spoke one word that gave the answer to all Abram's concerns. Abram did not live to see the bondage of the children of Israel, but he believed God. He knew that if God spoke it, then it will come to pass; he had that surety.

We are blessed to inherit the promises of God; but much too often we find ourselves wondering how those things will come about. Sometimes we confess faith; but go in our own efforts trying to make things come to pass. But when we allow **'surety'** to be the answer God speaks to us; this hope is an anchor for the soul. God's promises are sure and stedfast: He is faithful to His word. Then there are some who profess faith under the glory of another man's labor. God is not deceived by these impieties. The heart issues forth that which is in it; whether good or evil. The word must be kept; like a garden that is kept. All unclean things are not to fester and grow in the heart. Consider Moses and the priesthood; God required all gifts and offering to be clean and holy. Therefore allow God's word "surety" to have its perfect work in the heart: it will surely bring to pass his promises.

Abram was a man with great faith in the word of God. His growing in the knowledge of God was because he obeyed God. This should be the life of the word abiding in us; the word will produce fruit. Jesus said, *"For a good tree bringeth not forth corrupt fruit; neither doth a corrupt tree bring forth good fruit. For every tree is known by its own fruit. For of thorns men do not gather figs, nor of a bramble bush gather them grapes. A good man out of the good treasure of his heart bringeth forth that which is good: and an evil man out of the evil treasure of his heart bringeth forth that which is evil: for of the abundance of the heart his mouth speaketh."* **Luke 6:43-45.** The good pleasure of the Father is that men abide in his word that it may bringforth his fruit. The Jews in Jesus day laid claim on Abraham and his teaching, but didn't know Abraham's promised seed was Christ. If faith had been in their hearts, they would have "of a surety" known Christ. *"Jesus answered them, Verily, verily, I say unto you, whosoever committeth sin is the servant of sin.* "I speak that which I have seen with my Father: and ye do that which ye have seen with your father. They answered and said unto him, Abraham is our father. Jesus saith unto them, If ye were Abraham's children, ye would do the **works** of Abraham. But ye seek to kill me, a man that hath told you the truth, which I have heard of God: this did not Abraham."* Jesus said to them, *"Ye do the deeds of your father.* Then said they to him, we be not born of fornication; we have one Father, even God. "Jesus said unto them, If *God were your Father, ye would love me: for I proceeded forth and came from God; neither came I of myself, but he sent me."* **John 8:34-42**

Abraham's faith should teach us what faith is. And learning what faith is, we should be able to comprehend the exceeding great reward of faith. Everyone may desire to receive the reward, but there is a journey to experience which will bring us to the inheritance promised. This journey is laid out by God: the "way" is Christ. We must learn of him; follow his light, partake of his bread and drink of his cup. He is the Way, the Truth and the Life. If we seek to enter into the kingdom, faith is access to his grace.

Abram knew the outcome of his seed: Farmers may follow the almanac, the seasons and weather forecasts to predict the yield they will have from their crops. With Abram, God spoke to him of the bondage that his seed would experience. The word of God gives insight into the events of the future. The word has already determined the end and the course by which those things are accomplished. God's word assured Abram that his seed would be delivered with great substance. Therefore Abram had no cause to feel grieved about the future of his children. It is a wonderful thing to know that your children are set free from sin and that they will come forth with the blessings of God. For these blessings were promised to Abraham and to all who are of faith. They are blessed with faithful Abraham. He was chosen to inscribe and fashion upon the ages of men what faith is. For God is the author and the finisher of our faith in him. By faith and through faith we shall inherit the promises.

The plan of God unfolding in the life of Abraham is not without his measure of Grace. Even in this vision of Abram, God would give unto the children of Israel "Little Space Grace" This vision came to pass four hundred years after Abraham. God ordained salvation long before man began to know his word. The scriptures tell us that before the foundations of the world, God predestinated man unto the adoption of children by Jesus Christ. Seeing into the future, Abram viewed the bondage and the servitude his seed would endure. The fulfilling of the vision revealed God's word tended to his plan and purpose for man. After the death of Joseph, the children of Israel fell in straits, because they knew not the God of Abraham at that time. The deliverance out of bondage of Egypt turned Israel's attention to the one God and creator of all things. They had spent four hundred years among the Egyptians. The Egyptians were heathen people with many gods. The Egyptians gods had no power, no compassion and no blessings to bestow upon the children of Israel. God heard their cry and his "little space grace" brought deliverance to the children of Israel.

The House of God: the PRISON place: In all things pertaining to the work of God; it was Wisdom with God, establishing his place to dwell in. We know that, in *the beginning was the Word (wisdom), and the Word was with God and the Word was God. The same was in the beginning with God. All things were made by him; and without him was not anything made that was made."* **John 1:1-3**

The insight God gave about the future servitude of the children of Israel show wisdom activity. *"Wisdom hath builded her house,"* **Proverbs 9:1.** Wisdom started this process of building "her house," to dwell in; by men becoming hearers and doers of the word. The plan of God fashioned and structured faith in the life of Abraham. All the men of God after Abraham were chosen to serve his purpose.

By the determinant counsel of God's will, the children of Abraham would be strangers in the land of Egypt. The children of Israel resided in the land of Goshen. The exact location of Goshen is uncertain. The fact that Joseph met his father Jacob, who was traveling from Canaan, may indicate that Goshen was east of Egypt. The time of the Pharaohs, Goshen was the place the king's flocks were kept. It was a land fertile for Israel to pasture their flocks. After a period of time, another Pharaoh who knew not Joseph brought on ill favor towards Israel. The initial captive of the children of Israel was Joseph. The prison place of Abraham seed became an actual experience at the time the son of Jacob was sold into Egypt. Joseph was the great grandson of Abraham; who was despised of his brothers. His brothers sold him to the Ishmeelites for twenty pieces of silver: and they brought Joseph into Egypt. Eventually, after seventeen years, Joseph was reunited with his father and brothers. The children of Israel multiplied greatly. Later a decree went out to the Hebrew midwives by the king saying, *"When ye do the office of a midwife to the Hebrew women, and see them upon the stools; if it be a son, then ye shall kill him: but if it be a daughter, then she shall live. But the midwives feared God, and did not as the king of Egypt commanded them, but saved the men children alive."* **Exodus 1:15-16.** After suffering for four hundred years, God sent Moses to be a Deliverer to the children of Israel. The number of children of Israel had greatly increased in that period of time. At first after Joseph imprisonment in Egypt only seventy souls entered. Here the word fulfilled which was spoken by God to Abram. The activity of God's word fulfilling his plan and purpose.

The question might be asked, why a need to go into Egypt? The answer Abram was given was, *"for the iniquity of the Amorites is not yet full."* **Genesis 15:16.** The Amorites were of the seven nations ruling in the land of Canaan. Canaan was the land that was promised to the children of Israel. The Amorites were governed by many independent rulers or kings. They were a powerful people and they had strong cities. The morality of the Amorites was that they were profane, wicked and idolatrous. The situation which developed over a period of years, allowed time for the seed of Abram to first become great in number. After becoming a great nation, God used the children of Israel to drive the Amorites out of the land of Canaan. By the time King Solomon ruled Israel, the Amorites were brought into bondage. During Solomon's reign, it is written, *"And all the people that were left of the Amorites, Hittites, Perizzites, Hivites, and Jebusites, which were not of the children of Israel. Their children that were left after them in the land, whom the children of Israel also were not able to utterly destroy unto those did Solomon levy a tribute of bondservice unto this day."* **1 Kings 9:20-21.** With God, his plan and purpose worked through time, place and the circumstances of Israel's life. The right time was after four hundred years of bondage. The right place was the land of Canaan. The right circumstance was after the children of Israel wilderness experience, and the entering into the land of Canaan. God prepared Israel with his commandments, laws, statues, ordinances and judgment; equipping them for victory.

The prison place was for the purpose of preparing the children of Israel through suffering physically, emotionally and the spiritual bondage. They were acquainted with hardship, being destitute, abused, and without hope. The suffering in Egypt, Israel had little substance, food, clothing and shelter: basic needs for any people. The suffering of grievous hard forced labor stripped Israel of rest, comfort and strength. And having no voice to be heard gave Israel no power nor hopes to find deliverance. Before the children of Israel suffered, Abram could comprehend the severity of suffering. He suffered the famine of Canaan; the bondage of Sarai and the power of God that delivered him out of his straits. A prisoner has no liberal rights; being without liberty to go in and out by choice. The prisoner is usually malnourished, and must submit to the laws of the governors. The children of Israel were as prisoners; but they had not offended in the law of the land. As servants of Pharaoh, Israel was made to submit to that government. Pharaoh feared the Hebrews would become a multitude of people and turn against him in the time of a war. He saw them as a threat to his power and control. Therefore, he put taskmasters over Israel to afflict them. Their servitude was an extreme degree of imprisonment or bondage. Israel suffered hard labor; being punished without mercy, stripped of human dignity, and in bonds to heavy burdens. It is written, when Israel cried, *"And their cry came unto God by reason of the bondage. And God heard their groaning, and God remembered his covenant with Abraham, with Isaac and with Jacob, and God looked upon the children of Israel, and God had respect unto them."* **Exodus 2:24-25.** God considered their cry, and his deliverance for them came as a measure of "little space grace."

A SMOKING FURNACE and a BURNING LAMP: Abram made an altar and placed the heifer, she goat, the ram, the turtledove and a young pigeon upon it. God revealed to him concerning his seed being in servitude in a strange land. *"And it came to pass, that when the sun when down, and it was dark, behold a smoking furnace, and a burning lamp that passed between those pieces."* **Genesis 15:17.** In the law, the ministry of the priest offerings were made by fire. Fire represents the judgment of God. A living sacrifice is presented in total submission to the will of God. A sure sign of a fire is smoke. By the term 'smoking furnace' make it to be understood that the offering was by fire. The judgment of God will purify and refine the soul of men; when they allow the flesh to die. This kind of sacrifice is the living sacrifice, holy and acceptable unto God, which God is pleased with.

Malachi prophesied, that Jesus will come and, *"he shall sit as a refiner and purifier of silver: and he shall purify the sons of Levi, and purge them as gold and silver, that they may offer unto the Lord an offering in righteousness."* **Malachi 3:3.** This verse refer to the ministry of Christ. He is the Great High Priest, called of God a high priest after the order of Melchisedec. He sits on the right hand of the throne of Majesty in the heavens. Paul said, *"A minister of the sanctuary and the true tabernacle, which the Lord pitched, and not man. For every high priest is* *ordained to offer gifts and sacrifices: wherefore it is necessary that this man have somewhat also to offer."* **Hebrews 8:2.** Fire is the means by which gold and silver is purified. God's judgment is more than to pronounce a sentence; it is his divine law, his determination, discretion and ordinances. The things of the OT, especially concerning the priestly work, truly foreshadowed the work of Christ. It is his word abiding in us, and his word that wash and cleanse us from all unrighteousness and sin.

When Isaiah spoke of the future of Jerusalem in his day, he said, *"When the Lord shall have washed away the filth of the daughter of Zion, and shall have purged the blood of Jerusalem from the midst thereof by the <u>spirit of judgment</u>, and by the <u>spirit of burning</u>. And the Lord will create upon every dwelling place of mount Zion, and upon her assemblies, a cloud and a smoke by day, and the shinning of a flaming fire by night: for upon all the glory shall be a defense. And there shall be a tabernacle for a shadow in the daytime from the heat, and for a place of refuge, and for a covert from storm and from rain."* **Isaiah 4:4-6**

The wisdom of God was establishing his plan in the words of the prophets and in the laws that were practiced by the Levitical priesthood. His Word is line upon line and precept upon percept: like as a house being built by a master builder. Every dimension and framing of the house must line up; being fitly joined together by the wisdom of God. The Builder and Maker of his people Zion (the city of God), is Christ. He is the chief corner stone that became the head of the corner. He is the head of the church, the body of Christ. By Christ, the prophets and the law are fulfilled. Jesus said, *"Think not that I am come to destroy the law, or the prophets: I am not come to destroy, but to fulfill."* **Matthew 5:17.** Moses, in the law said, *"And the priest shall burn all on the altar, to be a burnt sacrifice, an offering made by fire, of a sweet savor unto the Lord."* **Leviticus 1:9.** Abram's offering was a sweet savor unto the Lord. It signified Christ being the ultimate sacrifice for sin; and acceptable unto God. *"And walk in love, as Christ also hath* *loved us, and hath given himself for us an offering and a sacrifice to God for a sweet smelling savor."* **Ephesians 5:2**

The furnace was designed for smelting, melting or used for baking bread. God said to Abram, *"Know of a* **surety** *that thy seed shall be a stranger in a land that is not theirs, and shall serve them and afflict (Israel) four hundred years."* *Egypt* was compared to as an iron furnace; implementing harsh treatment on the children of Israel. Moses said unto the people, *"But the Lord hath taken you, and brought you forth out of the iron furnace, even out of Egypt, to be unto him a people of inheritance, as ye are this day."* **Deuteronomy 4:20.** "For the Lord's portion is his people; Jacob is the lot of his inheritance." **Deuteronomy 32:9** *"For the Lord hath chosen Jacob unto himself and Israel for his peculiar treasure."* **Psalm 135:4.** *"But thou, Israel, art my servant; Jacob whom I have chosen, the seed of Abraham my friend."* **Isaiah 41:8**

THE COVENANT GOD MADE: The time God first spoke to Abram, he spoke promises. The word covenant first was spoken after Abram's vision from the Lord. *"In the same day the Lord made a covenant with Abram, saying, Unto thy seed have I given this land, from the river of Egypt unto the great river, the river Euphrates."* **Genesis 15:18** The Hebrew word for covenant is **beriyth:** — defined (in the sense of *cutting*); a compact (because made by passing between pieces of flesh): confederacy, league.

Along with the covenant, then come activity; the 'cutting' and the 'passing between.' This is what happened after Abram made the altar. God, himself provided the smoking furnace and the burning lamp. It is his judgment and his light that must pass between the pieces. Abram had divided the heifer, the she goat and the ram into; as the sacrifice. The flesh thereof, lay upon the altar; then the smoking furnace and the burning lamp passed between those pieces. The burning lamp foreshadowed Christ in the midst of the offering. He is the light of the world, the Son of God in the midst of the seven candlesticks. Reading from the Book of Revelations, in John's vision the candlesticks are the seven churches. Jesus revealed these things to John, and said, *"The mystery of the seven stars which thou sawest in my right hand, and the seven golden candlesticks. The seven stars are the angels of the seven churches: and the seven candlesticks which thou sawest are the seven churches."* **Revelation 1: 20**

There was a great period of time from the life of Abraham and the time of John the Revelator; but the light of the lamp that shines always is Christ. In the wilderness, the priests were to let the lamp burn always in the tabernacle. God said to Moses, *And thou shalt command the children of Israel, that they bring thee pure oil olive beaten for the light, to cause the lamp to burn always,* "it shall be a statue forever unto their generations on the behalf of the children of Israel." **Exodus 27:20-21**

THE CUTTING: With every act of sacrifice, the animal flesh was divided, the blood drained and the inwards also washed and burned by fire. *"And he brought the ram for the burnt offering: and Aaron and his sons laid their hands upon the head of the ram. And he killed it; and Moses sprinkled the blood upon the altar round about. And he* **cut the ram into pieces***; and Moses burnt the head, and the pieces, and the fat. And* <u>he washed the **inwards**</u> *and the legs in water; and Moses burnt the* <u>whole ram</u> *upon the altar; it was a burnt sacrifice for a sweet savor,* <u>and an offering made by fire</u> *unto the Lord; as the Lord commanded Moses."* **Leviticus 8:18-21.** Cutting is to divide; to divide is to separate; and to separate sanctify the sacrifice. It is written, "sanctify yourselves and be ye holy for God is Holy." We are cleansed by the word; his word is also his judgment. The Spirit of God is a consuming fire. His Spirit cleanses and sanctifies those who present themselves unto him as a living sacrifice. True sanctification is in this process of sacrificing. God accepts the sacrifice that his judgment and light is upon. As to the cutting of the sacrifice, the instrument for cutting is the sword. The scripture speaks of the Word of God as a sword; *"For the word of God is quick, and powerful, and sharper than any two-edged sword, piercing even to the dividing asunder of soul and spirit, and of the* *joints and marrow, and is a discerner of the thoughts and intents of the heart."* **Hebrews 4:12**

A BURNING LAMP PASSED BETWEEN: Abram obeyed God by cutting of the sacrifice; but the passing between the pieces was by the Spirit of God. The smoking furnace and the burning lamp passed between the pieces. When the word passing is used in a statement, it is an activity in process. But passed, termed the activity as already happened. Therefore, "passed between" meant that God established and preordained man's salvation before he created man. God is the Eternal, having no beginning of days or end of life; he is not limited to time. With him, all things are; and when he speaks to man, he speaks in the term of already is. Men may hope for the things of tomorrow, but God is Tomorrow. In this scripture, *"and a burning lamp that **passed** between those pieces,"* God has already determined man's deliverance through Christ. There is no remission of sin without the shedding of blood; a death or a passing comes first.

The Hebrew word for **passed** is abar, —defined; to cross over; used very widely of any transition (lit. or fig.). To cover, *bring over,* bring through, carry over, overcome, come over, convey over, current, *deliver,* do away, enter, escape, gender, *cause to proclaim,* perish, provoke to anger, put away, remove, set apart, *cause to make sweet smelling,* take away, *translate.* The italicized words are to draw attention to the ministry of Jesus Christ redemptive act. By the shedding of his blood; he died that we might be translated unto the adoption of sons. In other words God was giving Abram the answer to his question, "Whereby" shall I know that I shall inherit it?"

God made a covenant with Abram: and the vision illustrated deliverance from bondage as symbolized in the words *passed between.* Crossing over is a transition period; understood when people die. Mankind is appointed unto death; but after that the judgment of God. The spiritual change in man is a crossing over as well. The apostle Paul wrote, *"Know ye not, that so many of us as were baptized into Jesus Christ were baptized into his death? Therefore we are buried with him by baptism into death: that like as Christ was raised up from the dead by the glory of the Father, even so we also should walk in newness of life."* **Romans 6:3-4**

The word of God to Abram was proclaiming the gospel of Jesus Christ. *"The Spirit of the Lord is upon me, because he hath anointed me to preach the gospel to the poor; he hath sent me to heal the brokenhearted, to preach deliverance to the captives, and the recovering of sight to the blind, to set at liberty them that are bruised: "To preach the acceptable year of the Lord."* **Luke 4:18.** The bondage of the children of Israel illustrated the condition sin brought upon man. But every condition of bondage men are in, Jesus proclaimed the good news. The Jewish leaders of Jesus day should have realized this deliverance in the words of Jesus, *"To preach the acceptable year of the Lord."* The Pharisees and the scribes knew concerning the Passover, the feast of weeks and the feast of tabernacle. Every year, the seventh month on the Jewish calendar, the priests made atonement for the sins of himself and the people. Only once a year the high priest was allowed to enter the Most Holy place behind the veil. *"And this shall be a statute forever unto you: that in the seventh month, on the tenth day of the month, ye shall afflict your souls, and do not work at all, whether it be one of your own country, or a stranger that sojourneth among you. On that day shall the priest make atonement for you, to cleanse you, that ye may be clean from all your sins before the Lord.'* **Leviticus 16:29-30.** Jesus fulfilled this law because he entered in once to take away sin. When God commanded Moses in the building of the tabernacle, he said, *"And thou shalt hang up the veil under the tacks, that thou mayest bring thither within the veil the ark of the testimony: and **the veil shall divide unto you between the holy place and the most holy."*** **Exodus 26:33.** To the world, the sign of Jesus entering in to the most holy place, was when the veil was rent in the midst, *"And when Jesus had cried with a loud voice, he said, Father, into thy hands I commend my spirit: and having said thus, he gave up the ghost."* **Luke 23:45-46** Jesus is the High Priest, who did not enter into the holy places made with human hands. For we know that the tabernacle was made by Moses; which was the figure of the true dwelling place of God. But Christ entered into the presence of God, which is the Most Holy place. Therefore Christ once entered in the presence of God to bear the sins of many. He is the Lamb of God which taketh away the sins of the world. Christ as a lamb without any blemishes and without spot; foreordained before the foundation of the world. God gave him glory that our faith and hope might be in God through purifying our souls in obeying the truth.

A Biblical type of the CROSS OVER was when the death angel passed over the houses in Egypt. Moses said to the elders of Israel, *"Draw out and take you a lamb according to your families, and kill the Passover. And ye shall take a bunch of hyssop and dip it in blood that is in the basin, and strike the lintel and the two side posts with blood that is in the basin: and none of you shall go out at the door of his house until the morning. For the Lord will pass through to smite the Egyptians; and when he seeth the blood upon the lintel, and on the two side posts, the Lord will pass over the door, and will not suffer the destroyer to come in your houses to smite you."* **Exodus 12:21-23**

Note the command was by the shedding of blood. The night God delivered Israel out of Egypt; they were not to go outside the door of their houses. Those that remained in the house were saved because of the blood was spread upon the lintel and side posts. God's light and judgment passed between the pieces: a picture of Israel's deliverance out of Egypt. The shedding of blood that was spread upon the door of their houses symbolized Christ blood upon his dwelling place. As the children of Abram, we are saved by the blood of Christ. To reemphasize this point; the Hebrew word which defines shield, means DOOR. And faith is the shield that protects us against the fiery darts of the devil. Jesus said, *"I am the **door**: by me if any man enters in, he shall be saved, and shall go in and out and find pasture."* **John 10:9.** The door gives access to the grace of God: and this is by faith. What is given is 'little space grace' a measure of God's grace. To "find pasture" provides growing in grace and the knowledge of God. We pray, "Give us day by day our daily bread" because life is in the word of God. Bread is the substance of life: therefore man shall not live by bread alone, but by every word which proceedth out of the mouth of God.

Returning back to Abram's vision, he was shown these things. God revealed the covenant promise and a glimpse into the process by which it would happen. God foreordained this mystery which was once hidden. The mystery revealed so that men may know God is the author and finisher of their faith. No man can take this glory, because the wisdom of God established and accomplished this. Furthermore, the vision of the smoking furnace and the burning lamp passed between the pieces has come. The cutting (sacrifice) that Abram presented in the covenant God made with him is fulfilled. The cutting, is a dividing, and a separation; therefore to set apart or to sanctify. A covenant is an agreement made between two or more parties. Abram's part of the covenant was to offer a clean sacrifice unto God. God would in return accept the sacrifice according to his smoking furnace (judgment) and a burning lamp (truth). The New Testament revealed and fulfilled this vision of an acceptable sacrifice. The voice which spoke from heaven, said *"Thou art my Beloved Son, in whom I am well pleased."* **Mark 1:11.** God accepted the sacrifice who is Jesus the lamb slain for the sins of the world.

What a profound word of promise given to Abram; and his faith was just as profound. The will of God revealed to Abram made his faith sure, stedfast and comforting. Knowledge was a virtue of faith Abram obtained by the hearing of the Word. Abraham's knowledge of the will of God expelled darkness, brought clarity to confusion, gave direction, exercised judgment, answered all things and gave hope to all things. "Know of a surety" were the words of faith and hope Abraham heard from God.

21

WISDOM OBTAINED CHILDREN

WISDOM hath built her House: FAMILY! One of the synonyms for the Hebrew word which defines 'built' is FAMILY. As we continue to learn about the sojourner of faith, we will see the virtues that were added to his faith. But first let us learn how wisdom established Abraham's faith through family. In other words, wisdom obtains children. At the time God's covenant was made, Abram was childless. He was about eighty-five years old, and his wife Sarai, was past the years of childbearing. The word of promise created hope in Abram's heart as to a child from his own bowels. But in his time there was a practice that granted a married man to beget children from a handmaiden. The story of Sarai's handmaid, Hagar is well known with Biblical teachers. The man of faith did sire a son by Hagar; and the nation of people came from that seed. But keeping in line with the activity of God's plan for redeeming man; the wrestle between the seed of the free woman versus the seed of the bond woman began. Abram lived in the second millennial day from creation, but the oppositional forces of two natures were already known. The seed of the woman mentioned in the OT, was in opposition with the seed of the serpent. They are at war; the hostile nature of flesh against the spirit. Enmity always bringforth conflict, warfare and death; this is of the carnal flesh nature of men. But the Spirit of God brings forth life and good.

The dual nature of man since Adam is seen in many accounts in the scriptures. God made a distinction of the two seeds when he made judgment against the transgression of Adam. *"And the Lord said unto the serpent, Because thou hast done this, thou art cursed above all cattle, and above every beast of the field: upon thy belly shalt thou go, and dust shalt thou eat all the days of thy life: And I will put enmity between thee and the woman, and between thy seed and her seed: it shall bruise thy head, and thou shalt bruise his heel."* **Genesis 2:14-15.** God put a divide between Satan and Christ. Enmity is hatred, or hostility. It is opposition between another person and kind. Hostility is the birthplace of war: it is an antagonist, unfriendly spirit; non-hospitable, and is resistance of thought or in principle. Hostility is the very nature of an enemy.

When the serpent beguiled Eve, he was cursed and lowered to the position of crawling on his belly. The symbolism depicts Satan in the flesh nature of man; he is a spirit that can dwell in flesh. The bitter curse was to denounce violently and to declare the serpent evil. He was damned and anathematized or execrated. The ultimate curse is to be without hope; having no place for mercy or grace to be given. Completely annihilated and cut off from any and everything that may spare the life. God's sentence will destroy Satan works; therefore rendering him ineffective and producing nothing. Jesus said, *"I beheld Satan as lighting fall from heaven. Behold, I give you power to tread on serpents and scorpions, and over all the power of the enemy: and nothing shall by any means hurt you. "Luke* **10:18.** The apostle Paul wrote to the saints in Rome, and said, *And the God of peace shall bruise Satan under your feet shortly. The grace of our Lord Jesus Christ is with you. Amen."* **Romans 16:20**

<u>The Serpent's HEAD:</u> The control center for all actions of the body is governed by the head. The head is at the height of the body; the top part. God said to the serpent that the seed of the woman, which is Christ, would bruise his head. A bruise is an injury the body undergoes from pressure or pounding. The body that is bruised will give indication as to the position of the body.

The deadly force of the serpent is in his mouth; the fangs excrete venom when the serpent strikes its prey. Satan's voice carries the law of sin and death. Anyone who adheres to his voice is deceived. He is the father of a lie; a thief, murderer and a destroyer. His charm or cunning attack is by bruising the "heel:" a manner of tripping to make one fall. But the promise of God covers and protects men from the power of Satan through Jesus Christ. David expressed God's protection through Christ, by saying, *"For he shall give his angels charge over thee in all thy ways. They shall bear thee up in their hands, lest thou dash thy foot against a stone. Thou shalt tread upon the lion and adder: the young lion and the dragon shalt thou trample under feet. Because he hath set his love upon me, therefore will I deliver him:" I will set him on high, because he hath known my name."* **Psalm 91:11-14.** Notice the word <u>adder</u>, which is the serpent (Satan) that will be treaded upon by Christ. The language of scripture is prophetic; and word came to pass; *"And Jesus came and spake unto them, saying, all power is given unto me in heaven and in earth."* **Matthew 28:18.** *"As thou hast given him power over all flesh, that he should give eternal life to as many as thou hast given him."* **John 17:2**

God put enmity between the seeds; from this we should understand more about his plan of salvation. From the time of Adam, the battle of good and evil is present in every generation of mankind.

Jesus gained power over all the works of Satan. The serpent is the symbolic image of Satan, who was once called Lucifer, "daystar." The prophet Isaiah wrote, *"How art thou <u>fallen</u> from heaven, O Lucifer, son of the morning! How art thou <u>cast down to the ground</u>, which didst weaken the nations! For thou hast said in thine heart, I will ascend into heaven, I will exalt my throne above the stars of God: I will sit also upon the mount of the congregation in the sides of the north: I will ascend above the heights of the clouds; I will be like the most High."* Isaiah 14:12-14. Isaiah spoke of Satan as fallen; because he was cast down from heaven by God. Lucifer desired to be exalted above the angels of God; to preside over the congregation of God, and even to rule above the witnesses (clouds) that ascend to God. It was in the heart of Satan to sit in God's [temple] dwelling place, which is man. His subtle and cunning works are to rule men and portray himself as God. Eve failed victim to Satan deception; *"And the serpent said unto the woman,* *ye shall not surely die. For God doth know that in the day ye eat thereof, then your eyes shall be opened, and ye shall be as gods, knowing good and evil."* **Genesis 3:4-5**

It was Adam and Eve's choice to partake of the tree of knowledge of good and evil. It was God's judgment to allow men to see the contrast of what they had done. Enmity is the contrasting difference from obeying the law of Spirit. At first, Adam only knew what was good; but following the voice of the serpent through Eve, their eyes were opened. They knew that they were naked; in other words, their conscience of evil was awakened. Adam then understood God's laws were their covering: His laws are garments of righteousness. Adam and Eve were disrobed, ashamed and they hid themselves. When children were born of their union, the enmity strand of DNA of the sin nature is stamped on every person born on earth. But by His mercy, God provided for man redemption from the bondage of sin.

With Abraham, the foundation of God's plan was in the making. Earlier with Cain, God's rebuke was to direct him in the right way. God foreordained salvation for the whole world, including Cain's kind also. God didn't change his purpose to make man in him image and after his likeness. His wisdom was working the plan through visions, through his word, and through the lives of the men chosen to deliver his counsel. Abraham was part of the great plan of salvation.

HAGAR: Sarah's maid: In the process of time, Abram followed the practice of concubine or a surrogate wife. Hagar was an Egyptian and the handmaid of Abram's wife. Sarai said unto Abram, *"Behold now, the Lord hath restrained me from bearing: I pray thee, go in unto my maid; it may be that I may obtain children by her. And Abram hearkened to the voice of Sarai. And Sarai Abram's wife took Hagar her maid the Egyptian, after Abram had dwelt ten years in the land of Canaan, and gave her to her husband Abram to be his wife.* **Genesis 16:2-3.** As a maid, Hagar was a servant to Sarai. She was a bondwoman, in submission to the demands of her mistress, Sarai. Hagar had no liberal expressions outside of the guidelines Sarai would impose. Because Hagar had dwelt with Abram for years in Canaan, it is believed that Hagar was among the servants who Pharaoh gave to Abram. Since Sarai was in Pharaoh's palace while in Egypt, it is also possible that Hagar was Sarai's maid in Egypt. For ten years, Hagar had close contact with Sarai; a trusting relationship apparently developed between Sarai and Hagar.

Sarai believed God would bless Abram to be a father of many. Apparently Sarai was contemplating within herself that perhaps God would give Abram a child by her maid. She endeavored to make this happen by the way she knew was possible. There was no law to restrain or judge man if he should go in to his maid to beget children. Abram wasn't bound to a law: and Sarai did not put before him a law to adhere to. Sarai gave Hagar a position to serve as her surrogate. The law given by Moses was like unto a surrogate, until the time for the promise of God to fulfill.

The apostle Paul wrote concerning Isaac and Ishmael, and said, *"Tell me, ye that desire to be under the law, do ye not hear the law? For it is written, that Abraham had two sons, the one by a bondwoman, the other by a freewoman. But he who was of the bondwoman was born after the flesh; but he of the freewoman was by promise. "Which thing is an allegory for these are two covenants; the one from the Mount Sinai, which gendereth to bondage, which is Agar. (Hagar)* **Galatians 3:21-24.** The spiritual picture of Hagar, show the restriction the law had over the flesh. She represented the limitation of the law. No matter how many children that could have been born to her by Abram, none would become heir to the promise of God. Only the son of the freewoman could receive God's promise. The account of Sarai and Hagar is told like an allegory, so that it may be understood the bondage of the law. Abram lived four hundred years before the law. ***"For if the inheritance be of the law, it is no more of promise: but God gave it to Abraham by promise."*** Galatians 3:18.

SARAI, Despised by Hagar: *"And he went in unto Hagar, and she conceived: and when she saw that she had conceived her mistress was despised in her eyes."* **Genesis 16:4.** When a person despise another person, it is very likely the person who is despised will be harmed. To put a space between the two parties will reduce the despite, disrespect, and scorn; a wise action. The wise man Solomon said, *"For three things the <u>earth is disquieted</u>, and for four which it cannot bear: For a servant when he reigneth: a fool when he is filled with meat; for an odious woman when she is married: and <u>a handmaid that is **heir** to her mistress."</u>* **Proverbs 30:21-23.** This scripture highlights the attitude of Hagar toward her mistress, Sarai. The word *disquieted* is → to take away the peace or tranquility of: DISTRUB, to be uneasy. Also in this verse, the word **heir**, is the Hebrew word **Yarash**, defined as: To seize, *take possession*; to inherit; *to occupy*; to drive away, expel. To be an heir; to dispossess, is dispossessed; to become poor, make poor, to devour.

The earth is disquieted by a maid that is an heir, in the sense of devouring or taking possession; because she despises her mistress. Hereto, Sarai had no peace after Hagar conceived. Hagar looked down on Sarai in dishonor; for she disdained her. To be Abram's wife for the sake of childbearing made Hagar feel above her mistress. She became lifted up with a proud heart. Hagar was not the only maid servant that was in Abram's house; he had more. But Sarai selected Hagar because she apparently favored Hagar above the rest.

<u>**SARAI rebuked Hagar**</u>: *"And Sarai said unto Abram, **My wrong be upon thee**: I have given my maid into thy bosom; and when she saw that she had conceived, I was despised in her eyes: the Lord judge between me and thee. But Abram said unto Sarai, Behold thy maid is in thy hand; do to her as it pleaseth thee. And when Sarai dealt hardly with her, she fled from her face."* **Genesis 16:5-6.** It is interesting to note that Sarai saw her wrong to be charged to Abram. Seemly he would bear the repercussion of the action Sarai had made. But he dealt with Sarai according to knowledge, considering her as the weaker vessel who

was also joint heir to the grace of God. Abram did not ridicule Sarai for her giving Hagar unto him. He did not show favor towards Hagar for the disrespect toward Sarai. His soft answer to Sarai turned away wrath and allowed Sarai to do "as it pleaseth thee." The man of faith exhibited temperance. *"Delight is not seemly for a fool; much less for a servant to have rule over princes. The discretion of a man deferreth his anger; and it is his glory to pass over a transgression."* **Proverbs 19:11-2.** Abram had self-control over the matter with Sarai and Hagar: he passed over the transgression. His discretion was the virtue called temperance. A principle of this word is to let wisdom have her perfect work. And to cover a multitude of faults is the wisdom of love.

When the earth is troubled by the discontent and the disregard men put upon it, the earth answers back with sore judgment. Natural wildlife, the atmosphere, the rivers and lakes are some of the many things affected by man's abuse to the earth. The earth is disquieted more so with the disrespect men have towards one another. Truly Hagar had become disrespectful toward her mistress. And with Sarai, it was in her hands to do as it "Pleaseth thee."

Pleaseth, the Hebrew word is **towb,** defined: as *Good,* (in the widest sense used), or good thing, (well) best, beautiful, better, bountiful, cheerful be in favour, fine, graciously, joyful, kindly, lovingly, most pleasant, precious, prosperity, sweet, be (well) favoured.

"And when Sarai dealt hardly with her, she fled from her face." Sarai was righteous and kind to Hagar: she had only sought children of her. She did not send Hagar away at that time; Hagar fled from her mistress. Sarai first examined her own heart and submitted to God's judgment before she rebuked Hagar. It pleased Sarai to rebuke and correct Hagar. The severity of the rebuke brought shame to Hagar. Shame reacted with the dropping of the head, turning of the face or fleeing from the presence of the judgment. Hagar fled from Sarai's face because she was shamed. Hagar fled from her face, which showed that Sarai, her mistress didn't send her away.

To keep Hagar around her, inferred that Sarai had forgiven her of her disrespect. Sarai was the freewoman; and as Paul said of Sarai, *"But Jerusalem which is above is free, which is the mother of us all, For it is written, Rejoice thou barren that beareth not; break forth and cry, thou that travaileth not: for the desolate hath many more children than she which hath a husband."* **Galatians 3:26-27.** The promise upon Sarai was to become the mother of nations. Ishmael was the son of the bond maid, but Sarai had claim over Ishmael because Hagar was her surrogate.

How could Sarai as a Hebrew woman become the mother of other nations? Sarai was joint heir to the same promise God gave to Abram. The wisdom of God was establishing this promise in the actions of Sarai and Hagar. Some men preach concerning Sarai and Hagar, but they condemn the act of Sarai. This kind of preaching gives no understanding to the fact that the word of God was accomplishing his promise. The works of God are according to his purpose in righteousness: for his judgments are true. In this account with Sarai and Abram, temperance was added to Abram's faith. Temperance is a fruit of the Spirit: it is a product of the law of God working in the believer. Abram governed the dilemma Sarai faced by being temperance. He trusted Sarai to do the right thing concerning Hagar. Sarai wasn't ignorant to the teaching and godly life of Abram; she knew from his lifestyle what was right to do. He walked by faith, because the light of God was a lamp unto his feet. There was no cause to stumble or to be misguided.

Those who live by faith, also adds to faith, virtues. God has given all things that pertain unto life and godliness. This is done through the knowledge of Christ, who hath called us unto virtue and glory. *"Whereby are given unto us exceeding great and precious promises that by these ye might be partakers of his divine nature, having escaped the corruption that is in the world through lust."* **2Peter 1:4.** Abram's faith gave him access to the promises, because he gained knowledge of him who is eternal. Little Space Grace was God's favor to him. After many generations now passed, Abraham's glory and virtues are taught. The Jews of Jesus day highly esteemed him as father Abraham; and taught the covenant God made with him. Faith pleases God; Abram was called the friend of God.

The accounts and the experiences in Abram's life are more than stories told. They are the parables, and dark saying of old; in them are the hidden mysteries of God's will. The events were literal; but the messages lay before us the foundation of salvation and the glory that will be revealed in God's appointed time.

HAGAR fled from her mistress: As stated earlier, shame was why Hagar fled from the presence of Sarai. *"And the angel of the Lord found her by a fountain of water in the wilderness, by the fountain in the way to Shur."* Genesis 16:7. The cause of Hagar's shame was her disrespect towards her mistress. This painful emotion was a conscious guilt: a condition of humiliating disgrace Hagar felt. God showed mercy unto Hagar: it illustrated his outreach hand to other nations of people. Remember, Hagar was an Egyptian: with no bloodline to an inheritance. God worked in Abram in whom the promises were given; and through his work, fulfilling the conditions of the covenant. God said unto Abram, *"And I will bless them that bless thee, and curse him that curseth thee: and in thee shall all families of the earth be blessed."* Genesis 12:3.

Hagar soon learned that to flee offered her no hiding place from the Law of God. The angel of the Lord found her *"by a fountain of water in the wilderness."* It could be asked, can you imagine a fountain in the wilderness? The idea of a wilderness is to picture a land undeveloped. The wilderness is a place where wild beast roam; and scarce vegetation for human consumption. The land is uninhabited or a place where few people might live. And a place dry and not well watered. The Hebrew word for *fountain* is **ayin,** it is the analogy of a fountain; used to express a condition rather than a literal reservoir. Defined as, an *eye (lit. or fig) by analogy, a fountain,* as the eye of the landscape) —*affliction, outward appearance, countenance, displease, humble, look, (not) please, resemblance, yourself.* The definition shine light on the emotional condition Hagar was in. She was in a place to see herself; her countenance or appearance was saddened by her guilt. The scripture also points out that she was "*by the fountain in the way to Shur.*" To be "by a fountain" and to be "<u>by the fountain</u>" made distinction of the two places. The first fountain does not specify a particular source for water. The second fountain identifies the source, being located in a certain place. The wilderness of Shur is the certain place; known by others who had travelled the land. Years later "<u>*by the fountain in the way to Shur*</u>" it is the place Moses brought the children of Israel to. "*And when they came to Marah, they could not drink the waters of Marah, for they were bitter: therefore the name of it was called Marah.*" **Exodus 15:23.** The wilderness place offered no life for Hagar. The angel asked her, "*Whence comest thou? And whither wilt thou go? And she said I fled from the face of my mistress Sarai.*" She answered the first question; but the second question the angel asked he sought to know her choice. The advice the angel gave her, "*Return to thy mistress, and submit thyself under her hands.*" Repentance is the first course of action, so that shame and guilt are taken away. To know the truth is the liberty wherewith Christ hath made us free. The chains of bondage which is sin are broken with repentance. By definition, to repent is to turn about or from: to feel regret. The angel instructed Hagar to repent.

The prosperity of ISHAMEL foretold: "*And the angel of the Lord said unto her, I will multiply thy seed <u>exceedingly</u>, that it shall not be numbered for multitude. And the angel of the Lord said unto her, Behold, thou art with child, and thou shalt bear a son, and shalt call his name Ishmael; because the Lord hath heard thy affliction.*" *And he will be a wild man: his hand will be against every man and every man's hand against him; and he shall dwell in the presence of all his brethren.*" **Genesis 16:10-12.** God heard Hagar's affliction: he considered her broken emotional state. In other words, God forgave Hagar and ordained for her a son. He revealed to her the <u>name</u>, <u>number</u>, and <u>notoriety</u> of her son. *"I will multiply thy seed exceedingly."* To go beyond the implied limit, is exceedingly. That which is increased by multiplication is empowered, strengthened, and enriched. Ishmael would be powerful, strong and rich upon the land. He would be a man with a defined character: "a wild man." A wild man is one who is without restraints to natural laws. A wild man is un-controlled in all manner of cultures, traditions and established systems. His work will be in opposition to every man: creating enemies instead of allies. And every man's work will be against Ishmael. Endless conflict and warfare will be in his prosperity. But his habitation will be in the presence of all his brethren; this implies an acceptance of only his own. He will show respect of persons; a racist toward anyone that is not his brethren. He will only be supported by his brethren.

A spiritual application as to Hagar and Ishmael is as follows. Hagar is the bond woman; the maid of the free woman. She was kept in bondage until she repents and submits to truth; the free woman. Hagar is called Mount Sinai, because from that mount came the law. To be in sin a person is bound under the law. To be free from sin comes by grace and truth. The Seed of Hagar, who was Ishmael, produced many more children than she that was the free woman. Sin multiplies, becomes powerful, strong and enriched by what it masters in the earth. Sin is like the wild man; opposing everything that is not of its nature.

Sin only dwell among all its kin; that which is of the same nature. The contrast of good and evil is known in every generation of man. The enmity is the spiritual warfare of good and evil. Satan works to trip men; causing men to fall by his deception. Then in Christ, the spirit of truth takes authority over the works of the devil; rescuing man from the bondage entrapment of Satan. The nature and character of Ishmael portrays the contrast of the two seeds of Abraham. In the years proceeding Ishmael's birth, the promised seed of Abraham will verify this contrast.

Hagar acknowledged God's mercy: *"And she called the name of the Lord that spake unto her, Thou God seest me: for she said, Have I also here looked after him that **seest** me?* Genesis 16:13. Hagar took heed to the voice of the Lord by acknowledging *"Thou God **seeth** me."* To have the awareness of God taking notice of her affliction gave comfort to her. To realize God "seeth" captures a picture of Hagar's yesterday, today and her tomorrow.

Seest is a present tense vision; Seeth is a continual vision. The Hebrew word for both seest and seeth is, **roiy,** (ro-ee) derived from the word **raah,** (raw-aw). **Roiy** means, sight: *abstr,* vision (a spectacle); gazing stock, look to. But **Raah,** mean > to see—*advise self,* discern, approve, *behold,* consider, make to enjoy, have experience, gaze, take heed, look on, be near, present, provide, regard, have respect, shew self, think, view, visions. The word of the angel also caused Hagar to see herself; *"Have I also here looked after him that seeth me?"* Hagar had a change of heart as indicated in her words. Her affliction would have led her to death in the wilderness if she had not repented. But the word of God brought faith, hope and life. God's, "little space grace" was given to Hagar before the promise came to pass.

Next, the name was given to the unspecified fountain: the name means, **Well of the Living One Who Sees Me.** *"Wherefore the well was called Beer-lahai-roi: behold it is between Kadesh and Bered."* Genesis 16:14. The location of the place Hagar was in the wilderness, the name was given. The location was between Kadesh and Bered. The word **Kadesh, is,** Holy Place. **Bered,** means, Hail: this word is a word of salutation; to *greet* or summon by calling. That is to greet with enthusiasm. These words illustrated the experience and life change that happened with Hagar. It wasn't the land that made it a Holy Place: it was the presence of God through his word that Hagar experienced. She called on the Lord that "seest" and she received life; the Living Water. *"And Hagar bare Abram a son: and Abram called his son's name, which Hagar bare, Ishmael. And Abram was fourscore and six years old, when Hagar bare Ishmael to Abram."* Genesis **16:15-16.** When

Hagar bare Ishmael, the promise of having a son and his name came to pass. Abram named the son Ishmael, the name that the angel had given to Hagar. Abram unwavering faith in the promises of God was seen in the name given to his son. Ishmael means, *God will hear.*

WISDOM acted to materialize the word of God: The promise to Hagar foreshadowed the plan and will of God. *"For the Scriptures, foreseeing that God would justify the heathen through faith, preached before the gospel unto Abraham, saying, In thee shall all nations be blessed."* Galatians 3:8. Abraham's son by Hagar was the way by which other nations through Abraham were blessed. Hagar was an Egyptian; and Ishmael was the son of Abraham, who was Hebrew. Some ministers preach this scripture, condemning the act of Abraham with Hagar; But God was acting on His plan to bring salvation to mankind. The wisdom of God must obtain children. God's word actively performs his will; it accomplishes what he pleases and prospers where unto it is sent.

It was the word of God which appeared unto Abraham in the land of Ur. He was given the promise of a Seed; by which all nations will be blessed through him. In a vision, the word of God came to Abraham, and promised him a seed; saying if he could number the stars, so shall his seed be. And by the word of God, an angel spoke with Hagar in the wilderness place; giving promise to her son's prosperity. The word of God is his wisdom; the same was with him when the foundation of the earth was established.

22

The Cutting Away

Wisdom "hath builded" HEWN OUT: It was stated earlier that *"wisdom hath builded her house, she hath hewn out her seven pillars:"* Proverbs 9:1. The Hebrew word *"hewn"* is **chatsab,** and defined as follows: to *cut* or crave (wood, stone or other materials); by impl. To *hew,* split, *square, quarry, engrave:—cut, dig, divide,* grave, *make,* maso*n.* The Builder who makes or constructs a building, will use in the process, a cutting or hewing out of his work. In fashioning out the temple of God, which is "God's House" wisdom hath hewn or cut out also. The question which may be asked is, what have wisdom hewn out? In the Book of Proverbs, Solomon said, "her seven pillars." One of the pillars wisdom hewn out is FAITH.

Abraham continued to experience the word of God in his life. He carried the covenant sign of his faith, which was <u>circumcision</u>. At the age of ninety-nine, *"the Lord appeared to Abram, and said unto him, I am the Almighty God; walk before me, and be thou perfect."* Genesis 17:1. Over a period of twenty four years, from the age of seventy-five, Abram heard the voice of God. When he was called to leave his kindred, his country and his father's house, Abram obeyed the voice of God. In a vision, the word of God came to him to show him "whereby" he would inherit the promises. God appeared unto him. The expression, "Almighty God" further advanced Abram's knowledge of God. As God Almighty, Abram learned the power of God; the one who could utterly destroy, control, and waste. He learned the impregnable God; the Almighty God incapable of being taken by an assault: God is unconquerable. Therefore, God embarked upon the covenant agreement with Abram. No greater one can make this oath and swear by it but God.

WALK BEFORE ME: Part of the terms of the contract with Abram was to *"walk before me, and be thou perfect."* In the Old Testament two men are recorded in Abram's history that "walked with God." The first man was Enoch, the seventh generation from Adam; and later Noah, the tenth generation of Adam. With Enoch, *"By faith Enoch was translated that he should not see death; and was not found, because God had translated him: for before his translation he had this testimony, that **he pleased God.**"* Hebrews 11:5. The number seven symbolizes perfection: and Enoch was the seventh generation from Adam. His sign of faith was that he walked with God; which is the perfect walk. Enoch appeased God: he afforded joy, satisfaction, and an agreeable fulfillment of God's desire and will. The Hebrew writer said, ***"But without faith it is impossible to please him; for he that cometh to God must believe that he is, and that he is a rewarder of them that diligently seek him."*** Hebrews 11:6. God remunerated Enoch for his faith: he received the equivalent pay for his faith. The scripture called his reward, "translated." And by definition, it is to convey to heaven or to a non-temporal condition without death.

The apostle Paul wrote to the saints at Colosse, saying, *"As ye also learned of Epaphras our dear fellowservant, who is for you a faithful minister of Christ: Who also declared unto us your love in the Spirit. For this cause we also, since the day we heard it, do not cease to pray for you, and to desire that ye might be filled with the knowledge of his will in all wisdom and spiritual understanding; That ye might **walk** worthy of the Lord unto all pleasing, being fruitful in every good work, and increasing in the knowledge of God; Strengthened with all might, according to his glorious power, unto all patience and longsuffering with joyfulness; giving thanks unto the Father, which hath made us meet to be partakers of the inheritance of the saints in light: Who delivered us from the power of darkness, and hath translated us into the kingdom of his dear Son: In whom we have redemption through his blood, even the forgiveness of* *sins.*" Colossians 1:7-14. The account of Enoch was left for the sojourners of faith to know that they also will be translated into the kingdom of God: having walked before God.

Noah is the other person in Abram's lineage who "walked before God." The father of Noah was Lamech; and at one hundred and eighty-two years old he begot a son. *"And he called his name Noah, saying, this same shall comfort us concerning our work and toil of our hands, because of the ground which the Lord hath cursed."* Genesis 5:29. After a period of years, it is written, *"These are the generations of Noah: Noah was a just man and perfect in his generations, and Noah walked with God."* Genesis 6:9. To be just is to exemplify a righteous behavior; which attest to one's faith. This was the character of Noah; he was perfect in his generations. He walked before the Lord which singled Noah out above all of his relatives in his day. Righteousness exalts a nation: and Noah was exalted above the rest. Noah "walked with God" which showed his relationship, fellowship and friendship with the Father.

Abram's covenant terms with God were for him to **"walk before"** God. To walk is a moving forward, to move backward or move from side to side. The entire circumference of his life was to be before God. Walk is directional, with a purpose; to which a person can arrive at a viewed goal. Walk is measurable by time, space and distance. Walk is governed and dependent on strength, endurance and to be unwavering (not to sway). These are the things that define walk. But with Abram, God centralized his walk by saying "before me."

"Before me" It is understood in that the word before is the position of being in front of. Abram was to be governed by the jurisdiction or commandments of God. He was to be at God's disposal. Not only as a man of faith, but Abram was first in the time element of God's plan of salvation. His faith illustrated and exemplified how righteousness pleases God. Abraham walk was with the sign of circumcision; the token of God's covenant with him. It is not found or recorded prior to Abram, the sign of circumcision as God's covenant with any man before Abraham.

Abram's walk moved him forward: He left the land of Ur, his father's house, his country and kindreds. It was a period of time and a great distance from Ur when he arrived in Canaan. At no time did he waver in his faith toward God; especially through the things he suffered. His faith brought him to Canaan; faith directed him through the land. His faith caused him to drive out the kings of the land; all the way to Syria. Faith set him aside from his nephew Lot; having stood on the law of brotherly love to solve strife between the herdsmen. His walk was before God: he did what was pertained in the law of righteousness and was justified by his faith. Abram kept the terms of the covenant God made with him. The right direction and do the right thing is justifiable.

But to fulfill the will of God is "to be perfect." By keeping the terms of the covenant of God, Abraham was obeying the law of righteousness. This alludes to steadfastness, endurance and to continue on the right course. Abraham's walk before God moved him to another position and place of faith. To walk before the Lord, allowed him to grow in the knowledge of God; and to receive the grace of God. The status he acquired was because of his faith walk. Abraham took the right stand and held to the word of God. His attitude was to firmly hold to what God had revealed to him. In doing so, Abraham was of himself the locale to the where the promises of God would be found. Therefore godliness was added to Abraham's faith. The full measure of God in man is for man "to be perfect." Godliness is that measure Abraham gained through obedience. Godliness is to be pious; a loyal reverence for God. And to be pious is to appease God in devotion and divine worship.

Then God said, *Be thou perfect.*" Perfection completes the work of God which Abram was to adhere to. At that point, Abram's life had fulfilled the meaning of his name, "exalted father." God raised him from the place he was in, to a position of being highly honored and of a notable reputation. He was recognized among the people of his day. Abram was a father to Lot; later he fathered Ishmael, his son by Sarai's bond maiden. He was proven to be a father to His brethren and to a servant's son.

God's terms of the Covenant: *"As for me, behold, my covenant is with thee, and thou shalt be a father of many nations. Neither shall thy name any more is called Abram, but thy name* **shall be Abraham**: *for a father of many nations have I made thee." And* **I will make** *thee exceeding fruitful, and* **I will make** *nations of thee, and kings shall come out of thee, I will establish my covenant between me and thee and thy seed after thee in their generations for an everlasting covenant, to be a God unto thee, and to thy seed after thee. And I will give unto thee and to thy seed after thee, the land of Canaan, for an everlasting possession; and I will be their God,* "Genesis 17:4-8. The first position of change was to have a new name. His name, *"Shall be Abraham" which* is a father of many nations. His name would be wide spread, which speaks of greatness; to be noble, rich, fruitful, having abundance and a possessor of much. God told Abraham, *"I will make thee exceeding fruitful, and I will make nations of thee and kings shall come out of thee."* Genesis 17:6.

The word **make** is an authorized act of creating or bringing forth that which is desired. Questions could be asked, how can one be made fruitful? The fruit is the end result of a seed that was planted and kept in its seasons. Abraham heard the voice of God and kept his words. Then, how are nations made? They are made through the process of time, growth and development of the people of the earth. Through social interactions, relationships and kinsman-ship kept alive. Nations are made by language, cultures and traditions practiced among their kind. And how are kings made? Many kings acquired their rule through much conquest and conflict; having gained victory over their enemies. Kings are also born of a blood line; in which their offspring's are ordained to become inheritors of the kingdom. God spoke to Abraham the entire scope of his (seed) children's history. Abram 'name became great; nations and kings came out of his lineage. Before these things came to realization, the word of God had established it. "Wisdom hath builded her house, she hath hewn out her seven pillars."

The apostle Paul said, *"Having made known unto us the mystery of his will, according to his good pleasure which he hath purposed in himself: that in the dispensation of the fullness of times he might gather together in one all things in Christ, both which are in heaven and which are on earth; even in him: In whom also we have obtained an* **inheritance,** *being predestinated according to the purpose of him which worketh all things after the counsel of his own will."* Ephesians 1:9-11

The Sign of the Covenant is CIRCUMCISION: The contract required a <u>sign</u> to seal the agreement between God and Abraham. The engraving or hewing out which wisdom placed upon the pillar of faith was circumcision. A seal or signature stamped or written upon a document makes it legal; therefore circumcision was that seal. This Covenant became the law to regulate, permit, protect, and provide goods expected. Thus far Abraham was justified by faith; but he had to fulfill or perfect the law given to him. Once the covenant was made, Abraham was obligated to perfect or fulfill his part of the covenant.

Abraham was already given the right course of actions to follow; to <u>"walk before God and to be thou perfect."</u> He did not question God as to why God would have him to circumcise every man child in his house. The reason is in knowing that **"a token"** is the sign which assures that the directive grants an attainable end. Signs represent laws; conveying messages and pointing to specified directions to follow. The law of God was illustrated in Abraham's walk: his godliness was the image of God's law that he obeyed. Conformity to the image of God's dear Son is obedience to the word of God. Paul the apostle of Jesus Christ said, *"And we know that all things work together for good to them that love God, to them who are the called according* *to his purpose. For whom he did foreknow, he also did predestinate <u>to be</u>* <u>*conformed to the image of his Son*</u>*, that he might be the firstborn among many brethren."* Romans 8:28-29. And Jesus prayed to the Father, and said, *Neither pray I for these alone, but for them also which shall believe on me through their word: That they all may be one; as thou, Father, art in me, and I in thee, that they also may be one in us: that the world may believe that thou hast sent me. And the glory which thou gavest me, I have given them; that they may be one, even as we are one: I in them, and thou in me,* ***<u>that they may be made perfect</u>*** *in one; and that the world may know that thou hast sent me, and hast loved them, as thou hast loved me.* Jesus prayed, *"Father, I will that they also, whom thou hast given me, be with me where I am; that they may behold my glory, which thou hast given me: for thou lovedst me before the foundation of the world."* John 17:20-24

To **"be thou perfect"** was exercised in Abraham's obedience to the terms of the covenant to circumcise. *"This is my covenant, which ye shall keep, between me and you and thy seed after thee; every man child among you shall be circumcised. And ye shall circumcise the flesh of your foreskin; and it shall be a token of the covenant between me and you. And he that is eight days old shall be circumcised among you, every man child in your generations, he that is born in the house, or bought with money of any stranger, which is not of thy seed. He that is born in thy house, and he that is bought with money, must (needs) be circumcised: and my covenant shall be in your flesh for an everlasting covenant. And the uncircumcised man child whose flesh of his foreskin is not circumcised, that soul shall be cut off from his people; he hath broken my covenant."* Genesis 17: 10-14

Abraham first circumcised the males who received the sign; those not determined by age; "every man child." Then God said, *"And he that is eight days old shall be circumcised among you, every man child in your generations, he that is born in the house, or bought with money of any stranger which is not thy seed."* (V.12) God established his plan of salvation for all people through the sign of the <u>covenant of circumcision</u>.

Believers are made perfect through the word of God they receive and obey. God's word conform the Believer into the image of Christ. This is the sign of the covenant of God, called circumcision. Circumcision was evidence that a covenant was made between God and Abraham. It is the cutting away, the hewing out, the engraving or writing upon the heart of men God's laws. The foreskin had to be removed to channel in righteousness; to make clean the pathway of godliness. This is the glory of God revealed in the Believer; the sign that the covenant is fulfilled or "perfected" in them. The command was for man to allow the cutting away of the foreskin. The male is the gender of the one that is capable of begetting children; without him there would be no offspring. It was imperative for Abraham's household, and his servants to be circumcised. Then God said, *"And he that is eight days old shall be circumcised among you, every man child in your generations, he that is born in the house, or bought with money of any stranger which is not thy seed."* (V.12) God established his plan of salvation for all people through the sign of the <u>covenant of circumcision.</u>

The word <u>token</u> in Hebrew is, **owth,** *oth,* and defined; (in the sense of appearing); a signal (lit. or fig.) As a flag, beacon, *monument,* omen, *prodigy, evidence.* A mark, miracle (en-) sign, token. The sign of the covenant was to be kept by Abraham and his seed after him.

<u>EIGHT DAYS OLD</u>: God marked a time; a determined season, or an age upon the keeping of his Covenant. The covenant wasn't to be abolished, ratified or done away with. The number eight secures His law. But what does the number eight mean as to the spiritual things of God? Some say that it signifies 'new beginnings' in which it does bring newness to life. The number eight represents an eternal cycle; it speaks to that which is forevermore, everlasting, always, and eternal. To connect the word **"Days old"** further defines the eternal cycle of God's word; in this respect, the keeping of circumcision. The carnal understanding of a man is to see circumcision as a ritual rather than a sign. Circumcision is an indicator of what the desired end is. It leads in the way of holiness. Wisdom established the highway of holiness, long before Jeremiah said, *"Behold the days come, saith the Lord, that I will make a new covenant with the house of Israel and with the house of Judah: Not according to the covenant that I made with their fathers in the day that I took them by the hand to bring them out of the land of Egypt; although I was a husband unto them, saith the Lord."* The covenant to the fathers is the law of God written with his own finger on stone. *"But this shall be the covenant that I will make with the house of Israel; I will put my law in their inward parts, and write it in their hearts; and I will be their God, and they shall be my people."* Jeremiah 31:31-33. How will this be performed? Jeremiah said, *"Circumcise yourselves to the Lord, and take away the foreskins of your heart, ye men of Judah and inhabitants of Jerusalem: lest* my *fury come forth like fire, and burn that none can quench it. Because the evil of your doings."* Jeremiah 4:4. Giving no room to carnal thinking or logic; but with spiritual understanding, *Paul* said, *"For circumcision verily profiteth, if thou keep the law: but if thou be a breaker of the law, thy circumcision is made uncircumcision. Therefore if the uncircumcision keeps the righteousness of the law, shall not his uncircumcision be counted for circumcision? And shall not uncircumcision which is by nature, it fulfill* (perfect) *the law; judge thee, who by the letter and circumcision dost transgress the law? For he is not a Jew, which is one outwardly, neither is that circumcision, which is outward in the flesh. But he is a Jew, which is one inwardly; and <u>circumcision is that of the heart, in the spirit, and not in the letter</u>; whose praise is not of men, but of God."* Romans 2:25-29

These things were illustrated in the life of Abraham; he kept the sign of the covenant. God said unto Abraham to circumcise every man child; those in his house, born in his house, the ones bought with money and the ones of eight days old. Those in Abraham's house were not all Hebrews; and this is the same message Paul taught the Roman church: *"if the uncircumcision keep the righteousness of the law; shall not his uncircumcision be counted for circumcision?"* God's plan of salvation is for all people; the Jews and the Gentiles.

Wisdom was establishing the ways of God before Moses wrote them as the laws of God. The sojourner's faith highway was to "walk before:" God and his walk preserved him. Those who are of the faith journey, travel the highway of holiness. God commanded Abraham to walk before him and be thou perfect. Abraham was before Moses day. He was the law giver to the children of Israel, Moses said, *"Circumcise therefore the foreskin of your heart, and be no more stiffnecked."* Deuteronomy 9:4. Circumcision is the token of the covenant of God: a sign for others to see the life of the faithful. Circumcision shows others the righteousness of God's law being kept by the believer. Obeying the word of God reflects the glory of God and his righteousness.

When the Hebrew children were born; on the eight day they were circumcised. The newness of life must carry the token of God's covenant. Salvation was ordained before the birth: therefore making known to man the foreknowledge of God. The birth of Jesus marked the newness of life for fallen man. *"And when eight days were accomplished for the circumcising of the child, his name was called JESUS, which was so named of the angel before he was conceived in the womb."* Luke 1:21. When Mary, the mother of Jesus brought him to the temple for dedication, the scripture said, *"And behold, there was a man in Jerusalem, whose name was Simeon; and the same man was just and devout, waiting for the consolation of Israel: and the Holy Ghost was upon him ".* And it was revealed unto him by the Holy Ghost, that he should not see death, before he had seen the Lord's Christ."* vv.30-31 *"For mine eyes has seen thy salvation, which thou hast prepared before the face of all people; a light to lighten the Gentiles, and the glory of thy people Israel."* Luke 2:25-31. Jesus fulfilled this custom of the law; which was the token God gave unto Abraham. Every man child was to be circumcised at eight days old. This was an early example in the life of Jesus, that he fulfilled what was written of him. Jesus said, *"Think not that I come to destroy the law or the prophets,"* Before he was born, the word concerning him was being fulfilled. For an example, Isaiah prophesied saying, *"Therefore the Lord himself shall give you a* *sign; Behold, a virgin shall conceive, and bear a son, and shall call his name Immanuel" Isaiah* 8:14. This prophecy was fulfilled in the New Testament. *"But while he thought on these things, behold, the angel of the Lord appeared unto him in a dream, saying, Joseph, thou son of David, fear not to take unto thee Mary thy wife; for that which is conceived in her is of the Holy Ghost. And she shall bring forth a son, and thou shalt call his name JESUS: for he shall save his people from their sins. Now all this was done, that it might be fulfilled which was spoken of the Lord by the prophet, saying, Behold, a virgin shall be with child, and shall bring forth a son, and they shall call his name Emmanuel, which being interpreted is God with us."* Matthew 1:20-23

The Stipulation for being Uncircumcised: *"And the uncircumcised man child whose flesh of his foreskin is not circumcised, that soul shall be cut off from his people; he hath broken my covenant."* Genesis 17: 14. With every law given, there are penalties that incur suffering or hardship if not obeyed or honored. In no prior time was it known whether that God placed a stipulation on his word. The father of faith was inspired to teach the law of circumcision to others. Abram's faith was moving him forward among the people as a courier of truth. Thus the ability to lead others is the activity of a teacher. A teacher will guide others in knowledge; giving them a course to follow and a discipline to adhere to. But if they should error or stray from the right course, then will they experience dire consequences. God is the law giver with authority to exact punishment. He is holy and just; and his judgments are righteous and true.

The stipulation placed on the uncircumcised taught a principle; to show that there is a difference between the clean and the unclean. God said unto Abram, *"...that soul shall be cut off from his people: he hath broken my covenant."* The cutting off of that soul exposes them as not carrying the sign of circumcision. To be disobedient and to resist the will of God is to be stiffnecked. This introduced to Abram the knowledge of those that are seen as law breakers. Later the time came when the children of Israel were called a stiffnecked people. A behavior of being stiffnecked is when a person is unwilling to be turned or governed by God. The person, who is uncircumcised of heart, is the soul who will be cut off. Like as with Adam's transgression; sinful man will suffer and become acquainted with sorrows. That soul will lose the blissful presence of God.

23

JOINT-HEIRS

SARAI' name was changed: God changed the name of (Abram) "exalted father" to Abraham; God changed Sarai name also. The name change imputed a new nature; and this change insured a new role. There was a time in Sarai' life, when she had the tenacity to be wearisome; her patience and tolerance exhausted. What is known of Sarah is like the spiritual barren condition of many. But God's word to her created expectation: for his word produces life. The promised blessings God made to Sarai were comforting words of hope. She was no longer to be barren, but with expectation of a son. This was her life changing account. Her former attitude was like the typical trait that was seen in the life of children of Israel. God ordained and chose Israel as a peculiar treasure out of the earth. But "little Space Grace" assisted Israel through their time of exhaustion. They could trust and have hope in the word that comforted them along the way. These words lead Israel in the pathway to life. Isaiah said, *"Hear ye now, O house of David; Is it a small thing for you to weary men, but will ye weary God also? Therefore the Lord himself shall give you a sign; Behold, a virgin shall conceive, and bear a son, and shall call his name Immanuel."* Isaiah 7:13-14. The sign of salvation fulfilled in the day of Mary. *"And she shall bring forth a son, and thou shalt call his name Jesus: for he shall save his people from their sins."* Matthew 1:21. Immanuel is God with us; therefore the spirit of heaviness or wearisome is done away with. A newness of life takes the place of the barren life. God blessed Sarah to become the mother of nations. Sarah's name is defined as being a noble female; a princess or queen: Sarah depicts the spiritual mother "New Jerusalem, or the City of God. The apostle Paul said, *"But Jerusalem which is above is free, **which is the mother of us all**, for* is written, Rejoice, thou barren {Sarah} that bearest not; break forth and cry, thou that travaileth not: for the desolate hath many more children than she who hath a husband. Now we, brethren, as Isaac was, are the children of promise. "Galatians 3: 26-28. Sarah was the free woman; the promise concerning Sarah was, "I will bless her, and she shall be a mother of nations," Genesis 17:16

The children of promise were those God promised Abraham would be the father of. And Sarah, Abraham's wife was the mother of the children of promise as well. Sarah represents spiritual Jerusalem, the mother of us all. The physical location of Jerusalem is in the land of Palestine: also known as the land of promise. Jerusalem was the capital city of Palestine: and the name Jerusalem means, **founded peaceful**. The very meaning of the name Jerusalem is a promise of overcoming the barren and weary life once known in Sarai. God has ordained this peace for the children of faith.

The wisdom of God was establishing his "House" and Sarai name change signified the fashioning of the New Jerusalem; which shall be revealed. "And John saw the holy city, New Jerusalem, coming down from God out of heaven prepared as a bride adorned for her husband." Revelation 21:2. God's city is his people, Jerusalem; and Sarah portrayed this city of God. Her name defines a member of a royal family. Sarah is the esteemed woman of sovereign power.

Spiritually so, Sarah is the consort of a prince. She bonds to the spiritual consort, who is Christ: for he is the Prince of Peace. "And there came unto me one of the seven angels which had the seven vials full of the seven last plagues saying **Come hither, I will show thee the bride, the Lamb's wife.** And he carried me away in the spirit to a great and high mountain, and showed me that **great city, the holy Jerusalem,** descending out of heaven from God." Revelation 21:9-10

By the holy prophets, God sent his words of comfort to his people. "And I have put my words in thy mouth, and I have covered thee in *the shadow of mine hand, that I may plant the heavens, and lay the foundations of the earth, and say unto Zion, thou art my people."* Isaiah 51:16. The shadow of God's hand, speaks of the works he wrought for the children of Israel. His purpose is to plant, or sow spiritual things of himself in the earth {man}, and say to Zion, "thou art my people." God is possessor of heaven and earth; the same message spoken to Abraham by Melchizedek, priest of the Most High God.

Gospel choirs may sing the song, "I Have a New Name Over in Zion' the nature change and the behavior change in the believer takes on a new name. In the Book of Revelation, John wrote, *"Him that overcometh will I make a pillar in the temple of my God, and he shall go no more out: and I will write upon him the name of my God, and the name of the city of my God, which is new Jerusalem, which cometh down out of heaven from my God: and I will write upon him my new name."* Revelation 3:12. God predestined the salvation of man before the foundations of the world. The faith life of Abraham introduced God's plan of salvation. God's plan began to develop in the life and history of all men that He chose and placed his name.

Abraham's walk wasn't by sight or by human logic; but he trusted and relied on the covenant God made with him. *"As it is written, I have made thee a father of many nations, before him whom he believed, even God, who quickeneth the dead, and calleth those things which are not as though they were. Who against hope believed in hope, that he might become the father of many nations, according to that which was spoken, so shall thy seed be. And being not weak in faith, he considered not his own body now dead, when he was about a hundred years old, neither the deadness of Sarah's womb: He staggered not at the promise of God through unbelief; but was strong in faith, giving glory to God; and being fully persuaded that, what he had promised, he was able also to perform."* Romans 4:17 20. Abraham was justified by his faith in God. Paul said, *"For what saith the Scriptures? Abraham believed God, and it was counted unto him for righteousness." "And he received the sign of circumcision, a seal of the righteousness of the faith which he had yet being uncircumcised: that he might be the father of all them that believe, though they be not circumcised that righteousness might be imputed unto them also: And the father of circumcision to them who also walk in the steps of that faith of our father Abraham, which he had being yet uncircumcised.?* "Romans 4:3 & 10-12. God said unto Abraham that Sarah will bear him a son, *"and thou shall call his name Isaac: and I will establish my covenant with him for an everlasting covenant with him and his seed after him."* Genesis 17:19

ISAAC, the son of promise: The name Isaac means, "laughter" mockery. Isaac was merriment to his old aged parents. The promised son, "Laughter" would cause Abraham and Sarah to have joy, to experience, take heed too, look on, or upon; to mark, perceive, present, provide, regard, respect, and to know the vision of God's covenant plan. The things Abraham experienced were etched in his faith walk, which the Wisdom of God hewed out. They were the substance of things hoped for, and the evidence of things not seen. When God spoke to Abraham, *"Then Abraham fell upon his face, and laughed, and said in his heart, Shall a child be born unto him that is a hundred years old? And shall Sarah, that is ninety years old, bear?* Genesis 17:17 Abraham's first response was that he fell on his face and he laughed. Before the promise came to be, laughter was in his heart. It was not a mockery that Abraham was making; but merriment to the fact that at a hundred years old he would have a son. This wasn't an expression of disbelief; Note, he said, *"Shall a child be born unto him that is a hundred years old?* At the beginning of this scripture, {Genesis 17:1} it is written, *"And when Abram was **ninety years old and nine**, the Lord appeared to Abram, and said unto him, I am the Almighty God; walk before me, and be thou perfect."* In calling out the age of a hundred years old, Abraham was actually speaking prophetic. A short time later after this, the Lord visited Abraham at his tent's door. He told him that about that time the next year, Sarah will have a son. In the next year, Abraham was a hundred years old when Isaac was born.

A man of one hundred years old would be viewed as foolish to expect to beget children. To an unbeliever he would make mockery of the promise God made. But with Abraham, his laugher was in the sense the merriment and joy of the news. The father of faith became the father of all that believeth in God to the saving of their souls. We know that a child is born of only one father. But the mystery revealed is knowing faith included all as children of Abraham. Abraham's name change placed him in a new role. Form "exalted father-Abram" to "the father of many nations" have God made him. Faith caused the impossible with man, to be the possible with God.

Wisdom established faith as a pillar in God's House; his dwelling place. Faith strengthens the house of God. Faith can bare, endure, hope and believe all things. Faith is the access door to the Grace of God; providing man with the things hoped for. That is why, "all things are possible to him that believeth." To all people, Faith cometh by hearing, and hearing by the Word of God. His word made all things and by it all things are made possible by the Word.

Every time faith pleases God, a measure of "little space grace" is given. Then there are virtues that accompany each experience of faith. Having a new name, the covenant of circumcision and the blessing of parenting added to Abraham's faith. After hearing the promise, Abram prayed that his son Ishmael would live before God. This prayer showed a compassionate heart which reflected the virtue called **charity**. Abraham sought God to bless Ishmael also. It mattered not that Ishmael was the son by Sarah's bond maiden; Abraham desired Ishmael's life to be blessed also. "Charity, *Seeketh not her own, "Charity, Beareth all things, believeth all things, hopeth all things, endureth all things."* 1Corinthians 13:5. The father who loves his children, will demonstrate his love by the work of charity. Charity tends to the love affection the father has for his children. The law of God's commandment is love. Before God commanded men to love one another, faith was tending to his law. Abraham was bearing the cross of Ishmael; he believed God would bless Ishmael also. His hope was in knowing God had promised an inheritance; and his faith was stedfast in those promises.

The promise God made and the prayer of Abraham concerning Ishmael was answered years later. Ishmael was blessed with the natural things of the earth. He became fruitful; he multiplied exceedingly; twelve princes were begotten of him; God made him a great nation. But the covenant promise was established with Isaac. After God had finished talking with Abraham, he went up from Abraham. Then Abraham performed the words of the Lord by circumcising himself, Ishmael and those of his house, as God had commanded.

THE COMMUNION

GOD Appeared unto Abraham in the plains of Mamre: Abraham heard the voice of God in Haran. He heard the word of the Lord in a vision; and next Abraham experienced the visitation of God in the door of his tent. *"And the Lord appeared unto him in the plains of Mamre: and he sat in the tent door in the heat of the day. "And he lifted up his eyes and looked, and, lo, three men stood by him: and when he saw them, he ran to meet them from the tent door, and bowed himself toward the ground."* Genesis 18:1-2. Abraham was sitting in his tent's door. Abram was in state of relaxing in his temporary dwelling place; but not asleep. This illustrated a man waiting and unoccupied with labor. Again faith continued to be defined in and through Abraham. The virtue added to Abraham's faith was patience. And patience is a fruit of the Spirit of God. Patience portrayed in this scripture as the time to tarry or wait on the vision to fulfill. Since the time of his circumcision, Abraham remained stationary in readiness and expectation. His "Faith was the substance of things hoped for" Circumcision was the token of the covenant between Abraham and God he adhered to. Abraham was ninety-nine years old when he was circumcised. He spent twenty four years of living steadfast, from the time of leaving his father's house, kindred and country. He was steadfast in faith; overcoming trails, adversities and difficulties despite of opposition. At times, the faith journey places us in a waiting state. But let patience have her perfect work. God's "little space grace" shows up along faith's journey. The prophet Isaiah said, *"But they that wait upon the Lord shall renew their strength; they shall mount up with wings as eagles; they shall run, and not be weary; and they shall walk, and not faint."* Isaiah 40:31

Picture a man ninety nine years old, running to meet his guest? Apparently, Abraham had vigor [strength] to be able to make haste. Like as in the previous verse of scripture; they that wait on the Lord shall renew their strength. The Lord showed up or appeared at Abraham's tent. <u>Shall</u> is the promise word to mount up with wings as an eagle. The promise of God will cause the person to to ascend or soar above. His patience enabled him to run and not become exhausted in strength, nor lack in endurance or vigor. It takes more energy to run than to walk. But God included in his promise to those that wait upon him, "they shall walk and not faint." They will not lose courage, become weak, or be lacking in strength or vigor. <u>Faint</u> is a feeling of a mental and oppressive state; a lack of courage. Note the word usage for the word <u>wait</u>: it is not alluding to physical strength or weakness. It is stated to give a clear thought that patience does not attack or affect a person's physical strength. *"For the vision is yet for an appointed time, but at the end it shall speak, and not lie: though it tarry, wait for it; because it will surely come, it will not tarry."* Habakkuk 2:3.

When Abraham saw the men, he made haste to invite them to visit with him. Abraham spoke this in terms of extending friendship to strangers. He had recognition of who the stranger was; he called him "My Lord." He desired this visitation from God; therefore he pleaded with the men to not pass from him. Earlier experiences with the Lord came by God's word spoken to Abraham; And by the vision, Abraham saw of his seed in a strange land. He was exercised in knowing the voice of God, and the vision of God. These experiences led Abraham in being able to recognize the presence of God. In his own eyes, Abraham saw the Lord; and when Abraham saw the three men, he ran to meet them. Abraham bowed to the ground, showing humbleness and his wiliness to service. *"And said, My <u>Lord, if now I have found favor in thy sight, pass not away, I pray thee, from thy servant.</u>"* Genesis 18:3. To experience a visitation from the Lord was like knowing the "One," *"Who satisfieth thy mouth with good things; so that thy youth is renewed like the eagles'."* Psalm 103:5

"IF" *I now have found favor in thy sight"* these words expressed the conditions of the covenant that were met thus far; now in exchange, pass not away. Recall, Abraham followed the command of the Lord to circumcise all the male children of his house. Obedience is rewarded with the favor of God. At this visitation, Abraham was given the time his son would be born. He was showing himself merciful to his guest: therefore he obtained mercy. Abraham was pure in heart: therefore he was blessed to see God.

Some people may question whether or not Abraham saw God. Some Theologians might say that this theophany appearance of God to man is believed to have been Christ. The argument would be that "no man has seen God." To understand the meaning of the word *appeared* may shine light on who Abraham entertained. Appeared in Hebrew is >**raah,** and **defined;** to see, (lit. or fig). Also appeared means to advise self, appear, approve, <u>behold</u>, <u>consider</u>, discern. This definition does not give any hint of an apparition or some ghostly figure. It seems difficult for the human mind of some people to comprehend God coming in the form of a man. But the Scripture said, "The word was made flesh" which is Jesus Christ; and he dwelled among men. God created all things; but with some men, they refuse to believe God can make himself known visibly also.

Moses wrote, "And the Lord appeared unto him." Earlier than with Moses, the Lord appeared unto Abraham. God is the author and finisher of our faith; and God made Abraham the father of faith. First faith had to become originated in the man that would produce the children of faith. Each event of Abraham's life was part of the way in which wisdom was establishing faith. Understanding the structural design of faith; it was defined in the very life of Abraham. In the process of salvation, God first established faith, then later the law came by Moses: Next followed the prophets, God's name being a memorial, the judgment of God and the horn of Salvation. Not necessarily in this order; but faith came before other pillars of wisdom were established.

"And the Lord Appeared unto him," Notice that Abraham was exercised in hearing the word of God. When the word is heard, the word reveals God; in other words the Lord appears. The location of God appearing was, "in the plains of Mamre." Spiritually, Mamre is a place of spiritual strength and vigor. Faith brought Abraham to this place in his life. His faith pleased God; and this gave him favor. The Appearing or presence of the Lord will happen for the believer who heareth and doeth the will of God. When the Lord appears, there appeareth **three**. *"For there are **three** that bear record in heaven, the **Father**, the **Word**, and the **Holy Ghost**: these three are one."* 1 John 5:7

Abraham saw the Lord at the tent door. Three bear record; **meaning,** in Greek, **martureo, defined**: *to be a witness*, i.e. to testify. Give [evidence]; bear record, having obtained a good or honest report. Give testimony, witness.

The Humility of Abraham: Virtues reflected in the character of Abraham were meekness, goodness and gentleness. These are portrayed in the manner of how Abraham hosted and befriended his guest. First, Abraham provided water for the Lord to wash his feet; and he provided a place for his rest. *"Let a little water, I pray you, be fetched, and wash your feet, and rest yourselves under the tree:" v. 4.* Travelling by foot was the main course of transporting self from place to place. With travel, sandals worn can cause the feet to become dusty; and water is needed to wash the feet. In ancient times it was essential and an obligatory expression of hospitality for the householder to offer water to his guest. This is a type and shadow of the priestly order; and finished work of Christ.

In the law, the high priest removed is shoes as he performed the duties in the tabernacle; he served barefoot in the temple. *"And the Lord spake unto Moses, saying, Thou shalt also make a laver of brass, and his foot also of brass, to wash withal: and thou shalt put it between the tabernacle of the congregation and the altar, and thou shalt put water therein. For Aaron and his sons shall wash their hands and their feet thereat: When they go into the tabernacle of the congregation, they shall wash with water, that they die not; for when they come to burn offering made by fire unto the Lord: So they shall wash their hands and their feet, that they die not: and it shall be a statue forever to them, even to him and to his seed throughout their generations."* Exodus 30:17-21

Reading the account about Moses pulling off his shoes, for the place he stood on was "holy ground." God called Moses to be a leader and a deliverer to his people, Israel. *"And Moses said, I will now turn aside, and see this great sight, why the bush is not burnt. And when the Lord saw that he turned aside to see, God called unto him out of the midst of the bush, and said, Moses, Moses. And he said, here am I. And he said draw not nigh hither: put off thy shoes from off thy feet, for the place where on thou standest is holy ground."* Exodus 3:3-5. God called Moses to be holy before the Lord. He was charged by God with a new direction or path to follow.

To remove the sandals or shoes signified that the priest must disrobe his former walk; by washing the feet. His walk was to be a holy walk. There was no need for wearing sandals in the temple: this alludes to men own doctrines, judgments and directions. It was God who appointed and ordained every vessel in the tabernacle for the service of the priesthood. With Abraham, he was already keeping the laws that Moses taught, contained in ordinances. He offered unto the Lord a clean offering; signified by the water. The washing of the Lord's feet foreshadowed the High Priest entering the tabernacle clean and holy. Therefore he entered the tabernacle of Abraham's dwelling with washed feet.

The shadow of Christ as Abraham's guest is revealed in the New Testament. *"Now of the things which we have spoken this is the sum: We have such a high priest, who is set on the right hand of the throne of the Majesty in the heavens; A minister of the sanctuary, and of the true tabernacle, which the Lord pitched, and not man."* Hebrews 8:1-2. The Lord visited Abraham in his (tent) tabernacle. As the Lord, who is the Great High Priest, also washed his feet and rested under the tree. Abraham honored the Lord by faith: he offered water for the Lord to wash his feet. Faith was ahead of the law given by Moses. The Law came four hundred years later that pertained to the ministry of the Levitical priesthood. *"For if that first covenant had been faultless, and then should no place have been sought for the second. For finding fault with them, he saith, Behold, the days come, saith the Lord, when I will make a new covenant with the house of Israel and with the house of Judah: Not according to the covenant that I made with their fathers in the day when I took them out of the land of Egypt; because they continued not in my covenant, and I regarded them not, saith the Lord. For this is the covenant that I will make with the house of Israel after those days, saith the Lord; I will put my laws into their mind, and write them in their hearts: and I will be to them a God, and they shall be to me a people."* Hebrews 8:7-10

Abraham kept the law of God in his heart; and this was why he could offer the Lord water and rest. God was pleased with his faith. Jesus taught about the washing of the feet. *"When Jesus knew that his hour was come that he should depart out of this world unto the Father, having loved his own which were in the world, he loved them unto the end." After that he poureth water into a basin, and began to wash the disciples' feet; And to wipe them with the towel wherewith he was girded. Then cometh he to Simon Peter: and Peter saith unto him, Lord, dost thou wash my feet? Jesus answered and said unto him,* Jesus said, *"What I do thou knowest not now; but thou shalt know hereafter."* John 13:5-7. The example Jesus showed the disciples was in preparation of them becoming ministers of Christ; they must serve as ministers with a clean walk. To walk clean is to walk in humility. An effective ministry and the acceptable services to God are to be humble. Peter's problem was pride; he thought to resist having his feet washed. Peter later learned what foot washing meant, as Jesus had said unto him. From Peter's on teaching after he became truly converted, he taught about the work of a minister: he said, *"Feed the flock of God which is among you, taking the oversight thereof, not by constraint, but willingly; not for filty lucre, but of a ready mind; Neither as being lords over God's heritage, but being examples to the flock. And when the chief Shepherd shall appear, ye shall receive a crown of glory that fadeth not away. Likewise, ye younger, submit yourselves unto the elder. Yea, all of you are subject one to another,* **and be clothed with humility:** *for God resiseth the proud, and give grace to the humble. Humble yourselves therefore under the mighty hand of God, that he may exalt you in due season."*1Peter 5:2-6. Peter learned that to effectively work and love God's people was to do it in humility.

Jesus is the only example to follow. He is name "God with us," *"made himself of no reputation, and took upon the form of a servant, and was made in the likeness of men. And being found in fashion as a man, <u>he humbled himself,</u> and became obedient unto death, even the death on the cross. Wherefore God also hath highly exalted him, and given him a name which is above every name: That at the name of Jesus every knee should bow, of things in heaven, and things in earth, and things under the earth: And that every tongue should confess that Jesus Christ is Lord, to the glory of God the Father."* Philippians 2:8-11

The example Jesus gave his disciples as to foot washing taught humility. The statement Abraham made, *"let a little water be fetched,"* has a message that resonated humility and honor. A little in amount was the measure of water needed to wash the feet. The feet are the members of the body. The feet may be thought of as less honorable; but they are necessary. They are the body's comely parts in which God has fashioned the body with. The feet are then given more abundant honor because they lack. The hospitality Abraham showed his guest by fetching water to wash the feet is the abundant honor he showed unto the Lord *"A man's pride shall bring him low: but honor shall uphold the humble."* Proverbs 29:23

Furthermore, using the word <u>fetched</u>, which is in past tense; it is therefore already done. Abraham spoke in prophetic terms, because Christ work had not yet being glorified by the Father. But, *"let a little water be fetched"* was the substance of his faith. The thing hoped for, and evidence of what had not yet came to pass. The Old Testament foreshadowed the work of Christ. The prophet Malachi prophesied about the work of Christ: *"Behold, I will send my messenger, and he shall prepare the way before me: and the Lord, whom ye seek, shall suddenly come to his temple, even the messenger of the covenant, whom ye delight in: behold, he shall come, saith the Lord of hosts. But who shall abide the day of his coming? And who shall stand when he appeareth? For he is like a refiner's fire, and like the fuller's soap: And he shall sit as a refiner and purifier of silver: and he shall purify the sons of Levi, and purge them as gold and silver, that they may offer the Lord and offering in righteousness."* Malachi 3:1-3. This passage of scripture stated, "the messenger of the covenant" This points to Abraham's guest. The Lord visited Abraham and gave him the covenant promise of a seed. Christ is the messenger of the covenant. Jesus once said to the people, *"Your father Abraham rejoiced to see my day: and he saw it, and was glad. "Verily, verily, I say unto you, before Abraham was, I am."* John 8:56-58. Christ humbled himself; and received honor and glory from the Father. When John the Baptist baptized Jesus, the heavens opened and the Holy Ghost descended in a bodily shape like a dove, and the voice from heaven said, *"Thou art my beloved Son: in thee I am well pleased."* Luke 3:22

The Rest of the Lord reveals Faith: *"and rest yourselves under the tree:"* Rest is to be without labor; for labor is to work. The rest of God is found under the tree; a foreshadowing that Christ completed all he was sent to do on earth. Now he sits on the right hand of the Father making intercession for man. Christ fulfilled the promise God made with Abraham. "And *I will make thee exceeding fruitful, and I will make nations of thee, and kings shall come out of thee. And I will establish my covenant between thee and thy seed after thee."* Genesis 17:6-7. In the New Testament, Paul wrote, *"Now to Abraham and his seed were the promises made. He saith not seeds, as of many; but as of one, and to <u>thy Seed, which is Christ</u>. And this I say, that the covenant that was confirmed before of God in Christ, the law, which was four hundred years after, cannot disannul, that it should make the promise of none effect."* Galatians 3:16-17. Christ suffered the death on the cross, and completed his work. *"Christ hath redeemed us from the curse of the law, being made a curse for us: for it is written, Cursed is every one that hangeth on a tree."* Galatians 3:13. Hanging on the tree [synonymous for the CROSS] a *symbol* of death. In the law it is written, *"And if a man have committed a sin worthy of death, and he be to be put to death, and thou hang him on a tree: His body shall not remain all night upon the tree, but thou shalt in any wise bury him that day; for he that is hanged is accused of God; that thy land be not defiled which the Lord thy God giveth thee for an inheritance."* Deuteronomy 21:22-23. The curse of the law carried the sentence of death for those that greatly offended in the law. Jesus became the curse for man that they would be redeemed by his blood which he shed. He redeemed man from under the law. *"Is the law then against the promises of God? God forbid: for if there had been a law given which could have given life, verily righteousness should have been by the law. But the Scripture hath concluded all under sin that <u>the promises by faith of Jesus Christ might be given to them that believe</u>. But before faith came, we were kept under the law, shut up unto the faith which should afterwards be revealed. Wherefore, the law was our schoolmaster to bring us unto Christ, that we might be justified by faith."* Galatians 3:21-24

The life of Abraham and his faith walk foreshadowed the faith that was revealed in the New Covenant. Abraham desired that the Lord rest under "the tree" and the Lord did so. Jesus entered into his rest by his death on the cross. *"When Jesus therefore had received the vinegar, he said,* **it is finished:** *and he bowed his head, and gave up the ghost."* John 19:30. The Lord rested under the tree: he ceased from his work because he finished what he was sent to do. The form of execution for the offenders was to be hung on a tree. Jesus fulfilled the shadow of Abraham's offer "to rest under the tree." His death caused a ceasing of his work on earth. It is finished as he spoke this on the cross; his words were proclaiming his rest.

Faith bringeth men to the rest of God. Now faith is revealed in the New Testament; man can enter into the rest of God by ceasing from his own labor. Faith stands on the hearing of the word of God: His voice must be attended to. The Day of the Lord is the Today if ye will hear his voice, harden not your hearts. *"For he that is entered into his rest, he also hath ceased from his own works, as God did from his. Let us labor therefore to enter into that rest, lest any man fall after the same example of unbelief."* Hebrews 4:10-11. The children of Israel erred in their hearts; they murmured and provoked the Lord in the wilderness. Israel's evil heart was the sin of unbelief and departing from the living God. They were a stiffnecked people; becoming hardened through the deceitfulness of sin.

The rest of God makes distinction between the person of faith and those of unbelief. God's rest is the Believer's assurance that his word is established and will come to pass. His rest grants trust, peace, confidence and a reliance on his word. The Believer walk by faith, expecting the reward promised. Patience must have her perfect work; and what is promised will fulfill. The true faith walk is not by sight; but a reliance on the word that leads. The faithful believes in God and that he will fulfill his word in due season.

With the children of Israel, many died in the wilderness because of their unbelief and inciting others to disobey also. The people rebelled: *"And the entire congregation lifted up their voice and cried; and the people wept all night. And all the children of Israel murmured against Moses and against Aaron: and the whole congregation said unto them, Would God that we had died in the land of Egypt! Or would God we had died in the wilderness."* Israel made complaints to Moses and Aaron concerning their wives and children becoming prey; and the fear of falling by the sword. Joshua and Caleb tried to plead with the children Israel, by reminding them that the land they went to search out was exceeding good land.

Joshua spoke as a man of faith, and said, *"If the Lord delight in us, then he will bring us into this land, and give it us; a land which floweth with milk and honey. ONLY rebel not ye against the Lord, neither fear the people of the land: for they are bread for us: their defense is departed from them, and the Lord is with us: fear them not..."* Numbers 14:1-2; 8-9 But the reactions of the children of Israel were calling out to stone Joshua and Caleb.

Words to rebellious Israel: *"And the Lord said unto Moses, How long will this people PROVOKE me? And how long will it be ere they believe me, for all the signs which I have showed among them?* Numbers 14:11. Moses pleaded for the children of Israel that God would not disinherit them; or kill all this people. Moses did not want the other nations to make light of the work of God. *"Now if thou shalt kill all this people as one man, then the nations which have heard the fame of thee will speak, saying, Because the Lord was not able to bring this people into the land which he sware unto them, therefore he hath slain them in the wilderness. And now I beseech thee, let the power of the Lord be great, according as thou hast spoken, saying, The Lord is longsuffering, and of great mercy, forgiving iniquity and transgression, and by no means clearing the guilty, visiting iniquity of the fathers upon the children unto the third and fourth generation. Pardon, I beseech thee, the iniquity of this people according unto the greatness of thy mercy, and as thou hast forgiven this people, from Egypt even until now."* Numbers 14:15-19. In the Book of Hebrews, notice Israel's murmuring, complaining, and unbelief moved God to wrath. *"For some, when they had heard, did provoke: howbeit not all that came out of Egypt by Moses,"* *"And to whom sware he that they should not enter into his rest, but to them that believed not?"* Hebrews 3:16-18 *"Let us therefore fear, lest a promise being left us of entering into his rest, any of you should seem to come short of it. For unto us was the gospel reached, as well as unto them: but the word preached did not profit them, not being mixed with faith in them that heard it. For we which have believed do enter into my rest: although the works were finished from the foundation of the world."* Hebrews 4:1-3. Men must believe that God is, and that God is a rewarder to them that diligently seek him. [Hebrews 11:6] *"There* *remaineth therefore a rest to the people of God. For he that is entered into his rest, he also hath ceased from his own works, as God did from his. Let us labor therefore to enter into that rest, lest any man fall after the same example of unbelief."* Vv. 9-11

The Lord rested under Abraham's tree; signifying that his work is done. God had given Abraham the covenant and the promises. First the word went forth from God. He spoke unto Abraham in the land of Ur. The word of the Lord came unto him in a vision after the slaughter of the kings. Next the covenant of circumcision was made with Abraham when he was ninety-nine years old. Shortly afterward, the Lord visited Abraham in the plains of Mamre.

"...A MORSEL of BREAD," After water was fetched to wash the feet, Abraham said, "And *I will fetch a morsel of bread,* "He offered food for the Lord to partake of at his tent. When Jesus walked on earth to do the will of God, he fulfilled all things that were written of him. The Lord visited Abraham's house, illustrating his salvation is come. In the New Testament, this sign was fulfilled. *"And Jesus entered and passed through Jericho. And behold, there was a man named Zacchaeus, which was the chief among the publicans, and he was rich. And he sought to see Jesus who he was; and could not for the press, because he was little of stature. And he ran before, and climbed up into a sycamore tree to see him: for he was to pass that way. And when Jesus came to the place, he looked up, and saw him, and said unto him, Zacchaeus, make haste, and come down; for today I must abide at thy house." And Jesus said unto him, this day is salvation come unto this house forsomuch as he also is a son of Abraham. For the Son of man is come to seek and to save that which was lost."* Luke 19:1-5; vv. 9-10

The magnitude of the seed of Abraham is counted as the stars of heaven; and the sand of the sea. God was establishing his word of promise in Abraham before the seed came forth. The faith of Abraham was shown in his hospitality to his guest. He made **communion** with the Lord. The word fetch, in the presence tense, is the activity of receiving, or seizing upon the blessing from the Lord. Therefore, he said, *"I will fetch a morsel of bread,"* meaning, he will go after bread. The Lord came to his house to bless him with the gospel. Before his son Isaac was begotten, Abraham's faith was his assurance of obtaining the promise.

When the Lord visited his house; honor, meekness and humility were shown the Lord. Next, Abraham demonstrated <u>communion</u> with the Lord by fetching a morsel of bread. The blessing that came to Abraham's house included Zacchaeus of the New Testament. Salvation was preordained long before Christ came to fulfill the covenant promise made with Abraham. *"Truly my soul waiteth upon God; from him cometh my salvation."* Psalm 62:1. *"How excellent is thy lovingkindness, O God! Therefore the children of men put their trust under the shadow of thy wings. They shall be abundantly satisfied with the fatness of thy house; and thou shalt make them drink of the river of thy pleasures.* (Psalm 37:22) *For such as be blessed of him shall inherit the earth;"* Psalm 36:7-10. And Jesus said, *"Blessed are the meek: for they shall inherit the earth."* Matthew 5:6

The previous scriptures inferred the blessings of Abraham because of his faith in God's word. From the time of Abraham to Moses, and even all the righteous men thereafter, put their trust "under the shadow of God's wings." SHADOW is a sign that the body is near: and the body is Christ. Signs and wonders were wrought by God for his people Israel; showing his protection and mercy over them. Moses spoke unto the children of Israel concerning God's love: *"Ye have seen what I did unto the Egyptians, and how I bare you on eagles' wings, and brought you unto myself."* Exodus 19:4. And in another place, Moses said, *"As an eagle stirreth up her nest, fluttereth over her young, spreadeth abroad her wings, taketh them, beareth them on her wings: So the Lord alone did lead him, and there was no strange god with him."* Deuteronomy 32:11-12

The guest that visited Abraham is like a visionary glimpse of salvation coming to Abraham's house. The apostle Paul taught that the covenant was confirmed before of God in Christ; which was four hundred years before the law came by Moses. {READ: Galatians 3:17} This scripture affirms that Christ was in Abraham's day; and he is the guest that visited Abraham in his tent.

Sarah Prepared Bread: To make Bread involves a time element; along with the knowledge of measures, ingredients and temperature. The baker must have all necessary items to make bread. For bread to be bread there is a mixing together of the ingredients. The simplest mix the baker will need is flour {wheat} oil, water and salt. The kneading of the dough must be skillfully done for the best results. All the ingredients of natural bread portray what the scripture speaks of as Christ. He is the Anointed One [oil], *"The Spirit of the Lord is upon me, because he hath anointed me to preach the gospel to the poor;"* Luke 4:18. Jesus referred to himself as the Savior: *"Ye are the salt of the earth; but if the salt have lost his savor wherewith shall it be salted?"* Matthew 5:13. *"For unto you is born this day in the city of David a Savior, which is Christ the Lord."* Luke 2:11

Jesus is the water of life; *"Jesus answered and said unto her, If thou knewest the gift of God, and who it is that saith to thee, Give me to drink; thou wouldest have asked of him, and he would have given thee living water." But whosoever drinketh of this water that I shall give him shall never thirst; but the water I shall give him shall be in him a well of water springing up into everlasting life.* John 4:10, 14. *"And Jesus said unto them, I am the bread of life: he that cometh to me shall never hunger; and he that believeth on me shall never thirst." "And Jesus said unto them, I am the bread of life: he that cometh to me shall never hunger; and he that believeth on me shall never thirst."* John 6:35. Jesus referred to himself as "a corn of wheat" in a figure of speech. The grain is the main ingredient used in the making of bread. First the corn grain is grinded into fine flour. Christ is the SEED {grain of corn}, the word of life. He planted himself in the earth. Men must allow His word to be planted in their hearts. Without seed, there will be no plant life, animal life or human life. *"In the beginning was the Word, and the Word was with*

God, and the Word was God. The same was in the beginning with God. All things were made by him; and without him was not anything made that was made." John 1:1-3

"And *Abraham hastened into the tent unto Sarah, and said, Make ready quickly three measures of fine meal, knead it, and make cakes upon the hearth."* Genesis 18:6. There are four specifics that detail the process Sarah followed making bread. First, Sarah was to make ready quickly: Usually when bread that is not allowed to sit, also will not have time to become leavened. Therefore unleavened bread is the quality of the bread that was made by Sarah for Abraham's guest. The spiritual type points to Jesus; he ate the last supper with his disciples. The preparations for the Passover were by the disciple; it was done quickly. Read: Matthew 26:17-25. The time was at hand for Christ to eat the Passover and there was no delay. Read: Mark 14:12-21; 1 Like 22:7-14 With Moses, the children of Israel were given this commandment, *"And ye shall let nothing of it remain until the morning; and that which remaineth of it until the morning ye shall burn with fire. And thus shall ye eat it; with your loins girded, your shoes on your feet, and your staff in your hand; and ye shall eat it in haste: it is the Lord's Passover."* Exodus **12:9**-10. The Lord visited Abraham's house, and bread was prepared in haste. The bread was not allowed to become leavened.

Centuries later after Moses, "the Feast of Unleavened Bread" continued to be practiced. The Israelites were to tell their children after them about the sacrifice of the Lord's Passover. It was because the Lord passed over their houses and smote the Egyptians; but delivered Israel. As the shadow of the things God prepared for man's salvation; Abraham was literally expressing them in his faith walk. Faith is the substance of the thing {salvation} God desire to make known. With Abraham, the wisdom of God was establishing man's salvation and redemption to come. God's covenant was made with Abraham; and in this scripture, we see a glimpse of wisdom fashioning the things of God. It is God's ordaining for men to partake of the Bread of Life: for his bread is unleavened.

UNLEAVENED BREAD

The Hebrew word **matstsah, is (**from the word *matsats; a prime root; to suck, milk.*) Unleavened is defined >> in the sense of greedily devouring for sweetness; sweet: {I.e. not soured or bittered with yeast} an *unfermented cake or loaf, [eaten at Passover]* without leaven.

The night of the Passover in Egypt, the children of Israel were instructed by Moses to eat unleavened bread. They were to eat unleavened bread for seven days; the person that ate leaven bread would be cut off from Israel. This feast of unleavened bread was to commemorate Israel's deliverance from Egypt. *"Ye shall eat nothing leavened: and ye shall ye shall eat leavened bread. And ye shall observe this thing for an ordinance to thee and to thy sons forever. And it shall come to pass, when ye are come to the land which the Lord will give you, according as he hath promised, that ye shall keep this service. That ye shall say, it is the sacrifice of the Lord's Passover, who passes over the houses of the children of Israel in Egypt, when he smote the Egyptians, and delivered our houses. And the people bowed the head and worshipped."* Exodus 12:17-28

The ordinance of Passover was observed by the Jews in the time of Christ. The disciples of Jesus kept the Passover in his day. Jesus sent Peter and John to prepare the Passover that they may eat. The disciples said unto Jesus, *Where wilt thou that we prepare?* Jesus told the disciple to go into the city; they would meet a man carrying a pitcher of water. They were to follow him into the house where he entered. They said unto the Goodman of the house, *"The Master saith unto thee, where is the guest chamber, where I shall eat the Passover with my disciples? And he shall show you a large upper room furnished: there make ready. "And when the hour was come, he sat down, and the twelve apostles with him. And he said unto them, with desire I have desired to eat this Passover with you before I suffer. For I say unto you, I will not any more eat thereof, until it be fulfilled in the kingdom of God. "Luke 22:14-16. "As they were eating, Jesus took bread, and blessed it, and broke it, and gave it to the disciples, and said, Take, eat, this is my body. And* *he took the cup, and gave thanks, and gave it to them, saying, Drink ye all of it; <u>For this is my blood of the new testament</u>, which is shed for many for the remission of sins. But I say unto you, I will not drink henceforth of this fruit of the vine, until that day when I drink it new with you in my Father's kingdom."* Matthew 26:26-29

The prophet Jeremiah prophesied of the New Covenant, *"Behold, the days come, saith the Lord, that I will make a <u>new covenant</u> with the house of Israel and with the house of Judah: Not according to the covenant that I made with their fathers in the day that I took them by the hand to bring them out of the land of Egypt; which my covenant they broke, although I was a husband unto them saith the Lord. But this shall be the covenant that I will make with the house of Israel; After those days, saith the Lord <u>I will put my law in their inward parts, and write it in their hearts; and will be their God, and they shall be my people.</u>"* Jeremiah 31:31-33

Eating the Passover with the disciples signified Jesus' fulfilling the law and the prophets. Moses was given the law of Passover; the Lord commanded him to have the people prepare it. Now Jesus fulfilled this law. Read Exodus chapter twelve which further supports this truth that the law was fulfilled by Christ. By faith Moses kept the Passover; but the true Passover is Christ. In the New Testament, the apostle Paul said, *"Your glorying is not good. Know ye not that a little leaven leaveneth the whole lump? Purge out therefore the old leaven that ye may be a new lump, as ye are unleavened. For even Christ our Passover is sacrificed for us."* 1Corinthinas 5:6-8 The Passover feast was the partaking of unleavened bread and the slain lamb; the clean sacrifice. The command for keeping the Passover specified that the children of Israel eat it with unleavened bread. In the New Testament, Paul reveals the message concerning this sign when he said, *"<u>Therefore let us keep the feast, not with old leaven of malice and wickedness; but with the unleavened bread of sincerity and truth.</u>"* This should explain why the children of Israel were not to eat leavened bread. Eating leaven bread represented the nature of an insincere person; one who was unholy, and falsely worshipping God. The godly principle to learn is that men "must worship God in Spirit and in Truth, *"for the Father seeketh such to worship him."* John 4:23

The word <u>sincerity</u> means purity; *judged by sunlight.* It is clean being without mix or defilement. And the word <u>Truth</u> refers to the standard of God's word. Sincere worship is that of a righteous heart. Jesus is the way, the truth and the life: he is man's example of true worship. The Psalmist David sung a song of deliverance; *"He brought me up also out of a horrible pit, out of the miry clay, and set my feet upon a rock, and established my goings. And he put a new song in my mouth, even praise unto our God: many shall see it, and fear, and shall trust in the Lord,"* . . . *"Many, O Lord my God, are thy wonderful works which thou hast done, and thy thoughts which are to us-ward: they cannot be reckoned up in order unto thee: if I would declare and speak of them, they are more than can be numbered. Sacrifice and offering thou didst not desire; mine ears hast thou opened: burnt offering hast thou not required. Then said I, Lo, I come: in the volume of the book it is written of me. I delight to do thy will, O my God: yea, thy law is within my heart."* Psalm 40:2-8. To worship in Spirit and in Truth is the message Jesus illustrated and proclaimed. Jesus said, *"I am the Bread that came down from heaven,"* His bread is unleavened: for no guile or sin was in him. The man that partakes of his bread will live. Remember, Judas also partook of the Last supper; but Judas did it unworthily. This is the law Moses taught the children of Israel, *"For whosoever eateth that which is **leavened**, even that soul shall be cut off from the congregation of Israel, whether he be a stranger, or born in the land."* Exodus 12:19. After Judas betrayed Jesus, he later repented and brought the thirty pieces of silver back to the chief priest and elders. Judas said, *"I have sinned in that I have betrayed the innocent blood,"* And he cast down the pieces of silver in the temple, and departed, and went and hanged himself."* Matthew 27:4-5. Judas ate at the table with Jesus unworthily and his soul was cut off.

The specific order for Passover keeping commenced the first month, and tenth day of the month of the Jewish calendar. This feast day was the most important time of the year for the Jews. Passover was entered into the beginning of the Jewish year with the declaration of deliverance. Moses taught Israel teach their children and their children' children about God's redemption in Egypt. Today the first of the year is celebrated by most people; having arrived at a new beginning. Men seem to think that the New Year will bring deliverance from whatever bondage of life they are in. But the children of Israel were taught that it was a time to celebrate God for his deliverance: the end of bondage. Today, men festivities show mockery to the things of God. All sorts of evil practices are done the first of the New Year; in addition to many resolutions made by men. Their activities are filled with wickedness, illicit sexual conduct, drugs, intoxication and criminal behavior. Few people will make regard to celebrating a new year because they are delivered from the bondage of sin.

The Jewish New Year was entered into with the partaking of unleavened bread for seven days. The children of Israel prepared bread that had no leaven; in other words, no falsehood and sin. Bread is life for the natural man to live by. The Manna or word of life which came down from heaven, giveth life to those that obey the word of God. Truly, Israel was given life outside of Egypt. In their deliverance, the death angel passed over their houses. Only those in Egypt who had not the blood upon their door posts died. The Exodus happened and God sustained Israel forty years in the wilderness after coming out of Egypt.

Therefore, the ordinance of Passover was instituted by Moses as the Lord had commanded him. This ordinance signified or represented partaking of the word of life; the unadulterated truth. The sacrifices of men must be a holy offering unto the Lord. No defilement or mixing of the offering. The offering God accepts must be holy and clean. The Passover ordinance commanded for unleavened bread, to be pure and unmixed. God's word is holy and it is truth. As a spiritual type, the children of Israel's salvation and deliverance from sin came through Jesus Christ. The message of salvation is followed with receiving life and good. God has given us his provision for salvation in His the word. It is the good news Jesus proclaimed; which is the kingdom of God at hand. The kingdom of God is governed by the Holy Spirit; it will guide, reprove and judge the world of sin. The work of the Spirit leads in the path of righteousness through the hearing and doing of the word of God.

The way in which God dealt with the children of Israel is a history lesson for the church today. The events in Israel's life are examples or patterns for us today to follow and or not to follow. Many times God spoke to the forefathers; and now hath in these last days spoken unto us through his son Jesus Christ. The experiences Israel underwent served as a precedent and the model men can learn from. When God spoke to Israel, they had a choice to obey His commands. In doing so, Israel avoided the punishment that would have been inflicted on them if not disobeyed. Israel's obedience to God's commandments was the model God desired to illustrate throughout history.

The apostle Paul taught the Corinthian church concerning the partaking of the bread by reminding the church the account of the last supper. *"For I have received of the Lord that which also I delivered unto you, That the Lord Jesus the same night in which he was betrayed took bread: And when he had given thanks, he broke it and said, Take, eat: this is my body, which is broken for you: this do in remembrance of me. After the same manner also he took the cup, when he supped, saying, this cup is the new testament in my blood: this do ye, as oft as ye drink it, in remembrance of me. For as often as ye eat this bread, and drink this cup, ye do show the Lord's death till he come. Wherefore whosoever shall eat this bread, and drink this cup of the Lord unworthily, shall be guilty of the body and blood of the lord. But let a man examine himself, and so let him eat of that bread, and drink of that cup.* Paul said, *"For he that eateth and drinketh unworthily, eateth and drinketh damnation to himself, not discerning the Lord's body."* 1 Corinthians 11:24-29

Many church congregations today practice this sacrament in the form of worship. And many have no understanding to the spiritual implications for this form of worship. Men might practice this ordinance and yet be damned or cut off as the law stated. Moses said to the children of Israel; *"For the Lord will pass through to smite the Egyptians; and when he seeth the blood upon the lintel, and the two side posts, the Lord will **pass over** the door, and will not suffer the destroyer to come in unto your houses to smite you. And ye shall observe this thing for an ordinance to thee and to thy sons forever."* Exodus 12:23-23

Regarding the Lord's body, a person must understand that it is through his redemptive work men are saved. He is the Lamb of God slain. His bloodshed is the reason why death has no power over him. *"For the wages of sin is death, but the gift of God is eternal life through Jesus Christ our Lord."* Romans 6:23

The children of Israel were given life because the blood of the lamb upon the door posts of their houses in Egypt. Although Israel lived under the old covenant, Jesus expounded on the partaking of the word that bringeth life. Jesus taught concerning the leaven bread, that men may know what they should partake of. The leaven bread was not acceptable in the day of Israel's Passover. Leaven bread is not the acceptable form of worshipping God today. Israel was warned to not eat leaven bread in the commemoration of their deliverance from Egypt.

Jesus taught his disciples to be aware of the leaven of the Pharisees. *"Then Jesus said unto them, <u>Take heed and beware of the **leaven** of the Pharisees and of the Sadducees</u>. And they reasoned among themselves, saying, it is because we have taken no bread. Which when Jesus perceived, he said unto them, O ye of little faith, why reason ye among yourselves, because ye have brought no bread? Do ye not yet understand, neither remembers the five loaves of the five thousand, and how many baskets ye took up? Neither the seven loaves of the four thousand, nor how many baskets ye took up? How is it that ye do not understand that I spake it* *not to you concerning bread, that ye should beware of the leaven of the Pharisees and the Sadducees. Then understood they how that he bade them not beware of the leaven of bread, but of the doctrine of the Pharisees and of the Sadducees."* Matthew 16:5-12

From the practices of the Pharisees and the Sadducees, Jesus showed the disciples by example leaven bread. Therefore he was teaching that salvation is not gained by the doctrines of men. Israel's deliverance came by obedience to the word of God; which is the model every man can follow. The disciples were puzzled by this warning to them; therefore Jesus rebuked the disciples by saying, *"O ye of little faith,"* Having "little faith." The disciples had not yet understood the bread Jesus provided in feeding the five thousand was of a divine work. They were seeing by sight; which is not faith because human logic was trying to judge the matter. Their spiritual understanding at the time was darkened by natural sight. The disciples knew that twelve basket of the fragments were taken up; more than the five loaves originally given. With increase, there is also a life source from which the increase comes. The fragments of food that remained were the increase of the food. In the scriptures, Jesus told the disciples that he is the Bread of Life that came down from heaven. *"Verily, verily, I say unto you, Moses gave you not that bread from heaven; but my Father giveth you the true bread from heaven. For the bread of God is he which cometh down from heaven, and giveth life unto the world. Then said they unto him, Lord, evermore give us this bread. And Jesus said unto them, I am the bread of life: he that cometh to me shall never hunger; and he that believeth on me shall never thirst."* John 6:32-35

If men partake of this bread they will live forever. The manna Moses and the children of Israel partook of in the wilderness was not eternal life. The manna in the wilderness lasted forty years; and those who partook of it are all dead. The natural bread only could sustain the natural life in man for a period of time. The Bread of Life gives life to those that partake of it. Jesus teaching was to show that to partake of the leaven bread, or false doctrines of men, will not produce spiritual life.

Clearly, leaven bread or the doctrines of men are not the bread from heaven. Men might mix and alter the teachings of Christ to persuade others to follow their doctrines. There are many church leaders practicing the very thing Jesus taught his followers to beware of. All kinds of false teachings have entered the place of worship. God is not pleased with false religion. The church of today has become weak; waxen cold of loving one another; and going after the vanity that is in the world. These practices do not show forth the character of Christ or the gospel Jesus taught. Paul said "don't be unequally yoked together with unbelievers. Therefore, be no more *"Ye of little faith"* But be hearers and doers of the word, and abide in life.

In the scriptures, Jesus said, *"Beware, ye of the leaven of the Pharisees, which is hypocrisy. For there is nothing covered, that shall not be revealed, neither hid, that shall not be known. Therefore, whatsoever ye have spoken in darkness shall be heard in the light: and that which ye have spoken in the ear in closets shall be proclaimed upon the housetops."* Luke **12:1-3**. The Pharisees portrayed false worship and religion. The Greek word **hupokrisis** is the word hypocrisy: defined as *acting under a feigned part*, i.e. *deceit*– condemnation, dissimulation. Clearly the church is to beware of hypocrisy; deceitful doctrines and practices that are false worship. Hypocrisy exists today in the midst of some congregational churches. Excuses are made or having a deaf ear to turn away the truth. Rather, they give heed to the things that are falsely worshipped. But Jesus said to the disciples to be aware of the leaven of the hypocrites. Some may become defensive and say, we don't suppose to judge, or that nobody is perfect. Paul said, *"For the wrath of God is revealed from heaven against all ungodliness and unrighteousness of men, who hold the truth in unrighteousness."* Romans 1:18

Jesus word of TRUTH is the unleavened bread. Sarah made ready for Abraham's guest unleavened bread. The Lord visited his house and supped with him. The Lord ate of unleavened bread as a guest at Abraham's house. Communion with God is to worship Him in Spirit and in Truth: this was portrayed with Abraham. Several times it is mentioned in the Bible, Abraham made an altar: and he bowed down to worship God. Faith establishes the course of true worship. The father of faith demonstrated the course of true worship. The word of God said, *"Faith cometh by hearing, and hearing by the word of God."* Romans 10:17. Abraham heard the voice of God and he bowed down and worshipped God.

The children of Israel were Abraham's seed, and they adhered to the first Passover. They followed the command God gave unto Moses. This marked the beginning of Israel's true worship by God standards. Prior to the birth of Israel, God said unto Abraham, *"And also that nation, whom they shall serve, I will judge: and afterward shall they come out with great substance."* Genesis 15:14. The children of Israel, were under servitude of the Pharaohs until God sent them a Deliverer. The Passover feast was kept the night of their deliverance. Egypt was called the house of bondage; but spiritual bondage is sin. The children of Israel lives were made an example to the world. They were chosen by God to show forth His name in all the earth. God wrought great wonders in Egypt; but Pharaoh's heart was hardened until the death of all the first born in Egypt happened. The false beliefs of the Egyptians and their many gods were brought to judgment by the plagues God sent into the land. If the children of Israel had refused the Passover, they would have been destroyed as well. But a great multitude of people came out of Egypt because they obeyed the word of God that was spoken by Moses.

The wisdom of God was establishing the pillar of faith in Abraham. It would come the time when men will learn true worship. Unleavened bread is one of the doctrines of faith to learn. Man must worship God in Spirit and in Truth. As a spiritual type, Abraham instructed Sarah to make unleavened bread; this illustrated a true worshipper of God. Remember, Jesus said to the Pharisees in his day that Abraham rejoiced to see his day and he did. The Lord was Abraham's guest who came and supped with him that day. At a later time Lot offered his guest unleavened bread. But with Abraham, this is the first time recorded in the Old Testament concerning unleavened bread. His nephew Lot apparently learned about unleavened bread from Abraham's teaching. The same messengers that were at Abram's tent visited Lot also. *"And there came two angels to Sodom at even; and Lot sat in the gate of Sodom: and Lot seeing them rose up to meet them; and he bowed himself with his face toward the ground; And he said, Behold now, my lords, turn in, I pray you, into your servant's house, and tarry all night, and wash your feet, and ye shall rise up early, and go on your ways, And they said, Nay; but we will abide in the street all night. And he pressed upon them greatly; and they turned in unto him, and entered into his house; and he made them a feast, and did bake **unleavened bread**, and they did eat."* Genesis 19:1-3. Abraham was a man of faith; those of his household learned the course of true worship.

The believer's faith walk is to worship God in Spirit and in Truth. It may be called communion and illustrated as partaking of a morsel of bread; our "Daily Bread" Each day men only will eat a portion of bread. A loaf of bread would have the need to be stored. We know that natural bread will spoil if left over for a period of time. Fresh bread will sustain a person's health; but old bread that is spoiled by mold, causes illness if eaten. Therefore, the Lord will give us daily bread; it is fresh and nourishing to the body. *"Beloved, I wish above all things that thou mayest prosper and be in health, even as thy soul prospereth."* 3John (v) 2. In the Lord's Prayer, Jesus said, *"Give us day by day our daily bread."* Luke 11:3

Three measures of fine meal: *"And Abraham hastened into the tent unto Sarah, and said, Make ready quickly three measures of fine meal, knead it, and make cakes upon the hearth."* **Genesis 18:6** Abraham's instruction to Sarah detailed the fashion, the quality and the work given to the bread. He understood the process of making bread. First the amount was numbered as three measures. This revealed what Abraham had determined to be given to his guest. "Three measures" implied equality or that which is just without partiality. The bread would take on the same form, likeness, and taste quality; having undergone the same work to make it so: *"knead it."* The process that made fine meal was the milling of the grain. This was done by grinding the grain with flat stones; called millstones. Grain in its first form is the seed not broken for consumption. It must be broken and made digestible for it to make edible bread.

Four centuries after Abraham, the practice of bread making was the process the children of Israel used. They were sustained by eating the Manna God provided them in the wilderness. There was the time when the children of Israel murmured and said, *"But our soul is dried away: there is nothing at all, beside this manna, before our eyes.* ***And the manna was as <u>coriander seed,</u>*** *and the color thereof as the color of bdellium. And the people went about, and gathered it, and <u>ground it in mills or beat it in a mortar,</u> and baked it in pans, and made cakes of it: and the taste of it was as the taste of fresh oil."* Numbers 11: 6-8

Moses commanded the children of Israel to gather manna for six days; and on the sixth day they were to double that amount. Their lives sustained by the manna they gathered, and prepared. The manna was eaten as their 'daily bread" to them. Six days of gathering the Manna is a shadow of the six thousand years of man's history; sustained by bread. But the seventh day is the day man will sup with Christ in the kingdom. Jesus said to his disciples, *"With desire I have desired to eat this Passover with you before I suffer: for I say unto you, I will not any more eat thereof, until if be fulfilled in the kingdom of God."* Luke 22:15, 16. From the time of Adam, humans always eat from what is grown out of the earth to live. Over six thousand years men continue to eat to live. On the horizon is the seventh day that awaits the consummation of all things. This day is called the rest of God, which is the Sabbath. *"For the spake in a certain place of the seventh day on this wise And God did rest the seventh day from all his works. 'Again, he limited a certain day, saying in David, today, after so long a time; as it is said, and today if ye will hear his voice, harden not your hearts. For if Jesus had given them rest, and then would he not afterward have spoken of another day. There remaineth therefore a rest for the people of God."* Hebrews 4:4-9. Also read: Psalm 95:6-11; Psalm 79:13; Psalm 80:1-3; Today is the limited time for men to hear his voice and obey. From Christ's first advent until his return is the certain day limited. After a limited certain day, then another day, which is the seventh day, is the rest for the people of God.

Some theologians teach that this is mistranslated, "For if Jesus had given them rest," They say, it should be written, "For if Joshua had given them rest." Whether it is missed translated or not, the rest for the people of God yet remain to enter into the rest. As for Joshua, the children of Israel were led by him into the Promised Land. He had a charge to keep from the Lord after the death of Moses. *"...the Lord spake unto Joshua the son of Nun, Moses' minister, saying, Moses my servant is dead; now therefore arise, go over this Jordan, thou, and all this people, onto the land which I do give them, even the children of Israel. Every place that the sole of your foot shall tread upon, that has given unto you, as I said unto Moses." There shall not any man is able to stand before thee all the days of thy life: as I was with Moses, so I will be with thee: I will not fail thee, nor forsake thee. Be strong and of a good courage: for unto this people shalt thou divide for an inheritance the land, which I sware unto their fathers to give them. Only be strong and very courageous, that thou mayest observe to do according to all the law, which Moses my servant commanded thee: turn not from it to the right hand of to the left, that thou mayest prosper whithersoever thou goest. This book of the law shall not depart out of thy mouth; but thou shalt meditate therein day and night, that thou mayest observe to do according to all that is written therein: for then thou shalt make thy way prosperous, and thou shalt have good success. Have not I commanded thee? Be strong and of a good courage; be not afraid, neither be thou dismayed: for the Lord thy God is with thee whithersoever thou goest."* Joshua 1: 1-**9**

As a minister, Joshua was the commander who led military battles against the Amorites and other Canaanite people of the land. When

God spoke to Moses concerning his death; Moses prayed unto the Lord to set a leader over the children of Israel after him. *"Let the Lord, the God of the spirits of all flesh, set a man over the congregation, Which may go out before them, and which may go in before them, and which may bring them in; that the congregation of the Lord be not as sheep which have no shepherd. . . take thee Joshua, . . a man in whom is the spirit, and lay thine hand upon him; And set him before Eleazar the priest, and before all the congregation; and give him a charge in their sight."* Numbers 27:15-19

The things concerning Joshua are pointed out to show that he was called of God. As a servant of God, he was commissioned to lead, to survey and divide to Israel the land of promise. But in his leadership, the REST for Israel was not fulfilled: Joshua directed them to look for 'another day.' The scripture says, *"If Jesus had given them rest, then would he not afterward have spoken of another day."* Israel did not enter into the rest of God because of their unbelief. Their unbelief was that they tempted God; erring in their hearts after having known his works and his ways. One thing theologians and the people can agree on, and that is, Joshua is a type of Christ. His ministry illustrated the government of God upon the shoulder of Jesus. Upon Christ, the kingdom of God is established with judgment and justice; to bring in much people to God. But we see that Israel wasn't given rest in Joshua' day because the Rest of God would come after the work of Christ.

Also *"no rest given"* can be understood with the crossing over the River of Jordan. Twelve stones were taken out of the Jordan; Joshua pitched the stones in Gilgal, or made a memorial there. *"And he spake unto the children of Israel, saying, When your children shall ask their fathers in time to come, saying, what mean these stones? Then shall let your children know, saying, Israel came over this Jordan on dry land. For the Lord dried up the waters of Jordan from before you, until ye were passed over, as the Lord your God did to the Red Sea, which he dried up from before us, until we were gone over."* Joshua 4:20-23 The stones were set as a memorial. Past experiences that are remembered and a statue erected in a certain place is noted as a memorial. The reason for a memorial is to commemorate a certain event that happened. The memorial is a way of passing on historical accounts; often something which ended before a completion. The stones Joshua placed at Gilgal were a memorial forever. It stood as a sign to the people that "**another day**" points to the rest of God. The scripture said, "Having *spoken of another day.*" If it had been Israel's time for rest, then Joshua would not have commanded the people to tell future generations about the mighty works of God. The children of the people were told about the crossing over of Jordan; alluding to another day, or another time. This indicated that Joshua had not given them rest in that place. The sign of not having found a place of rest; is why Israel passed the knowing of their experience on to their children and children's children.

The River of Jordan signified the Holy Spirit coming down: which is a spiritual baptism man experiences today. With Moses, the children of Israel experienced an <u>Exemption</u> from death because the blood was applied upon the lintel and side posts of their houses. With Joshua, the people experienced <u>Transition,</u> because they "passed over" Jordan. The blood of Christ cancelled out the death penalty: exemption from death. By the Holy Spirit men will experience transition into the kingdom of God. In crossing Jordan, the Ark of the Covenant was carried in ahead of the people by the priests. The Ark of the Covenant was associated with the presence of God. *"And they commanded the people, saying, When ye see the ark of the covenant of the Lord your God, and the priests the Levites bearing it, then ye shall remove from your place, and go after it. Yet there shall be a space between you and it, about two thousand cubits by measure: come not near unto it that ye may know the way by which ye must go: for ye have not passed this way heretofore."* Joshua 3:3-4

Jesus is the Ark of the Covenant. He went the 2000-cubits, or Sabbath Day journey ahead of the church. The Jewish people practiced travelling one-half mile on the Sabbath; noted as a Sabbath Day journey. The things that transpired with Joshua and the children of Israel are fulfilled with Christ. Before Jesus ate the Passover with the disciples, Jesus went to pray, *"And he came out, and went, as he was wont, to the Mount of Olives; and his disciples also followed him. And when he was at the place, he said unto them, pray that ye enter not into temptation. And he was withdrawn from them about a stone's cast, and kneeled down, and prayed, Saying, Father, if thou be willing, remove this cup from me: nevertheless not my will, but thine be done."* Luke 22:41-43. At the time of Jesus ascension, Jesus *"Led them out as far as Bethany and he lifted up his hands, and blessed them. And it came to pass, while he blessed them, he was parted from them, and carried up into heaven."* Luke 24:50-52 The prayer of Jesus is mentioned to point out his location at that time: the place was Mt. Olives. This mount is a Sabbath day journey from Jerusalem; about 2000 cubits in distance. Recall, Joshua was to space the Ark of the Covenant 2000 cubits from the people. Jesus ascended back to heaven; therefore he's gone ahead of the people that will come after him. The space between the Ark of the Covenant and the people has a time factor. The time being the two days Jesus spoke of that the kingdom of heaven rules during the church age. The Holy Ghost, or Comforter was sent back to lead men into all truth. The 'other day' is the eternal rest for the people of God, when Jesus returns to set up his kingdom rule in the earth. Referring back to Abraham offering the Lord rested form his journey, typified the Lord will complete his work. Learning from this, we see Abraham's faith introduces to men the rest of God: the Lord's Sabbath. Jesus finished his work that he was sent to accomplish for salvation.

Jesus first advent was the Day of Atonement as prophesied in the Book of Isaiah; but he also spoke concerning the seventh day. Jesus came in the fourth millennial day from Adam. He spoke in his first advent, *"And he said unto them, Go ye, and tell that fox, Behold, I cast out devils, and I do cures today and tomorrow, and the third day I shall be perfected. Nevertheless I must walk today, and tomorrow, and the day following: for is cannot be that a prophet perishes out of Jerusalem."* Luke **13:32**-33 Jesus was not speaking of a literal 24-hour day. But in this scripture, [today and tomorrow] equals the two thousand years of the rule of the "kingdom of heaven. The kingdom of heaven refers to the church ruling of Christ in the earth. The Holy Ghost was sent to guide, reprove and lead man upon the earth. Not yet the rule of the kingdom of God: [the third day] which is the eternal rule of Christ on earth as "King of kings and Lord of lords.' ↔Revelation 19:16. He ascended back to the Father after his resurrection and left his work to go on until his return. *"Forasmuch then as the children are partakers of flesh and blood, he also himself likewise took part of the same; that through death he might destroy him that had the power of death, that is the devil;" For verily he took not on the nature of angels; but he took on him the seed of Abraham. Wherefore in all things it behooved him to be made like unto his brethren, that he might be merciful and faithful high priest in things pertaining to God, to make reconciliation for the sins of the people."* Hebrews 2:16-18

Jesus is the Bread of Life, he *gave "three measures of meal"* that men may partake of to live. The Bread God has given to men is a "**measure of faith**." **A measure of his Grace** according to the measure of the gift of Christ." And God has given the Holy Spirit; so that men will come in the unity of the faith, and the knowledge of the Son of God, unto the **measure of the stature of the fullness of Christ**. Faith was established with Abraham. And because he was faithful; he was given "little space grace" (a measure of) the Grace of God. A portion of Bread is the promised seed; another measure God has given. Abraham's Seed is Christ: the grain of wheat which came forth as resurrected life. And because of his death, burial and resurrection, the seed brought forth much fruit; the salvation of many. Faith starts the process of the gradual transformation of men into the image of Christ. And grace is God's token of approval that faith obtained the undergone transformation. The identifying quality of faith is the character of Christ it reveals. Each of the three measures is justly equal to each other. Therefore faith is the measure in the processing of the bread. Grace is the measure of bread made known. And spiritual Life is the measure of Christ given when men partake of his bread.

The TENDER Calf: *And Abraham ran unto the herd, and fetches a calf tender and good, and gave it unto a young man: and he hasted to dress it."* Genesis 18:7. True communion with the Lord is null when it is without a sacrifice made by the shedding of blood. Worship has no real validity if there's no legal force to bind it. *"For when Moses had spoken every precept to all the people according to the law, he took the blood of calves and of goats, with water, and scarlet wool, and hyssop, and sprinkled both the book, and all the people, Saying, This is the blood of the testament which God hath enjoined unto you. Moreover he sprinkled with blood both the tabernacle, and all the vessels of the ministry. And almost all things are by the law purged with blood; and without shedding of blood is no remission."* Hebrews 9:19-22. Christ, the promised seed of Abraham offered himself. Jesus said, *"For this is my blood of the new testament, which is shed for many for the remission of sins."* Matthew 26:28. A Testator's will is legally enforced by death.

The "tender calf" depicts a young calf: Tender because it is easy to chew or be broken. The "tender calf" nature is delicate, mild, gentle and kind. Inclined to submit or heed to the power of the other. Faith seeks for the nature of Christ to partake of. Abraham demonstrated faith through being a host to his guest. God covenant promise unto Abraham is the word Abraham believed in; which was the reason for his actions. His seed was not yet born at the time: because there must be the shedding of blood first. The meal Abraham prepared showed forth the thing hoped for; as evidence of the redemption-seed not yet revealed.

When the time came for the children of Israel's deliverance out of Egypt; God gave Moses command for Israel concerning the blood sacrifice. *"Your lamb shall be without blemish, a male of the first year: ye shall take it out from the sheep, or the goats: (v.7) and they shall take the blood, and strike it on the two side posts and on the upper door post of the houses, wherein they shall eat it."* Exodus 12: 5, 7

291

The father of faith; the forefather of the children of Israel exemplified the Passover. Abraham performed the righteousness of God long before the law was given by Moses. This stands out as a reason why God accounted Abraham's faith as righteousness. Paul said, *"He therefore that ministereth to you the Spirit, and worketh miracles among you, doeth he it by the works of the law, or by the hearing of faith? Even Abraham believed God, and it was accounted to him for righteousness."* Galatians 3:6, 7. Abraham offered the Lord water, unleavened bread, and next offered was the "tender calf." The tender calf is a type of Christ. John the Baptist called him *"the Lamb of God, which taketh away the sin of the world."* John 1:29. John was the messenger sent as the forerunner of Christ; heralding and preaching the kingdom of God was at hand. John witnessed the Spirit descending from heaven upon the Lord like a dove which sat upon Christ. God said to John, *"Upon whom thou shalt see the Spirit descending, and remaining on him, the same is he which baptizeth with the Holy Ghost. And I saw, and bare record that this is the Son of God."* John 1:33-34

The Holy Spirit coming down, was symbolized as the River of Jordan in Joshua's day; the Ark of the Covenant resting in the Jordan. The Holy Ghost descended and rested upon Chris when he was baptized of John. When God spoke unto Joshua, *"... Joshua set up twelve stones in the midst of Jordan, in the place where the feet of the priests which bare the Ark of the Covenant stood: and they are there unto this day."* **Joshua 4:9** The Spirit of God remained upon Christ; fulfilling the type when Joshua set the stones as a memorial after crossing Jordan. Why did it remain? First, Christ had to fulfill all the righteousness of God. To be right covers legal activities. Jesus shall baptize with the Holy Ghost, therefore, Christ the High Priest feet must stand in the Jordan. John the Baptist said," *I indeed baptize you with water unto repentance: but he that cometh after me is mightier than I, whose shoes I am not worthy to bear: he shall baptize you with the Holy Ghost, and with fire: "Then cometh Jesus from Galilee to Jordan unto John, to be baptized of him. But John forbade him, saying, I have need to be baptized of thee, and comest thou unto me? And Jesus answering said unto him, suffer it to be so now: for thus* *it becometh us to fulfill all righteousness.*" Matthew 3:11-14. Because Christ is Shiloh; the place God put his name. The stones remaining signified that wisdom established a memorial; the place God established his name in. The Name of God as a memorial is another pillar wisdom established in the building of God's house.

Moses taught the people, saying, *"For ye are not yet come to the rest and to the inheritance, which the Lord your God giveth you. But when ye go over Jordan, and dwell in the land which the Lord your God giveth you rest from all your enemies around about, so that ye dwell in safety; Then there shall be a place the Lord your God shall choose to cause his name to dwell there;"* Deuteronomy 12: 9-11. And Jesus said, *"I receive not my honor from men. But I know you, that ye have not the love of God in you. I am come in my Father's name, and ye receive me not: if another shall come in his own name, him ye will receive . . . But if ye believe not his writings, how shall ye believe my words?* John 6:41-17**.** His name is the memorial: one of the pillars wisdom hewed out for God's House; the dwelling place for his name.

"And he hasted to DRESS IT:" After Abraham fetched a calf "tender and good," he placed it in the hands of a young man. The charge to keep was to prepare the meat; he performed a service for his master. His youth portrayed him as physically and skillfully able to be trusted with the task. The word **"dress"** carries another spiritual type which speaks of Christ. The word has a broad sense and wide use of applications. In Hebrew DRESS is **asah;** a prime. root; to do or make—*to accomplish, advance, appoint, become, bear, bestow, bring forth, bruise, have the charge, commit, execute, fashion, finish, fulfill, furnish, gather, get, grant, govern, journey, keep, labour, occupied, offer, observe, bring, perform, prepare, provide, requite, sacrifice, serve, set, shew, work, yield.* The underlined words are to direct the attention of "beholding the Son of God" who came to do the will of the Father. Jesus ministry is the underlined words describing his work and much more. The words were also spoken by the prophets; proclaiming his work was fore-ordained. These words were inscribed in the Laws of

Moses; therefore his work foreshadowed in the ordinances of the law. In history, the men of God made known and witnessed his work; demonstrating the power of God. And in the wisdom books of the Bible, the work of Christ is the declaration of his truth, love and mercy.

Dress IT:" is the act of preparing, so that presentation of the sacrifice can be given. With any meal, the food must be prepared first. *"For he established a testimony in Jacob, and appointed a law in Israel, which he commanded our fathers that they should make them known to their children."* Psalm 78:5 Generations later the law of Passover was kept by Jesus and the disciples. This law was passed on to the children children's of Israel. In the New Testament, *"Then came the day of unleavened bread, when the Passover must be killed. And he sent Peter and John, saying, Go and prepare us the Passover that we may eat. And they said unto him, where wilt thou that we prepare?"* Luke 22:8- 9. Jesus came to fulfill the law and the prophets; not to do away with. Jesus said unto the disciples, *"For I say unto you, that this that is written must yet be accomplished in me, and he was reckoned among the transgressors."* In the Book of Isaiah, it is written, *"Yet it pleased the Lord to bruise him: he hath put on him a grief: when thou shalt make his soul an offering for sin, he shall see his seed, and he shall prolong his days, and the pleasure of the Lord shall prosper in his hand. He shall see the travail of his soul, and be satisfied: by his knowledge shall my righteous servant justify many; for he shall bear their iniquities. Therefore will I divide him a portion with the great, and he shall divide the spoil with the strong; because he hath poured out his soul unto death: and he was numbered with the transgressors; and he bare the sin of many, and made intercession for the transgressors."* **Isaiah 53:10-12.** Abraham's calf "tender and good" represented or symbolized the Lord; he was appointed, prepared and he accomplished his work.

READ the following scriptures to build on the knowledge of Christ's Work: Genesis 3:15; Jeremiah 23:5; Daniel 12:7; John 17:4; Proverbs 9:1; Matthew 22:10; Mark 14:15; Luke 22:12; Deuteronomy 30:3-4; Nehemiah 1:9; Psalm

50:5; 106:47; Isaiah 11:12; 40:11; 54:7; 56:8; Jeremiah 23:3; 29:14; 31:10; Ezekiel 20:41; 36:23-31;

Psalm 67:1-4; Ezekiel 37; 14

The GOOD Calf: Not only did Abraham specify "tender" which is the nature of the calf, he also said *"and good."* Good is a qualifying state of being righteous. To be righteous by definition is; *acting in accord with divine or moral law: free from guilt: morally right or justifiable.* Abraham was justified by his faith; therefore God accounted his faith as righteousness. He was acting out of the divine law of God concerning "the burnt offering." He followed the command of God to offer his son Isaac; which was the law given to him at the time.

Righteous and Good can be used synonymously to understand something about the nature of Christ. The fullness of the word of God through Jesus characterized Good by the radiance of his attributes. Everything God created in the beginning, God said "was good, and very good." In other words things, beautiful, best, better, bountiful, favoured, fine, glad, ease (as with liberty), gracious, joyful, kindness, living (life), merry, most pleasant, pleasing, pleasure, precious, prosperity, ready (wise or skilled), sweet (much loved or dear), and wealth (abundant; rich). These words identify the essence of Christ: his gift, his life and his work. Meditate on each of these words and see Christ in each of them. Jesus is esteemed as the beloved Son of God in whom God is well pleased. He is called the Righteous One, Good Master and the Good Shepherd. Jesus is the Word and the Word is Jesus, he is "The I Am."

There is no created thing void of the quality which God called or named it to be. That thing have become defiled or corrupted shows the nature of sin. God said in the beginning, "Let there be" and it was so. The story of creation started with the earth being without form, void and darkness upon the deep. God commanded by saying "let there be" then the earth received form [law], fullness [no more void] and Light [no darkness]. God instituted every law in the creation; in doing so, the earth was established to be inhabited. But any disobedience or breaking of his law causes damage, destruction and death.

The Lord is the *"tender and good* "calf who fits the requirements stated in the law of a burnt offering sacrifice. Moses came centuries later and was given these laws by God. The meal Abraham gave to his guest foreshadowed the law and the fulfillment of the law by Christ. Jesus came in the volume of the book it is written of him. In the Book of the Law written by Moses, is about Christ. The Good Calf was already predetermined by God to be the sacrifice. Man was in need of redemption from sin; and Christ was sent to fulfill the plan of God. From the beginning the word created all things GOOD; and the word of God through Christ will cause men the rebirth experience. That which became lame, bruised, poor and blind is restored: and men are reconciled to God through Jesus Christ. Instead of the wages of sin being death, God's Lamb gave his life, a ransom from the condemnation men were under. Jesus is the Good Shepherd, and the Lamb of God. He said, *"I am come that they might have life, and that they might have it more abundantly."* John 10:10

"He hasted to DRESS IT" For Abram's guest, a tender and good calf was fetched. Among the flock, the calf was selected. This calf symbolized Christ who is the Lamb of God, which taketh away the sins of the world. Abram lost no time in preparing the calf for the meal. He showed readiness, promptness and a wiliness to offer unto the Lord his fellowship.

FAITH makes Ready: Abram's readiness can be seen in that he "ran" to meet his guest. At the age of ninety-nine years old, his physical strength was good. The word of God in his heart made him mentally ready to entertain his guest. *"The slothful man roasteth not that which he took in hunting: but the substance of a diligent man is precious."* Proverbs 12:27. Walking in faith creates the readiness to serve the Lord. Abram was not inclined to be idle, lazy nor with an indolent attitude toward the strangers at his tent. A person who exhibits slothfulness has doubt, disbelief and restraints themselves of trusting. They are averse to activity, effort or movement; which tends towards treachery. A treacherous act is a violation of faith; this was not the attitude of Abram. In the parable of the "talents" Jesus said, *"Then he which had received the one talent came and said, Lord, I knew then that thou art an hard man, reaping where thou hast not sown, and gathering where thou hast not strewed..." His lord answered and said unto him, Thou wicked and slothful servant, thou knewest that I reap where I sowed not, and gather where I have not strewed."* Matthew 25:24. Jesus spoke this parable, teaching that a faithful and good servant is profitable to his Lord. The wicked servant was selfish, treacherous, and unfaithful in the things given unto him. He didn't trust in his lord; therefore he didn't serve his lord. *"For God is not unrighteous to forget your works and labor of love, which ye have showed toward his name, in that ye have ministered to the saints, and do minister. And we desire that every one of you do show the same diligence to the full assurance of hope unto the end: That ye be not slothful, but followers of them who through faith and patience inherit the promises."* Hebrews 6:10. But Abram gave; also he was faithful, and Abram was ready to serve his Lord. The wisdom of God's word established in Abram's heart this principle long before Paul wrote it. Abram made haste to dress the calf: showing a readiness to serve.

FAITH is Prompt: Not only does faith aid physical and mental ability for a readiness to serve the Lord; faith is prompt. Abram was instance, and quick to act as the occasion demanded of him. He knew that water, food and rest should be offered his guest. With no hesitation, water was fetched; a place to rest under the tree offered, while meat and bread were being prepared. Promptness eliminates the chance of missing out on what is desired. Promptness is organized, efficient and calculated action to offer as well as in receiving the thing hoped for. The immediate actions for all people is, *"Today if ye will hear his voice, harden not your hearts,"* Stated prior to this verse of scripture, says, *"For we are made partakers of Christ, if we hold the beginning of our confidence stedfast unto the end."* **Hebrews 3:14-15.** We see this action in Abram toward his guest: he was partaking of the fellowship of his Lord. Because he held fast his faith even unto the time when his son Isaac was born. Promptness brings no delay to the desire to fellowship with the Lord. Note in the scripture, it said, *"If we hold, our confidence stedfast unto the end."* It becomes a choice, the "OUR WILL" to serve the Lord.

<u>Faith is Wiliness:</u> God has offered salvation to all; but it is the wiliness to obey which fulfills the commitment. That which is offered is acceptable unto the Lord when the will in man is right. The word of God establishes faith in the heart of those who are willing to obey his voice. Remember, faith cometh by hearing the word; and God's word causes a renewing of the mind. The concepts, desires, beliefs are converted into the will of God. This conversion of the word of God becomes the will in the heart of men. It is no longer "my will" but His will in me. The conformity to the will is why faith can remain stedfast and faith fulfills the will of God. Jesus is our example of the Wiliness to obey the heavenly Father. Many times he said, "I come to do the will of Him that sent me." "I speak that which the Father gives me." "Not my will, but thou will be done." The Word was sent; and the Word accomplished the thing where unto it was sent. The Word prospered in the things of God, because it was the will of the Father that was kept. Faith in Abram demonstrated wiliness in preparing the meal. It is the will of the Father to have fellowship with man. Adam's transgression breached this fellowship in Eden. Before the fullness of time for Christ work of redemption, Abram typified the partaking of the body of Christ. The Tender good calf was slain; there was the shedding of blood. Abram served the Lord the prepared meal of unleavened bread, the tender good calf, also butter and milk. Jesus told his disciple that the unleavened bread was his body; and the cup was his shed blood. *"Then Jesus said unto them, verily, verily, I say unto you, Except ye eat the flesh of the Son of man, and drink his blood, he have no life in you. Whoso eateth my flesh, and drinketh my blood, hath eternal life; and I will raise him up at the last day...."* As

the living Father hath sent me, and I live by the Father: so he that eateth me, even he shall live by me. This is that bread which came down from heaven: not as your fathers did eat manna, and are dead: he that eateth of this bread shall live forever." John 6:54-58

Faith demonstrates readiness, promptness and wiliness to fellowship with the Lord. Faith is kept alive by the works of righteousness. The end of faith is the manifestation of the things hoped for. Abraham's hope was that the promise of God to manifest. Immediately after the meal, the Lord gave Abraham the time the promise of a son would come to pass. Abram was not weary in well doing: for in due season he obtained the promised because he fainted not.

The Fellowship Meal: *"And he took butter, and milk, and the calf which he had dressed, and set it before them; and he stood by them under the tree, and they did eat."* Genesis 18:8. After the food was made ready, Abram set the food before his guest and they did eat. Abram stood by under the tree; which signified he would await the promise of God. His Seed will bless all nations with salvation. Abraham did not live to see the redemptive work of Christ. He did not partake of the flesh and blood of Christ because he was passed on. But the word of God said, *"And these all, having obtained a good report through faith, received not the promise: God having provided some better thing for us, that they without us should not be made perfect."* Because Abraham believed God, it was accounted unto him for righteousness. The better thing God has provided is salvation for the heathens also. *"The Scriptures, foreseeing that God would justify the heathen through faith, preached before the gospel unto Abraham, saying, in thee shall all nations be blessed."* Galatians 3:8. Faith connected the fellowship of Abram with his guest. The relationship of his fellowship with the Lord is being "a Friend of God."

The thing about fellowship is the state of being a companion, partner or an associate with common interests. The meal was the means by which fellowship happened. The unleavened bread, the calf, butter and milk were eaten. Wisdom built her house, *"She hath killed her beasts: she hath mingled her wine; she hath also furnished her table."* Proverbs 9:2. What was known in Abraham's life depicted the plan and purpose of God materializing his promise of salvation. The word of God was establishing faith as the pillar of his house. With Abraham, faith connected God's presence at the table. For the true table is God's word or laws that men must partake of; this is true fellowship with him. Wisdom furnished her table with the slain beast, the unleavened bread and the drink. It is written that the salvation of men was preordained before the foundation of the world. Years before Christ came to earth; salvation for men was typified in the life of Abraham. *"Having predestinated us unto the adoption of children by Jesus Christ to himself, according to the good pleasure of his will, to the praise of the glory of his grace, wherein he hath made us accepted in the beloved. In whom we have redemption through his blood, the forgiveness of sins, according to the riches of his grace; Wherein he hath abounded toward us in all wisdom and prudence; Having made known unto us the mystery of his will, according to his good pleasure which he hath purposed in himself: That in the dispensation of the fullness of times* **he might gather together in one** (this is fellowship) *all things in Christ, both which are in heaven and which are on earth; even in him: In whom also we have obtained an inheritance, being predestined according to the purpose of him who worketh all things after the counsel of his own will."* Ephesians 1:5-11

To keep company with the Lord, relates to the fellowship. Abram said, *"My Lord, if now I have found favor in thy sight, pass not away; I pray thee, from thy servant:"* Genesis 18:3. How could favor be found in the sight of the Lord concerning Abram other than the Lord was mindful of Abram's faith? The grace of God is granted because of faithfulness. Therefore, Abram was a keeper of the word of God; he became a companion of God. Solomon spoke of the relationship of the beloved with the Beloved, by saying, *"Thou that dwellest in the gardens, the companions hearken to thy voice: cause me to hear it."* Song of Solomon 8:13. Abram was expressing this same desire to hear "his voice." Faith cometh by hearing the voice of God; and Abram heard his voice. Abraham's fellowship with the Lord made him a friend of God. *"And the Scripture was fulfilled which saith, Abraham believed God, and it was imputed unto him for righteousness: and he was called the Friend of God."* James 2:23. Consider why Abram was called the Friend of God. *"Know therefore that the Lord thy God, he is God, the faithful God, which keepeth covenant and mercy with them that love him and keep his commandments to a thousand generations,"* Deuteronomy 7:9. A true friendship is based on trust, commitment, being just, and serving others by the love of God. Jesus said, *"This is my commandment, that ye love one another, as I have loved you. Greater love hath no man that this, that a man lay down his life for his friends. Ye are my friends, if ye do whatsoever I command you. Henceforth, I call you not servants; for the servant knoweth not what his lord doeth: but I have called you friends; for all things that I have heard of my Father I have made known unto you. Ye have not chosen me, but I have chosen you, and ordained you, that ye should go and bring forth fruit, and that your fruit should remain: that whatsoever ye shall ask of the Father in my name, he may give it you."* John 15:12-16. Jesus taught the weightier matters of the law, which are judgment, mercy and faith. (Read Matthew 23:23) Abraham called himself the servant of the Lord: showing his just heart, mercy and faith to the strangers. God kept his covenant with Abraham, because Abraham kept God's commandment. The mercy of God is everlasting; through a thousand generations for those that fear him and keep his commandments. Grace was God's blessing to Abraham and to all people that are the children of Abraham through faith.

The meal at Abram's tent signified the fellowship of Christ. The tender calf life was given; a type of Christ life given for his friends who keepeth his commandment. This commandment is love that covers a multitude of faults. Every beast slain can yield from his body a 'hide' or garment to cloth another with. Many clothes are made of animal skin. Jesus was stripped of his robe at his time of trial and mockery. Nakedness which exposes sin was represented with Jesus. *"Then the soldiers of the governor took Jesus into the common hall, and gathered unto him the whole band of soldiers. And they stripped him, and put on him a scarlet robe."* Matthew 28:27-28. Jesus suffering and his taking on the sins of the world fulfilled the prophecy of Isaiah. *"He is despised and rejected of men; a man of sorrows, and acquainted with grief: and we hid as it were our faces from him; he was despised, and we esteemed him not. Surely he hath borne our griefs, and carried our sorrows: yet we did esteem him stricken, smitten of God, and afflicted. But he was wounded for our transgressions; he was bruised for our iniquities: the chastisement of our peace was upon him; and with his stripes we are healed. All we like sheep have gone astray; we have turned everyone to his own way; and the Lord hath laid on him the iniquity of us all."* Isaiah 53:3-6. *"For (God) hath made him to be sin for us, who knew no sin; that we might be made the righteousness of God in him."* 2Corinthians 5:21. All have sinned and come short of the glory of God. When Adam transgressed, he realized he was naked. To be naked is to be without a garment. The righteousness of God is the garment of salvation. And to love one another as Christ hath loved us: being clothed with his garment of righteousness. His desire is to gather together all things in Christ. Christ brought reconciliation, whereas men can become friends of God. He is the way that leadeth to life, bringing men into the paradise of God; that which Adam lost.

A friend will provide food, clothing and shelter: which may be both natural and spiritual blessings to others. Abram saw the need to provide his guest water, rest, and food while they were in his place. The inheritance Abraham shall receive is because he found favor with the Lord. If there is an inheritance, then the Testator must die in order for the heirs to will receive it.

The exceeding great reward is eternal life through Jesus Christ our Lord. Faith grants us the position of being joint-heirs with Christ. Through faith, we will inherit the same promise God spoke of to Abraham. When Jesus spoke concerning the future of his glory, he said: *"When the Son of man shall come in his glory, and all the holy angels with him, then shall he sit upon the throne of his glory:...Then shall the King say unto them on his right hand, Come, ye blessed of my Father, **inherit*** *the kingdom prepared for you from the foundation of the world. For I was hungry, and ye gave me meat: I was thirsty, and ye gave me drink: I was a stranger, and ye took me in: Naked, and ye clothed me: I was sick and ye visited me: I was in prison and ye came unto me.*" Matthew 25:31-36

... <u>BUTTER and MILK</u>: To complete the meal, Abram set before his guest butter and milk also. When butter is served with a meal; it is often eaten with the bread. Butter is softened or warmed by the fresh baked bread. Remember, Abram asked Sarai to bake the bread on the hearth. Fire or heat is necessary to cause the bread to be baked. It is no longer in the form of knead soft dough. The flavor and taste of butter on the bread is satisfying to the one that eats the bread. Butter is the fatness of milk or other foods such as nuts and fruits. But in Abram's day butter came from the beast that provided it. If butter had come from fruits and nuts, the time to extract the oil of nuts or fruits would have consumed more time in preparing the meal. But the butter and milk were already available for Abram's guest.

The substance of faith with Abraham's butter and milk is prophetic. Butter and milk speak of the fatness the children of Israel would receive in the land of promise. Faith is spiritual insight that reveals the will of God. Earlier, God had revealed to Abram the whereby that he would inherit the promises. In the vision from the Lord, Abram heard while in his deep sleep the word of God. He was told that his seed would be strangers in a land for four hundred years. Afterward, they shall come out with great substance. The children of Israel were enriched by the hand of God. In Moses song unto them, prior to his death, he said, *"For the Lord's portion is his people; Jacob is the lot of his inheritance. He found him in a desert land, and in the waste howling wilderness; he led him about, he instructed him, he kept him as the apple of his eye. As an eagle stirreth up her nest, fluttereth over her young, spreadeth abroad her wings, taketh them, and beareth them on her wings: So the Lord alone did lead him, and there was no strange god with him. He made him ride on the high places of the earth, that he might eat the increase of the fields; and he made him suck honey out of the rock, and oil out of the flinty rock; Butter of kine, and Milk of sheep, with fat of lambs, and rams of the breed of Bashan, and goats, with fat of kidneys of wheat; and thou didst drink the pure blood of the grape."* Deuteronomy 32:9-15

It is by the churning of milk that brings about butter. The pressure or wringing of milk is the ongoing process to make butter. The previous scriptures highlighted the process or experiences the children of Israel underwent. The Lord led them, and he instructed them in the wilderness that they may become fat. Israel waxed fat; in other words they grew or increased in the things of God. From trials and tribulations the outcome should be spiritual increase to the children of God. Abram gave butter and milk to his guest. *"And they did eat."* Milk is instructions the word of God gives to whosoever will partake of it. For a new born child, milk is the food that nourishes the child. Milk provides strength and growth to the child. With the children of Israel, they were as a child being nourished up in the laws of God.

Not only does the 'kine' provide the sacrifice to be offered unto the Lord. The 'kine' produces fatness, which symbolizes increase and abundance. The milk symbolizes nourishment: a food for babes to gain strength as well. The flock of God must be attended to; teaching his lambs and his sheep. All are fed the word of God in measures, so that they are able to receive it.

Isaiah prophesied concerning Christ, and said, *"Therefore the Lord himself shall give you a sign; Behold, a virgin shall conceive, and bear a son, and shall call his name Immanuel. **Butter and** honey shall he eat, that he may know to refuse the evil, and choose the good."* Isaiah 7:14-15 From the New Testament, after Jesus was dedicated in the Temple, in his young life, the scripture said of him, *"And the child grew, and waxed strong in spirit, filled with wisdom: and the grace of God was upon him."* Luke 2:40. In Abram's day, the Lord received butter and milk at the meal. Jesus exemplified the increase that came from the work of the word in him. He partook of the fatness {butter}. Honey was not part of the meal, because Jesus work did not come in Abraham's day. After his appearing, then the voice from heaven saying "This is my beloved Son, in him I'm well pleased." Pleasure is sweetness: Honey! It's Joy!

Jesus said the people, "I have meat that ye know not of" and in another place he said, "My meat is to do the will of him that sent me." Natural butter and honey cannot make a person know to refuse evil and choose the good. The prophet said, "butter and honey shall he eat," His words directed to a spiritual partaking of; and not natural food. Jesus spirit grew and waxed strong. Growth is increase; and strength empowers a person. A child nourished up on food is expected to grow and become strong physically. But a child who is taught the laws of God can know to refuse evil and choose the good.

The only one activity for butter; and that is to spread it. Jesus fulfilled the prophecy of Isaiah: he went throughout the land of Judea and Samaria spreading the gospel. He was filled with wisdom and the grace of God. Many heard him as he taught daily in the land. The miracles he performed were God's favor upon him. And what was the honey that he should eat? It was the pleasure of pleasing God. A joy that passest all understanding. For a pleasurable sensation is sweetness to the inner man. Butter and honey prophetically spoke of Jesus' work: to spread and to accomplish. He was the word sent from God. He obtained Joy for us. Men were lost without a Savior, but Jesus rescued men from the bondage of sin. Relief from any dilemma should bring pleasure and joy to the soul. The prophet Isaiah said in another place, *"For the Lord shall comfort Zion: he will comfort all waste places; and he will make her wilderness like Eden, and her desert like the garden of the Lord; __joy__ and gladness shall be found therein, thanksgiving and the voice of melody."* Isaiah 51:3. *"Therefore the redeemed of the Lord shall return, and come with singing unto Zion; and **everlasting joy** shall be upon their head: and __**they shall obtain gladness and joy**__; and sorrow and mourning shall flee away." {v.11}*

The occasion of Abram receiving and hosting the strangers illustrated several principles of the word of God. He was willing to offer the strangers water, rest and food. He did not forget to entertain strangers; for they were messengers of God. They hungered and thirst; and Abram gave them food and drink. Abraham was merciful; he obtained mercy. He was pure in heart; therefore he saw God in the likeness of the Lord that visited him. He found favor with the Lord, therefore gaining access to the grace of God. Faith made those things possible unto Abram because he believed in God.

25

FAITH PREVAILS THE LAUGHTER

When faith pleases God, the reward of faith is made manifest in due time. Immediately following the meal Abram provided for his guest, the Lord made known to Sarah and Abraham his purpose. He asked, *"Where is Sarah thy wife?* Genesis 18:9. Sarah was in the tent; *"And he said, I will certainly return unto thee according to the time of life; and lo, Sarah thy wife shall have a son. And Sarah heard it in the tent door, which was behind him."* v. 10. The scripture continued by stating that Abraham and Sarah were well stricken in age. At that time Abraham was ninety-nine and Sarah was eighty-nine years old. At their age in life, they were past the age of reproduction. Sarah laughed in response to this news: she contemplated seeing herself being an old woman becoming pregnant. Her laughter was of joy; a long awaited desire some barren women would love to experience. *"Therefore Sarah laughed within herself, saying, after I am waxed old shall I have pleasure, my lord being old also?* v. 12

With God all things are possible to them that believe. This statement is to verify the faith Abraham had. The impossible was to become the possible, because he believed. He hoped in the promise of a son; now the Lord told him that it would come to pass the next year. When a time is given which points to the fulfillment of the hope, the news heightens expectation. Such an assurance in the word of faith is difficult to prevail against. In the Book of Hebrews, it is written, *"For when God made promise to Abraham, because he could swear by no greater, he sware by himself. Saying, Surely blessing I will bless thee, and multiplying I will multiply thee."* What God revealed and established by his word, nothing can prevail against it.

<u>Unable to prevail Against:</u> What was the thing that couldn't prevail against faith? As to Abraham and Sarah, it was their age. To arrive at an old age meant that the body was living. But aging itself caused depreciation of the body: physical weakness, dimmed sighted, and all members declining in agility. These are the physical things that could not prevail against faith. The physical conditions of men are subdued by the word of faith. God sent his word to Abraham: the word came to accomplish the will of God. When Abraham heard, then the word became his hope. God was willing to show Abram the immutability of his counsel by confirming it with an oath. The promise the Lord made with Abram at his tent's door attested to the truth he had spoken. It was one thing for Abram to have heard the voice of God, and to see the word in a vision. But to be affirmed by an oath {TRUTH} sealed the deal. And the reason why this is so, it is because Truth is righteous, just and merciful.

Because his word is righteous; Abram had confidence that nothing would change it. If God's word could be changed, then truth is no longer truth. God cannot lie: and his counsels never change. God keeps his word and his oaths. For his word is just: therefore Abram wasn't deceived or misguided concerning the promise. And God's word is merciful: God has full charge and power to produce the reward of faith. Nothing can prevail against his word.

Wherefore did Sarah laugh: A person will laugh because of their thoughts; or the sight of things and the sound of things a person hear? With Sarah her thoughts and the words she heard from Abraham's guest caused her laughter. *"Therefore Sarah laughed within herself, saying, after I am waxed old shall I have pleasure, my lord being old also?"* **Genesis 18:12** It is not found in scripture that Sarah had no faith. The laughter was merriment in her heart; a joy to be told that she would have pleasure with her husband at her age. Remember Hagar, the handmaiden who had Abram's son Ishmael. Sarah was contended with knowing Abraham begot a son to pass on the blood line. It was thirteen years earlier when Ishmael was born. If Sarah was not contended with the present situation, there could have been other maidens to surrogate children for Sarah and Abraham also. This is said to bring clarity to Sarah's laughter. There are some who preach to show Sarah doubted the word of God and that her laughter was mockery. First the laughter came because of the words she heard from the Lord. Then laughter happened because of the thoughts within her heart. In order for the thoughts to enter her heart, Sarah first received the words in the heart that she heard. When the Lord spoke these words unto Abraham, the Lord wasn't standing in the presence of Sarah. She stood behind the tent's door, but the Lord discerned her laughter. He took notice of what was in her heart. What was in her heart may give a glimpse of her longing desire. Not only this, but God had already changed her name prior to the visit at the tent. When God made the covenant of circumcision, he changed her name and said, *"Sarah thy wife shall bear thee a son indeed: and thou shalt call his name Isaac: and I will establish my covenant with him for an everlasting covenant and with his seed after him.* "But my covenant will I establish with Isaac, which Sarah shall bear unto thee at this set time in the next year."* Genesis 17:19, 21. God found faith in Sarah's heart: and this kind of hope maketh not ashamed because the love of God was shed abroad in Sarah's heart. Love for God in the heart is because of faith in his word.

"And the Lord said unto Abraham, Wherefore did Sarah laugh, saying, Shall I of a surety bear a child, which am old? If something is unbelievable to a person, that person usually will ask for a sign. But sight is not the faith walk. In the case of Sarah, she did not ask for a sign to believe the words the Lord spoke. Signs are for unbelievers; for they trust not in the word God has given. The Lord also stated what Sarah's thought was: *"Shall I of a surety bear,"* the wording expressed the thought of her <u>adverse circumstance</u>; which was her old age.

Many of us today experience the same emotion as did Sarah. We hear the word of God concerning his promise, but we think of the natural laws that governs; then we ask "shall of a surety" It's not that we doubt his word; but we base our laughter on the yesterdays of life. Yesterday has ended the vision or hope; but we recite its history rather than hearing his voice, Today! Sarah's age was her yesterday: she recited it in her heart, and then she laughed at the adverse circumstance. Any woman of today at the age of Sarah when she heard the words of her guest would also laugh. They would see the adverse circumstance of age and the possible.

Sarah laughter could not prevail against the word of faith. God is the same yesterday, today, and tomorrow; it matters not the time of life we live in. He is sovereign and eternal. *"AH Lord God beholds, thou hast made the heaven and the earth by thou great power And stretched out arm, and there is nothing too hard for thee."* **Jeremiah 32:17**

The Lord said unto Abraham, *"Is anything too hard for the Lord? At the time appointed I will return unto thee, according to the time of life, and Sarah shall have a son."* Genesis 18:14. God affirmed his word by giving a time when he would return. His words reversed the circumstance of old age. For Abraham, the Lord introduced to him the possible which later manifested. God is God of tomorrow; therefore he rules over the impossible. Since old age was the adverse circumstance; at the appointed time God created and performed his marvelous work. The appointed time accomplished a great thing that age had no power over. The impossible distinguish the yesterdays, but the possible lay hold on tomorrow, the appointed time.

When Sarah heard the Lord's promise, *"Then Sarah denied, saying I laughed not: for she was afraid. And he said, nay; but thou didst laugh."* Genesis 18:15. Sometimes the faith of a person is assisted by the faith of another who has faith. Abraham was the head of his household who taught the people about God. His wife adhered to his teachings; therefore she was assisted in her faith by Abraham. *"Through faith also Sarah herself received strength to conceive seed, and was delivered of a child when she was past age, because she judged him faithful who had promised."* Hebrews 11:11. Sarah did not acknowledge having laughed which may indicate that she was embarrassed that the Lord revealed the secret of her heart. She denied having laughed, and the reason given was that she was afraid. Fear is a restraint that weakens the physical, mental and emotional status. With men, some things that hinder the impossible are the condition of age, concepts, strength and disbelief. With Sarah being afraid, in hearing the promise of bearing a son prevailed over the adverse circumstance of old age. To bear a child in her old age was life changing. The Lord corrected Sarah for denying that she laughed.

The word of God brings correction so that the believer can conform to the standard of his word. The Lord disputed Sarah's denying that she laughed. The word of God brings chastisement. The effect of his rebuke destroyed the fear. Then Sarah was no longer afraid because truth and mercy had met together. Nothing can prevail against the word; not even the spirit of fear. There is nothing too hard for the Lord. God has the power over the impossible.

REFLECTIONS:

God hears what is in the heart. Keeping us from transgressing his law, God rebukes us. His correction has a dual effect on us. Correction causes conformity to his truth and his correction show mercy. Faith established in Abraham virtues, truth, righteousness, and the love of God. He sojourned upon the land, experiencing every degree of what wisdom was establishing for the salvation of men. First, faith originated by the hearing of the word of God. Hearing demanded a response to what the word of God revealed. Along with his sojourning, 'little space grace' of God aided him. God's grace delivered him out of his straits. Little space grace empowered Abraham to overcome the attacks of his enemies. Faith was the substance of the will of God in his heart. And his faith witnessed the things unseen. He walked before the Lord because God was his guide. Abraham's walk before God perfected every command God gave him. He was chosen to be the father of faith. God authorized the course of life Abraham sojourned. Faith brought him to honor, to increase, riches, and the grace place of God. He did not seek after anything to prefer honor and glory upon himself; rather, he sought after the promise of God. *"He staggered not at the promise of God through unbelief; but was strong in faith, giving glory to God; and being fully persuaded that, what he had promised, he was able also to perform."* **Romans 4:120** Faith and Little Space Grace: the measure of the fullness of Christ. Faith connects us to Grace: and we that believeth on him hath everlasting life.

www.ingramcontent.com/pod-product-compliance
Lightning Source LLC
Chambersburg PA
CBHW020434130626

46549CB00001B/128